APR 05 1995
DISCARDED

LAW AND POLICY OF REGIONAL INTEGRATION:
THE NAFTA AND WESTERN HEMISPHERIC INTEGRATION
IN THE WORLD TRADE ORGANIZATION SYSTEM

NAFTA Law and Policy Series

VOLUME 1

Series Editors

Seymour J. Rubin, B.A., LL.B., LL.M.
*Professor of Law, Emeritus in Residence,
Washington College of Law, American University*

Dean C. Alexander, B.A., J.D., LL.M.
President, Septacontinentaux Corporation

The book series will include high-quality studies on different aspects of NAFTA, including legal analysis and commentary on the Agreement. Among the numerous areas that will be covered in the series are NAFTA topics as diverse as agriculture, dispute settlement, environment, intellectual property rights, investment, and labor. Contributors will be drawn form the legal profession, business, government, and the academic community. The series is designed to ensure that practitioners, corporate counsel, government officials, academics, and businessmen will gain a thorough understanding of the multi-faceted legal and economic implications of NAFTA.

Law and Policy of Regional Integration:

The NAFTA and Western Hemispheric Integration
in the World Trade Organization System

by

Frederick M. Abbott
Associate Professor of Law
Chicago-Kent College of Law

MARTINUS NIJHOFF PUBLISHERS
DORDRECHT / BOSTON / LONDON

Library of Congress Cataloging-in-Publication Data

```
Abbott, Frederick M.
    Law and policy of regional integration: the NAFTA and western
  hemispheric integration in the World Trade Organization system / by
  Frederick M. Abbott.
       p.      cm.
    ISBN 0-7923-3295-4
    1. Free trade--North America.   2. Western Hemisphere--Economic
  integration.   3. World Trade Organization.   4. Regionalism
  (International organization)   I. Title.
  KDZ944.A41992A73   1995
  341.7'54--dc20                                         94-42028
                                                              CIP
```

ISBN 0-7923-3295-4

Published by Martinus Nijhoff Publishers,
P.O. Box 163, 3300 AD Dordrecht, The Netherlands.

Sold and distributed in the U.S.A. and Canada
by Kluwer Academic Publishers,
101 Philip Drive, Norwell, MA 02061, U.S.A.

In all other countries, sold and distributed
by Kluwer Academic Publishers Group,
P.O. Box 322, 3300 AH Dordrecht, The Netherlands.

Printed on acid-free paper

All Rights Reserved
© 1995 Kluwer Academic Publishers
Kluwer Academic Publishers incorporates the publishing programmes of
Martinus Nijhoff Publishers.

No part of the material protected by this copyright notice may be reproduced or
utilized in any form or by any means, electronic or mechanical,
including photocopying, recording, or by any information storage and
retrieval system, without written permission from the copyright owner.

Printed in the Netherlands

To Stefan Riesenfeld

Scholar, Humanitarian and Friend

TABLE OF CONTENTS

Preface ix

Introduction and Overview 1

Chapter One -- The Political Economy of NAFTA Approval 7

Chapter Two -- The Basic Structure of the NAFTA 23

Chapter Three -- Regional Integration Arrangements in the WTO Framework 35

Chapter Four -- The NAFTA Trade in Goods Provisions 61

Chapter Five -- The NAFTA Provisions regarding Services, Investment and Intellectual Property 79

Chapter Six -- The NAFTA Regulatory Framework and Dispute Settlement Procedures 97

Chapter Seven -- The NAFTA and the European Union 119

Chapter Eight -- The NAFTA and Japan 139

Chapter Nine -- The NAFTA and the Rest of the World 153

Chapter Ten -- The Future of Western Hemispheric Integration 175

Appendix	189
1. GATT Article XXIV	189
2. Understanding on the Interpretation of Article XXIV of the General Agreement on Tariffs and Trade 1994	194
3. GATS Article V	199
Index	203

PREFACE

Regionalization of the international trading system is occurring against the backdrop of a new global multilateral trading structure. The creation of the North American Free Trade Agreement, the widening and deepening of the European integration process and the establishment of the World Trade Organization each raise a myriad of complex questions cutting across a host of disciplines -- economic, political, social and, of course, legal. Study of the relationship between these separate and interconnected regional and global integration processes becomes itself a discipline.

The purpose of this book is both to explore the new regional integration mechanism for North America -- the North American Free Trade Agreement (NAFTA) -- and to set it in the context of the World Trade Organization (WTO) that is taking the place of the GATT. Though the NAFTA is a largely self-contained integration system, it is very difficult to study and understand it without also studying and understanding the broader global regulatory context in which it sits.

Regional integration is not a new phenomenon. The modern idea of an economically integrated Europe grew up during the final phases of the Second World War and first took shape as the European Coal and Steel Community in 1951. Throughout the 1960s and 1970s the countries of Latin America fashioned regional integration arrangements to promote economic and political cooperative self-determination. The NAFTA is part of a continuum of regional integration efforts, though perhaps for reasons to be explored in this book, an especially important part. The process of regional integration will continue in the Western Hemisphere as the Northern and Southern Americas expand existing integration arrangements and create new ones. This book will explore the future of the Western Hemispheric continuum.

The international trading system is constantly evolving as it confronts changes in production and distribution technologies, as well as demands by individuals for progress in the sphere of social welfare. The integration of the global economy will continue as advances in industrial technologies lead, at an ever-increasing pace, to greater efficiencies and economies of scale. Business enterprises with enhanced production and distribution capacities will press to increase revenues and profits by penetrating expanded markets. The question with respect to the global economy is not whether markets will continue to integrate, but how. Present evidence strongly suggests that regional integration will be the driving mechanism for global market integration for the near to medium term. This lends an urgency to the study and understanding of regional integration mechanisms, not only because of their economic impact, but because of their broader effect on social welfare.

There are a number of individuals and institutions that I would like to thank for helping me with this book. Stefan Riesenfeld and Eric Stein both provided encouragement for my undertaking this project. Jochen Frowein at the Max-Planck-Institute in Heidelberg, Germany, arranged for a fellowship at the Institute which greatly facilitated my research on the situation in Europe. Meinhard Hilf and Thomas Oppermann in Germany also were particularly helpful in discussions on the European Union. Thomas Cottier generously shared the Swiss perspective on the NAFTA and GATT. In Japan, Mitsuo Matsushita and Ken Matsumoto were extremely helpful, both in sharing their perspectives and in assisting with local arrangements. John Schmidt (former U.S. Ambassador to the GATT) was kind enough to offer the participant's view of the Uruguay Round negotiations. Ernst-Ulrich Petersmann provided insight into the GATT and WTO processes. The GATT Secretariat and Office of the U.S. Trade Representative each were cooperative in providing information and documentation. The Chicago-Kent College of Law provided needed funding both from the Marshall D. Ewell Research Fund and the Norman and Edna Freehling Endowment Fund.

My principal research assistant on this project was Allyson Harris, a recent graduate of the Chicago-Kent College of Law. Ms. Harris found and reviewed back-up materials, edited footnotes, compared drafts, and otherwise supported the book. I am very grateful for her help. My wife, Cathy, performed a most useful final edit of the manuscript. Finally, my thanks to Selma Hoedt of Martinus Nijhoff Publishers for her continuing support and assistance.

Writing an analysis of developments in the modern field of international trade is made difficult by the nature of the field. The NAFTA and WTO charter documents, as examples of modern trade treaties, are voluminous and complex. They are supplemented by implementing legislation and administrative regulations, and by formal and informal decisions, reports and statements by government officials. The complexity of the interrelationships between all of the agreements and surrounding context means that, with respect to many areas, government officials, arbitral tribunals, lawyers and scholars will spend years, if not decades, creating more precise maps. New rules will be proposed, debated and adopted (or rejected). As a consequence of new information technologies, we will become aware of developments very rapidly. However, our ability to analyze and explain remains subject to the constraints not only of our thought processes, but to the constraints of the publication process as well. To create a timely analysis of developments in the field of international trade, a writer must stop time. Further developments must await the next edition.

Frederick M. Abbott
October 1994
Chicago

INTRODUCTION AND OVERVIEW

The North American Free Trade Agreement (NAFTA) is a phenomenon of great importance to the people of Canada, Mexico and the United States, and to the international community as a whole. The NAFTA is the second post-World War II regional integration effort among globally-important national economies, and the first such effort to be undertaken outside the shadow of violence. The NAFTA seeks to integrate the economies of the two most highly industrialized countries in the Western Hemisphere and the rapidly developing economy of a major Latin American political power. The NAFTA integration process will shape the structural evolution of the Western Hemisphere economy, affect the economic interests of countries outside the hemisphere, and inevitably have an important impact on political and social developments both within and outside of its territorial boundary.

The principal focus of the NAFTA is the removal of tariff and non-tariff barriers to trade in goods and services, and the provision of an open and secure environment for cross-border investment and the exchange of information and ideas. The commitments of the three NAFTA country parties (Parties) in these areas are extensive. Certainly in comparing regional integration efforts at the formation stage, the economic liberalization commitments of the NAFTA Parties are as or more extensive than any set of commitments previously undertaken among a regional group. The economic liberalization commitments of the NAFTA Parties are worthy of close study because of the impact they will have in and outside the NAFTA territory. A central focus of this book therefor will be to describe and analyze the legal framework of the NAFTA economic liberalization program.

The NAFTA establishes an institutional structure that is quite different from the institutional structure of the European Union. The major NAFTA institutions are essentially a setting for consultation and cooperation among the Party governments. The framers of the NAFTA assiduously avoided granting to regional institutions the power to make decisions which would directly bind the

Parties. These framers were operating in a historical and political environment far removed from that in which the framers of the European Economic Community operated in the 1950s, and these NAFTA framers doubtless perceived little enthusiasm in the body politic of any of the Parties for a transfer of governmental authority to a regional center. The NAFTA's consultative-cooperative institutional structure is of course of great interest because it is the mechanism by which the NAFTA will operate. The NAFTA institutional structure also defines the way in which the region will interact with multilateral institutions, including the World Trade Organization and European Union, as well as individual non-Party countries. The NAFTA again is quite different than its European Union counterpart in that it does not provide for the coordination of the external commercial policy of its Parties. The NAFTA institutional structure will be an important focus of attention in this book.

The NAFTA was first conceived as a mechanism for trade liberalization and not as a social charter. The NAFTA's limited provisions for the free movement of labor reflect the necessities of doing business across national boundaries and not the intention of creating a homogenous social environment. Nevertheless, the intense demands of individuals and interest groups concerned with the social consequences of economic integration, including those concerned with its impact on the physical environment, lead to the incorporation of provisions in the basic NAFTA charter which address in a minimum way some of the non-economic issues that the Parties and their nationals face, and lead to the adoption of two Supplemental Agreements which more extensively address labor- and environment-related issues. While the social provisions of the NAFTA remain rather limited at present, these provisions deserve attention because they are the foundation for the future evolution of the NAFTA's social framework.

The year 1993 was pivotal to defining the medium term structure of the international trading system for three reasons. First, the NAFTA was approved in the United States in the face of resistance from a nascent managed trade movement in the Congress. The political and economic backdrop of the NAFTA's approval are central concerns of this book. Second, the Maastricht Treaty on European Union was ratified in 1993 after exhaustive political debate on the future of European integration. Although the Maastricht Treaty is an incremental step in the European integration process, its failure would have signalled a turning away from the European integration ideal and would have created considerable uncertainty for the future. Third, the Final Act of the GATT Uruguay Round negotiations was approved, paving the way for the metamorphosis of the GATT into the World Trade Organization (WTO) in 1995.

The creation of the WTO as an institution is largely a symbolic event. The WTO will be formally recognized as an international organization replacing the less formally constituted General Agreement on Tariffs and Trade (GATT). More importantly, the WTO Agreement and its incorporated multilateral trade agreements will extend international trade law discipline to the new areas of trade in services, trade-related investment measures (TRIMS) and trade-related aspects of intellectual property rights (TRIPS), and will make important improvements to the mechanisms intended to assure the enforcement of WTO rules. In addition, WTO rules will generally be applied to the broad spectrum of WTO membership, giving a universal character to a set of rules which was previously applied in a multi-tiered manner.

The WTO Agreement contemplates the co-existence of the WTO and regional integration arrangements (RIAs) such as the NAFTA. It provides in GATT Article XXIV rules intended to govern the formation of RIAs with respect to trade in goods and it provides new and separate rules for regional services liberalization regimes in General Agreement on Trade in Services (GATS) Article V. In some important respects, however, such as in dealing with RIA changes to rules of origin, GATT Article XXIV continues to provide inadequate guidance. The new GATS Article V attempts to establish an objective standard for evaluating RIA services liberalization agreements, but it is not clear that the approach it takes is well suited to the difficult subject matter it governs. The WTO Agreement establishes a Working Party Review process to evaluate the conformity of RIAs with its rules. However, the Working Party Review process that is carried forward from GATT practice is hampered by a consensus decision-making procedure that is an obstacle to concrete action.

Despite the fact that the WTO Agreement foresees co-existence between the WTO and RIAs, including the NAFTA, the relationship between the WTO and RIAs is imprecisely defined, and conflicts between the WTO rule-system and the RIA rule-systems are inevitable. The WTO Agreement establishes the individual constituent countries of the RIA as responsible for compliance by the RIA with WTO rules, except in the special case of the European Union which shares direct responsibility with its Member States. The NAFTA Parties, however, agreed that their regional rules will take precedence over GATT rules as between themselves, and this rule of priority may extend to part or all of WTO rules. The NAFTA Parties in general may elect either WTO/GATT or NAFTA dispute settlement procedures to resolve conflicts arising under both agreements. In the case of environment-related disputes among the NAFTA Parties, the NAFTA dispute settlement process will ordinarily be used. NAFTA and WTO/GATT rules with respect to environment-related provisions are different in some important respects.

A principle objective of this book is to situate the NAFTA within the new framework of WTO rules, and to evaluate both the conformity of the NAFTA with these rules and the adequacy of the WTO rules themselves. The interplay between WTO/GATT and NAFTA rules and dispute settlement procedures is addressed. It is of paramount importance to the health of the multilateral trading system that the WTO and NAFTA be able to operate in relative harmony. While some modest level of tension between complementary rule systems is of course to be expected and may prove a useful stimulus to new ideas and approaches, there is a danger that conflict and tension between systems will eventually force the abandonment of one or the other. Though there is no such threat to the WTO or NAFTA on the immediate horizon, it will be well to consider the potential for conflict between the two systems.

The approval of the NAFTA contemporaneously with the approval of the WTO raises a host of interesting and difficult policy questions. From the end of the Second World War through the 1980s, the United States was the principal advocate of a multilateral approach to the governance of international trade. The WTO/GATT is the concrete embodiment of the multilateral trade ideal. Does the United States pursuit of the NAFTA represent a significant shift from multilateralism to regionalism in U.S. trade policy, or is the NAFTA perceived by U.S. trade policy-makers as a tool by which to accelerate the multilateral integration process? Are the European Union and NAFTA likely to become so strong as regional economic powers that the WTO will be marginalized? If the WTO is in fact marginalized, what will the consequences be for countries remaining largely outside formal regional frameworks, such as Japan, the People's Republic of China and Taiwan? This book examines the potential impact of the NAFTA on the WTO framework, as well as on some specific countries and regions outside its territory.

The NAFTA has been portrayed by the United States government as the first step toward a Western Hemispheric free trade area extending from Anchorage to Tierra del Fuego. Plans for extending the NAFTA already are under discussion. There are a variety of legal mechanisms which could be used to undertake this extension, including direct accession of third countries to the NAFTA, the merger of the NAFTA with existing or newly formed Western Hemispheric RIAs, or a "hub and spoke" arrangement with the United States and/or Mexico acting as hubs to which other countries join in free trade agreements as spokes. This book examines some of these potential arrangements, as well as the potential economic impact of a Western Hemispheric free trade area on countries outside the hemisphere.

Introduction and Overview

This book proceeds from an analysis of the NAFTA approval process and a brief description of the NAFTA's structure, to an examination of WTO rules which have evolved to deal with the RIA phenomenon, to a detailed examination of the NAFTA and its place within the global framework.

Chapter One reviews the strategy followed by the U.S. government in obtaining approval of the NAFTA and discusses the approval process. It describes the reaction of the third countries to its negotiation and conclusion. It reviews the factors that led to negotiation of the NAFTA in light of economic trends affecting the United States, Europe and Japan. It also considers the motivations of Mexico and Canada for entering into the NAFTA.

Chapter Two describes the basic features of the NAFTA as background for an in-depth discussion in Chapter Three of WTO rules affecting regional integration arrangements (RIAs). The legal relationships between the NAFTA and the Canada-United States Free Trade Agreement (CUSFTA) and between the NAFTA and the new WTO Agreement are examined. The lack of a NAFTA mechanism for the conduct of a common external commercial policy is studied in the light of the European Union's common commercial policy.

Chapter Three provides a detailed description and analysis of the treatment of RIAs by the GATT and WTO, including GATT Article XXIV, GATS Article V and the Working Party Review process. This chapter considers the potential for conflict between the WTO and RIA regulatory systems and what the consequences of conflict may be for the liberal global trading system.

Chapter Four provides a detailed description and analysis of NAFTA provisions affecting trade in goods, including rules of origin. It evaluates these provisions for their consistency with WTO rules governing RIAs and trade in goods. This chapter also discusses the NAFTA rules regarding technical standards and sanitary and phytosanitary measures. These are the rules that will largely determine the NAFTA's impact on the environment. The relationship between these rules and corresponding WTO rules is explored.

Chapter Five provides a detailed description and analysis of NAFTA provisions affecting trade in services, investment and intellectual property rights. As with Chapter Four, it evaluates these provisions for their consistency with WTO rules, including the new GATS Article V, and the TRIPS and TRIMS Agreements.

Chapter Six examines the regulatory framework of the NAFTA. It describes the dispute settlement procedures under the main agreement, as well as under the North American Agreements on Environmental and Labor Cooperation (NAAEC and NAALC). This chapter also more generally evaluates the NAFTA approach to the environment and labor.

Chapter Seven discusses the relationship between the NAFTA and European Union, principally from the economic and legal perspectives. It describes the formal views of the European Commission and Parliament concerning the NAFTA. This chapter looks at market access to the NAFTA and EU from a comparative perspective. It also discusses whether similarities between the NAFTA and EU may provide the basis for an inter-regional social welfare entente.

Chapter Eight discusses the Japanese view of the NAFTA based both upon published reports and the author's extensive discussions in Japan on this subject. This chapter explores the practical reasons why Japan has not pursued a formal Asian RIA and why it has instead become the major exponent of a rule-based WTO trading system.

Chapter Nine considers the impact of the NAFTA on the rest of the world. It reviews the state of the art in RIA economic analysis and examines the most current economic studies of the NAFTA's potential for trade creation and trade diversion. It suggests that RIAs must be evaluated as multifaceted organizations, from the political, economic and social perspectives. This chapter addresses the broad potential effect of the NAFTA and other RIAs on the WTO system.

Chapter Ten reviews the history of Western Hemispheric integration efforts and discusses important recent changes to Latin American perspectives on economics and trade. The prospects and possible legal mechanisms for future Western Hemispheric integration efforts are examined. The position of the U.S. government regarding the next steps in the integration process is considered, as is a study of the potential economic impact of a Western Hemispheric Free Trade Area.

The NAFTA is a phenomenon that deserves close and continuing study from the legal, political, economic and social perspectives. This book attempts to take an integrated approach to the NAFTA and its potential impact on the world trading system. Study of the NAFTA and the regional integration process may lead us to devise new approaches for helping to assure that the global multilateral trading system and the regional systems operate in relative harmony. The drafters of the GATT 1947 saw RIAs as steps in the process toward full integration of the world economy and material well being for the world's people. The NAFTA is an important step in this global process.

Chapter One

THE POLITICAL ECONOMY OF NAFTA APPROVAL

I. APPROVAL OF THE NAFTA AND RESPONSE OF THE GLOBAL TRADING COMMUNITY

The NAFTA was the subject of an intense public debate in the United States prior to its approval by the Congress.[1] The potential impact of the NAFTA on the U.S. labor market became a rallying point for U.S. labor unions which perceived and portrayed the NAFTA as an effort by U.S. industrial concerns, and particularly by the automobile industry, to undercut the negotiating strength and ultimately the wages and benefits of the American worker.[2] Many environmental interest groups characterized the NAFTA as an attempt by U.S. multinational business enterprises to obtain a platform for unregulated production in Mexico, and an attempt to fashion a lever by which U.S. environmental standards could be undermined through a process of downward harmonization with an unsatisfactory Mexican environmental regime.[3] Both the

---

[1] See Appendix I to this Chapter for technical details regarding the NAFTA approval process.

[2] See Katherine A. Hagen, *Fundamentals of Labor Issues and NAFTA*, 27 U.C. DAVIS L. REV. 917, 918-20 (1994); David A. Dilts & William H. Walker, Jr., *Labor Standards and North American Free Trade: Economic Dynamics or Dilemmas?*, LAB. L.J. 445 (July, 1993); William Cunningham & Segundo Mercado-Llorens, *The North American Free Trade Agreement: The Sale of the U.S. Industry to the Lowest Bidder*, 10 HOFSTRA LAB. L.J. 413, 428-435 (1993); Shellyn G. McCaffrey, *North American Free Trade and Labor Issues: Accomplishments and Challenges*, 10 HOFSTRA LAB. L.J. 450, 461-65 (1993); Gwen Ifill, *Clinton Defends Trade Pact to Skeptical A.F.L.-C.I.O.*, N.Y. TIMES, Oct. 5, 1993, at B10; Peter T. Kilborn, *Unions Gird for War Over Trade Pact*, N.Y. TIMES, Oct. 4, 1993, at A14; Anthony DePalma, *Vague Mexico Wage Pledge Clouds Free Trade Accord*, N.Y. TIMES, Sept. 29, 1993, at A1; Robin Toner, *In Auto-Making Country, Trade Accord is the Enemy*, N.Y. TIMES, Sept. 14, 1993, at A18.

[3] Environment-related issues were aired in the press. See, e.g., *Environmental Groups Line Up on NAFTA; Baucus Announces Support for the PACT*, 10 BNA INT'L TR. REPTR. 1577 (Sept. 22, 1993); *Some Environmentalists Fault Side Deal for What It Lacks Rather Than Provisions*, 10 BNA INT'L TR. REPTR. 1506 (Sept. 15, 1993). Michael McCloskey, *Rescue Nafta--Safeguard the Environment*, WALL ST. J., July 8, 1993, at A13 (comment by chairman of Sierra Club); William K. Reilly, *Nafta for a Better Environment*, WALL ST. J., July 30, 1993, at A9 (response letter from

U.S. environmental movement and labor unions traditionally had been hostile to Republican presidential administrations which espoused commitment to reduction in governmental regulation of business as the party platform. The Republican party had dominated the Executive Branch of the U.S. government since the withdrawal of the reelection candidacy of Democrat Lyndon Johnson in 1968.[4] Both the environmental movement and organized labor are aligned with the Democratic Party.

When Bill Clinton ran for the office of President in 1992 he endorsed the basic concept of the NAFTA, while proclaiming the need to make certain supplemental alterations in order to protect environmental and labor interests.[5] In the presidential election of 1992 the environmental and labor organizations had only a Republican candidate, George Bush, and a Democratic candidate who supported the NAFTA -- albeit with supplemental changes -- to chose between. When Bill Clinton won the presidency and continued to support the NAFTA, the environmental interest groups and labor unions found themselves in the anomalous position of opposing in the Congress the recently-elected President

---

former EPA Administrator); Mickey Kantor, *Nafta Maintains U.S. Environment Standards*, N.Y. TIMES, Sept. 23, 1993, at A26 (letter from USTR in response to Aug. 27 letter from Carol Clark).

Environmental issues were the subject of extensive congressional testimony by U.S. government representatives, interest group representatives and industry spokespersons. *See, e.g.,* Committee on Merchant Marine and Fisheries of the House of Representatives: Hearing on Environmental Implications of NAFTA, 139 Cong. Rec. D 1294 (daily ed. Nov. 10, 1993); Hearings before House Agriculture Committee, including testimony on environmental quality, *reported in* BNA Daily Report for Executives, Congressional and Presidential Activity, Oct. 8 and 18, 1993, Westlaw BNA-DER Database.

Environmental issues were the subject of numerous government and private studies and reports. *See Response of the Administration to Issues Raised in Connection with the Negotiation of a North American Free Trade Agreement* (transmitted to the Congress by the President on May 1, 1991); U.S. General Accounting Office, *U.S. - Mexico Trade: Information on Environmental Regulations and Enforcement*, GAO/NSIAD-91-227 (May 1991); Office of the United States Trade Representative, *Review of U.S. - Mexico Environmental Issues* (Draft, Oct. 1991); U.S. Environmental Protection Agency, *Summary, Environmental Plan for the Mexican - U.S. Border Area, First Stage (1992-1994)*, Feb. 1992; U.S. EPA, *Integrated Environmental Plan for the Mexican - U.S. Border Area (First Stage, 1992-1994)*; *Report of the Administration on the North American Free Trade Agreement and Actions Taken in Fulfillment of May 1, 1991 Commitments* (Sept. 18, 1992); Office of the USTR, *Review of U.S. - Mexico Environmental Issues* (Final, Feb. 25, 1992). The Sierra Club, *Environmental Concerns Regarding the North American Free Trade Agreement* (1993).

Environmental issues were the subject of litigation. *See* Public Citizen v. USTR, 5 F. 3d 549 (CADC 1993), *reversing*, 822 F. Supp. 21 (DDC 1993).

[4] The Republican Presidents in this period were Richard Nixon (1968-74), Gerald Ford (1974-76), Ronald Reagan (1980-88) and George Bush (1988-92). Jimmy Carter, a Democrat, was President during 1976-80. The Carter Administration was widely perceived as ineffective during the period of his presidency.

[5] *See Clinton Endorses NAFTA with Certain Reservations*, 9 BNA INT'L TR. REPTR. 1720, Oct. 7, 1992. *The 1992 Campaign, Transcript to 3d T.V. Debate between Bush, Clinton and Perot*, N.Y. TIMES, Oct. 20, 1992, at A20.

from the Democratic Party. President Clinton found himself in the equally anomalous position of depending on congressional support from the Republican Party to obtain approval of an agreement which his predecessor in office had initiated, negotiated and signed.

Throughout the lengthy public airing of NAFTA-related issues, the potential impact of the regional arrangement on countries other than Canada, Mexico and the United States was discussed principally in the context of potential trade-diverting consequences for small countries of the Caribbean, and to a certain extent for countries elsewhere in Latin America.[6] The NAFTA was portrayed as a means for improving America's competitive posture *vis-à-vis* Japan and the European Union, although this aspect of the arrangement did not become a major public selling point until the final stage of the approval process.

In the week or two prior to the scheduled November 17, 1993 House of Representatives approval vote, and with the conclusion of the GATT Uruguay Round scheduled for December 15, voting on the NAFTA was portrayed by the Clinton administration in the strongest possible terms as a three-way signal to the global community. First, the vote would generally demonstrate whether the United States was committed to open markets. Although it might well be argued that the NAFTA, as any regional arrangement, is a market restricting device as opposed to a market opening device,[7] in this particular case opposition to the NAFTA arose not from utopian global free traders, but rather from managed traders and protectionists. Thus rejection of the NAFTA might fairly have been viewed by the global community as a victory for market closing forces.[8]

Second, the Clinton Administration stressed that the NAFTA approval vote would constitute a vital signal as to whether the Congress would be prepared to approve the results of the GATT Uruguay Round negotiations. The Clinton Administration suggested that conclusion of the NAFTA would provide a major impetus for successful conclusion of the Uruguay Round by highlighting the risk of regionalization of the global community should the overall negotiations fail.[9] Moreover, according to the Clinton Administration, if Congress rejected the

---

[6] *See infra* Chapter Nine, text accompanying notes 7-9.

[7] *See* discussion of economics of regional integration arrangements, *infra* Chapter Nine.

[8] As the NAFTA approval vote drew near, the United States began to stress the desirability of commencing negotiations to admit new members, starting with Chile and proceeding through the Western Hemisphere. Although this had been an aspect of President Bush's Enterprise for the Americas Initiative (EAI), discussed *infra* Chapter Ten, this theme had not been emphasized until immediately prior to the approval vote date.

[9] The NAFTA was also portrayed as a safeguard measure in the event the Uruguay Round failed to successfully conclude.

NAFTA, the U.S. would lose its leverage at the GATT. If other countries believed that U.S. negotiators could not deliver what they promised there would be little point in making politically painful compromises with them.[10] Failure to pass the NAFTA would symbolize a United States which was an unreliable trade negotiator. Approval of the NAFTA, on the other hand, would relieve fears concerning the ability of the United States to conduct an effective foreign trade policy. To the extent that the NAFTA might discriminate against third country trade, third countries would be encouraged to bargain more seriously toward an effective market-opening GATT agreement in order to secure protection against discrimination.

Third and finally, President Clinton arranged a meeting of the Asia-Pacific Economic Cooperation (APEC) group in Seattle, Washington for November 18-19, 1993.[11] This meeting had initially been publicized as a forum where the APEC leaders could open a dialogue. It was also part of a U.S. policy-shift toward emphasizing the growing importance of the Asia-Pacific region and at least nominally shifting away from a Eurocentric policy. However, shortly before the meeting, U.S. officials began to suggest that it would be used to begin active work on an Asia-Pacific free trade arrangement on a more structured basis. This U.S. posture was *not* received favorably by other APEC governments (in general). Many indicated that APEC was not intended as such a forum. It was intended as a loose consultative arrangement to focus predominantly on Asian interests. Many of the APEC countries are in the early stages of industrial development and view interim protection as a vital component of establishing their local infrastructures. They are not necessarily anxious to accelerate market access commitments. There was a clear concern that the U.S. would attempt to dominate the APEC/Asian dialogue.

Regardless of the lukewarm to hostile reaction from members of the APEC group to the Clinton Administration's ambitious agenda for the APEC summit, the Clinton Administration characterized an affirmative NAFTA vote as critical to establishing U.S. credibility at the APEC meeting. From this standpoint, the outcome of the APEC summit was essentially irrelevant to the Administration,

---

[10] For example, why should the French government risk its political viability by sticking to the Blair House agricultural accord if the U.S. could not ratify the deal?

[11] Regarding the results of this meeting, *see* Paul F. Horwitz, *Looking to Asia for Growth, Clinton Vows to Open Markets*, INT'L HER. TRIB., Nov. 20-21, 1993, at 1. Paul F. Horwitz, *A Non-Starter in Seattle: Asian-Pacific Community*, *id.* at 1. As of the end of the meeting, members of APEC are the United States, Canada, Japan, PRC, South Korea, Hong Kong, Australia, New Zealand, Taiwan, Mexico, Papua New Guinea, Singapore, Malaysia, Indonesia, Brunei, Thailand and the Philippines. The latter six also are members of ASEAN. Chile was admitted to membership in APEC commencing in 1994.

and represented yet another effort to ratchet up the pressure on Congress in a high stakes political exercise.

On November 17, 1993, the NAFTA was approved by the U.S. House of Representatives by a vote of 234 to 200.[12] This was a substantially larger margin of approval than had come to be expected based upon stated commitments of Representatives up to the day before the vote. The Republican Party delivered 132 approving votes and the Democratic Party the remainder.[13] President Clinton made a number of political concessions to swing voters in the final few weeks before the approval vote was taken. These appear to have included an agreement not to raise federal livestock grazing land fees to appease western States cattle ranchers, deals to limit Mexican agricultural competition with Florida fruit and vegetable growers, protection for U.S. sugar producers and some arrangement to protect durum wheat (and other pasta-related wheat) growers from alleged Canadian subsidization, and an agreement to create a North American Development Bank.[14]

The official reaction of the European Commission to approval of the NAFTA was largely favorable. The Commissioner for External Economic Relations, Sir Leon Brittan, noted that completion of the NAFTA approval process would permit the United States to focus on the Uruguay Round negotiations. This reaction was reiterated by heads of government in a number of EU Member States.[15] Moreover, Sir Leon Brittan issued a formal statement noting that the

---

[12] On November 20, the NAFTA was approved by the U.S. Senate by a vote of 61 to 38. The Senate had long been expected to approve ratification of the agreement, and there was little of the public tension such as surrounded the House of Representatives vote. The North American Free Trade Agreement Implementation Act which approved the President's ratification is Pub. L. No. 103-182, 107 Stat. 2057 (1993), codified at 19 U.S.C. §§ 3311, et seq. (1994) [hereinafter NAFTA Implementation Act].

[13] See *North American Free Trade Agreement (NAFTA) Implementation Act*, Vote Report, Nov. 17, 1993, *available in* LEXIS, Legis Library, Votes file; *Nafta After the Victory*, N.Y. TIMES, Nov. 19, 1993, at A32.

[14] Douglas Jehl, *The Free Trade Accord: The Overview, Scramble in the Capital for Today's Trade Pact Vote*, N.Y. TIMES, Nov. 17, 1993, at A1; David E. Rosenbaum, *The Free Trade Accord: Both Sides Emphasize High Stakes of Trade Vote*, N.Y. TIMES, Nov. 15, 1993, at A14. See discussion of NADBANK, *infra* Chapter Two.

[15] See IPS Staff, *Trade: Now NAFTA Is Out of the Way U.S. and EC to Deal with GATT*, INTER PRESS SERVICE, Nov. 18, 1993 (LEXIS/NEXIS); P.H. Ferguson, *NAFTA Approval Hailed as Boost to Free Trade, Some Fear Closed Market*, Assoc. Press, Nov. 18, 1993 (LEXIS/NEXIS); Jessica Baldwin, *NAFTA Passage Hailed, Attention Shifts to World Trade Pact*, Assoc. PRESS, Nov. 18, 1993 (LEXIS/NEXIS); *U.S., Japan make GATT moves day after NAFTA vote*, FRANCE PRESS, Nov. 18, 1993 (LEXIS/NEXIS); Paul Taylor, *Balladur Rallies Coalition for GATT Endgame*, REUTER EUR. COMM. REP., Nov. 19, 1993 (LEXIS/NEXIS); *NAFTA, House NAFTA Approval Welcomed by EC, GATT Leaders and Japanese*, BNA INT'L TR. DAILY, Nov. 19, 1993 (LEXIS/NEXIS); *GATT: Geneva Talks Boosted by U.S. Congress Vote*, EUROPEAN REP., Nov. 20, 1993 (LEXIS/NEXIS). European Union trade officials praised the approval vote, particularly as a sign that open-market

EU did not consider the NAFTA to be problematic from the perspective of discrimination against third countries -- though cautioning that the fine print of the implementing legislation had yet to be published. Statements emanating from Japan, Thailand and South Korea were more cautious, indicating support on the basis that the prospects for successful conclusion of the Uruguay Round negotiations were enhanced, but noting that tariff preferences in favor of local producers would have a negative effect on their exports.[16]

Comments were made by a number of governments at or in connection with the APEC meeting following the NAFTA approval vote that at least initially suggested a philosophical attitude of acceptance of the inevitable. Among critical reactions, the Taiwan government indicated that NAFTA would have adverse effects and cause further shifts of production by its industries to the mainland People's Republic of China (PRC) in order to take advantage of lower wage rates.[17] At least initially the APEC bias was not to create a third bloc to compete with the EU and US/NAFTA blocs, but rather to stress the importance of completing the GATT Uruguay Round negotiations. To this end, additional -- though apparently not dramatic -- GATT market access offers were tabled in connection with the APEC meeting.

A major focus of media attention surrounding the APEC meeting was U.S. insistence that the PRC improve its human rights record as a condition of continuing to receive most favored nation (MFN) treatment. The PRC had in fact prior to the meeting made some concessions by indicating an intention to

---

forces had prevailed over protectionist forces. The timing of congressional approval of the NAFTA in the United States -- coming as it did less than a month before the scheduled conclusion of the GATT Uruguay Round -- highlighted the potential for the European Union to view the NAFTA as a U.S. bargaining lever for future trade negotiations.

[16] *See* reports, *id.*; note that a Japanese official is reported to have raised concern that NAFTA Party tariffs were scheduled to come down too slowly, thereby discriminating against third country producers.

> The official, however, expressed concern about tariff provisions of the agreement, which calls for eliminating tariffs among the NAFTA members over 15 years. He said those tariffs should go immediately when the agreement takes effect so that non-NAFTA countries will not be discriminated against.

See NAFTA Approval Welcomed, BNA INT'L TR. DAILY, *id.* The more rapidly the NAFTA countries lower their inter-Party tariffs, the greater the potential discriminatory effect on third countries. The Japanese official might be better understood to have been expressing concern with whether the NAFTA met the technical requirements of GATT Article XXIV. *See* discussion of Article XXIV and the NAFTA, *infra* Chapter Four.

[17] Paul F. Horwitz, *Looking to Asia for Growth, Clinton Vows to Open Markets*, INT'L HER. TRIB., Nov. 20-21, 1993, at 1; Paul F. Horwitz, *A Non-Starter in Seattle: Asian-Pacific Community*, *id.* at 1. More detailed discussion of the reaction of third country governments to negotiation and conclusion of the NAFTA is set forth, *infra*, Chapters Seven through Nine.

permit Red Cross visits to political prisoners. Although the U.S. and PRC governments attempted to deemphasize the issue at the meeting, it was certain that such focus played into the hands of APEC governments resistant to U.S. interference in their affairs.

Following the final APEC informal heads of state meeting on November 20, the Clinton Administration and U.S. media attempted to put an optimistic spin on the results.[18] They suggested the dawn of a new era in Asia-Pacific relations. The actual results of the meeting certainly were inconclusive. The meeting seemed to confirm the pre-meeting views expressed by most of the Asian countries, namely that they were not prepared to create a formal regional integration arrangement with the United States, though in the normal course of diplomacy they were willing to participate in discussions concerning regional economic interests. In the final analysis, the Clinton Administration appeared to have gotten out of the APEC meeting exactly what it had needed and bargained for -- a lever by which to influence the outcome of the NAFTA approval vote. The Administration had pursued a high risk strategy by emphasizing the adverse consequences to U.S. and global trade policy and interests which theoretically would have attended congressional rejection of the NAFTA. This high risk strategy paid off.

II. THE UNDERPINNINGS OF THE NAFTA

Although the specific structure of the NAFTA is unique among regional integration arrangements (RIAs), the NAFTA is part of a trend toward the structural regionalization of the international trading system that has been

---

[18] At the APEC meeting, Mexico and Papua New Guinea were admitted as new members. Chile was advised that it would be admitted in the following year. APEC members voted in favor of a three year moratorium on new membership so that the group could consolidate itself. There was agreement on a meeting of Finance Ministers in six months to consider macroeconomic policies. The representatives to the APEC summit:
1. Issued an "economic vision statement" that made an open international trading system a top priority;
2. Agreed that heads of state would meet in one year in Jakarta, Indonesia;
3. The U.S. and ASEAN "formed an alliance to improve trading relations. The group will seek to cooperate in financing, in trade among smaller companies and in removing bottlenecks in telecommunications, transportation, electric power and environmental technology;"
4. Agreed to create a non-binding code on investment and transfer of technology, and;
5. Created an APEC Educational Program to broaden intellectual exchanges.
See Paul F. Horwitz, *Clinton Cites Talks as Positive, But Divisions Remain*, INT'L HER. TRIB., Nov. 22, 1993, at 1; R.W. Apple, Jr., *No Missteps for President, But No Clear Gains Either*, id. at 1. *See also* Alexander Nicoll and George Graham, *Pacific rim ushers in 'brave new era for trade,'* FIN. TIMES, Nov. 22, 1993, at 1.

evolving since the end of the Second World War. The genesis of the major regional systems was quite different. The modern concept of an integrated Europe developed in the aftermath of World War II. The economies of the continental European countries had been devastated. Economic integration was viewed as a means to accelerate the rebuilding process by permitting European enterprises to take advantage of economies of scale. The modern European integration process also embodied the political goal of creating inter-state political linkages which would reduce the possibility of another conflict such as the two which had plagued Europe in the first half of the twentieth century. The history of the modern European integration process is very well documented and is the subject of a number of excellent studies.[19]

The NAFTA was founded in a much different historical environment than the European Union. Military conflict between the United States and Mexico is a part of their shared history. Although that conflict has influenced the modern

---

[19] The editors of INTEGRATION THROUGH LAW make the following observation about the thinking prevalent at the formation of the European Economic Community: "[T]he trauma of World War II - which was the immediate and powerful mobilizing vehicle for the integration movement - created, especially in the generation of the 'Founding Fathers,' a strong commitment to European integration as a meta-value in itself above any mundane cost-benefit analysis." Cappelletti, et al., *Integration Through Law: Europe and the American Federal Experience, A General Introduction*, in 1 INTEGRATION THROUGH LAW 3, 6 (Mauro Cappelletti et al. eds., 1986).
It has been observed that:

The idea of the 'United States of Europe'... which would be a faithful partner of the United States of America, could be seen behind the Marshall Plan, the American decision to take part in the defense of Europe (the Vandenbergh Resolution), and U.S. support for the process of neofunctional integration after 1950.

Elazar & Greilsammer, *Federal Democracy: The U.S.A. and Europe Compared, A Political Science Perspective*, in 1 INTEGRATION THROUGH LAW 71, 88.
THE FIRST REPORT OF THE EUROPEAN CUSTOMS UNION STUDY GROUP (Mar. 1948), prepared by 14 European countries considering the formation of a customs union (with the United States and several other countries participating as observers) concluded that it was not practicable to pronounce definitely on the advantages and disadvantages of such a union. *Id.* at 91, para. 217. However, the report observed:

Europe today, as a result of the upheavals caused by crises and wars, is a mosaic of different economic systems whose dissimilarities impede the achievement of equilibrium. Internal differences have been accentuated by the existence of traditional bonds between certain European and overseas countries or territories and, from a very different angle, by the distortion of European trade produced by the need to acquire hard currencies. . . .
Nevertheless, there exists between many European countries a close interdependence which might form the basis for an organic community.

Id. at 89, paras. 212-13. *See also* JOHN H. JACKSON, WORLD TRADE AND THE LAW OF GATT 580 (1969); F.A. Haight, *Customs Unions and Free Trade Areas Under GATT, A Reappraisal*, 6 J. WORLD TRADE L. 391, 392 (1972); Stefan A. Riesenfeld, *Legal Systems of Regional Economic Integration*, 22 AM. J. COMP. L. 415 (1974).

political and economic dialogue between the United States and Mexico, it is well enough in the past not to have played a critical role in the NAFTA formation process. The principal factor behind initiation of the NAFTA negotiations was a dramatic shift in Mexican economic policy. The government of Mexico had through the 1980s gradually turned away from central economic planning and trade protectionism toward a more liberal approach to economic development. Since Mexico had long restricted the opportunities of U.S. business enterprises within its borders, this shift in policy was viewed very favorably by the U.S. business sector and U.S. government trade policy officials. There would naturally from a U.S. business perspective be an advantage in attempting to lock in favorable developments in Mexican attitudes toward U.S. direct investment and exports. Initiation of the NAFTA negotiations presented the United States with an excellent opportunity to pursue a policy of protected export-driven growth.

A. ECONOMIC FACTORS AFFECTING U.S. NAFTA POLICY

The U.S. economy is mature from the standpoint of industrialization and is becoming saturated in terms of service supply to consumers. As productivity continues to be enhanced, the demand for workers is reduced. Yet employed workers are the consumers of goods and services. The government could tax businesses at a high level, provide substantial social welfare payments to marginal workers, and thereby attempt to maintain the consumer base.[20] Unfortunately, such a policy would cut into the productive capital available to business. Research and development, and plant and equipment expenditures, would be restricted. In the modern global economy, where businesses in countries with low social welfare payments are competing for cost advantages, a redistribution policy could not work over the long term.

An attractive alternative is to increase reliance on export markets as an outlet for both the manufacturing and services sectors. By penetrating markets which are not yet mature and saturated, the U.S. economy can generate local employment opportunities. The revenues generated by exports are no less useful to U.S. business enterprises than the revenues generated by local sales, and can just as well as be used to build and maintain a productive economic base.

---

[20] To a large extent this phenomenon can be seen in the social welfare policies of France, Germany and other European countries. *See* JOHN KENNETH GALBAITH, THE CULTURE OF CONTENTMENT (1992) for a discussion of deficiencies in the social welfare system in the United States.

The NAFTA can be viewed as an attempt by U.S. trade-policy makers and economic planners to stimulate export-led growth while limiting external access to the U.S. market. It is a limited export-led strategy involving a new second player, *i.e.* Mexico, which does not pose a significant threat to the U.S. high-valued industrial market. The U.S. has sought in a variety of ways -- though particularly by the use of restrictive rules of origin applicable to trade in goods -- to limit the benefits which the NAFTA will create with respect to Europe, Japan and other non-North American actors. The U.S. objective of limiting NAFTA access is certainly understandable in light of developments in the global economy.

Japanese and, to a somewhat lesser extent, European manufacturers, have become highly competitive with U.S.-high value-added manufacturers. The extent of deterioration in post-Second World War U.S. technological and infrastructure advantages *vis-à-vis* Japan and Europe is not fully agreed upon, and the United States apparently still maintains an overall productivity advantage.[21] Nevertheless, the dominant position that the United States maintained into the 1980s with respect to high value-added manufacuring is no longer present. The relative parity in manufacturing among the United States, Japan and Europe manifests itself in intense competition in the global export market. In Chapters Seven and Eight, merchandise trade flows involving the United States, Europe and Japan are examined in some detail.

The United States still maintains substantial advantages with respect to the supply of services. These advantages manifest themselves in substantial services trade surpluses for the United States, as detailed in Chapters Seven and Eight. U.S. advantages are based on a number of factors. The United States began its transition to a service-based economy prior to either Japan or Europe. Because of its large internal market, services businesses in the United States have been able to rapidly achieve economies of scale as compared, for example, with their

---

[21] For example, both LAURA D'ANDREA TYSON, WHO'S BASHING WHOM, TRADE CONFLICT IN HIGH TECHNOLOGY INDUSTRIES (1992) and LESTER THUROW, HEAD TO HEAD, THE COMING ECONOMIC BATTLE AMONG JAPAN, EUROPE AND AMERICA 45-51 (1992) argue that the United States has lost its competitive advantages in a number of important high technology fields. On the other hand, a 1992 productivity report by the Mckinsey Global Institute suggested that the United States maintains larger industrial productivity advantages than is popularly assumed. Sylvia Nasar, *U.S. Tops in Productivity Study, Service Sector Spearheads Lead over Japan, Germany*, CHI. TRIB., Oct. 14, 1992, Bus. Sec., at 2. These conclusions do not necessarily conflict, although the overall subjective impression conveyed by the studies is different. Another recent summary of economic data suggests that the United States continues to maintain substantial advantages in worker productivity and research and development, and that the United States position appears to be improving *vis-à-vis* European and Japanese competition rather than deteriorating. *See* Sylvia Nasar, *The American Economy, Back on Top*, N.Y. TIMES, Feb. 27, 1994, sec. 3, at 1, col 2 (Sunday edition).

European counterparts. The Japanese economy has largely ignored the potential requirements and demands of its consumer market as far as services are concerned, and thus an efficient services sector has yet to develop. Nonetheless, as the European economies continue to integrate and barriers to the transnational provision of services are removed in consequence of the 1992 Plan, European services providers should become highly competitive with the U.S. services providers in a fairly short time frame.[22]

As the NAFTA structure is presented in the following Chapters, note that the principal restrictions imposed on non-Party countries relate to imports of their manufactured goods. These restrictions are substantially tempered by the reality of the U.S. position in the global market-place. The United States could not afford to provoke retaliatory measures against its own exports.

Access to the NAFTA services market is by and large unrestricted. This may reflect existing U.S. superiority in the services sector. It may also evidence the fact that the European Union is largely open to U.S. services providers. The position of U.S. service providers in the EU market is very strong. The United States could not as a practical matter restrict the NAFTA services market without expecting that reciprocal restrictions would be imposed by the European Union. The United States would not gain from such an exchange.

B. SECONDARY U.S. OBJECTIVES

While it is clear that the principle motivation of the United States for negotiating and concluding the NAFTA was economic, there were secondary goals. The most important of these was to stem the tide of illegal immigration from Mexico which places considerable strain on the economies of important States such as California and Texas, and in doing so creates political tension both within these

---

[22] There is a relatively small capital requirement for the initiation of many services enterprises, unlike manufacturing enterprises which typically requires the large scale employment of capital in the start-up phase. Moreover, since much of the success of U.S.-based services firms is based upon the use of sophisticated computer programs coupled with an educated work force, European countries will have comparable access to resources. U.S. services firms which maintain operations within Europe rapidly diffuse their advantages into the local economy by training local employees. Therefore, the lag time between development in the manufacturing sector between the United States and Europe should not be seen in the services sector. The Japanese, facing both significant language barriers and a social structure less conducive to servicization are not likely to be highly competitive in the broad services market for some time. In certain sectors such as financing (where availability of capital is essential) they are and will remain very competitive.

The educated European work force is well-versed in the English language which to a large extent is the universal language of business. There is less facility with English among the Japanese. The importance of language barriers in the global services market should not be underestimated.

States and between the United States and Mexico.[23] From a U.S. perspective, if the NAFTA could accelerate economic growth in Mexico, it might reduce the incentives for Mexican emigration to the United States, and thereby ameliorate the illegal immigration problem at a minimal cost. The Bush Administration also suggested that the NAFTA would have the positive effect of solidifying and encouraging the political reform process in Mexico. While the NAFTA might indeed have such effect, it seems somewhat doubtful that this was a motivating factor of any great interest to the U.S. body politic.[24]

C. MEXICO'S INTERESTS

The motivation of Mexico for initiating the negotiation of the NAFTA also was principally of an economic nature. The Mexican government under the leadership of President Salinas was in the process of restructuring the Mexican economy to reduce its centrally planned character. It was gradually disavowing Mexico's long-standing policies of import substitution and antipathy toward investment by foreigners. Mexico had begun to see an acceleration of inward capital investment.[25] Nevertheless, the government recognized that if the transition to an open market economy was to succeed without causing the kind of political upheaval which frequently characterizes economic reform programs, it would have to do everything reasonably within its power to accelerate and aid that transition. By negotiating the NAFTA the government of Mexico would offer an incentive to U.S. enterprises to move more quickly into the newly opened market by providing both a form of investment guarantee and by offering a level of preferential treatment both with respect to imports and investment.

Mexico's limited policy of encouraging foreign investment in its border region under the Maquiladora program had succeeded in attracting substantial U.S. and other foreign investment, but had been a disaster from a social welfare standpoint. The program had resulted in large pockets of low-wage laborers

---

[23] *See, e.g.*, Robert T. Matsui, *Introduction*, 27 U.C. DAVIS L. REV. 791 (1994) (Symposium on Free Trade and Democratic Values: NAFTA's Effect on Human Rights); and Kevin R. Johnson, *Free Trade and Closed Borders: NAFTA and Mexican Immigration to the United States*, 27 U.C. DAVIS L. REV. 937 (1994).

[24] Suggesting the desirability of incorporating human rights goals in the NAFTA and other RIAs, *see* James F. Smith, *NAFTA and Human Rights: A Necessary Linkage*, 27 U. C. DAVIS L. REV. 793 (1994).

[25] *See* data on investment into Mexico in Chapter Seven, *infra* notes 23-26, and in references there cited.

living in unsuitable conditions in areas devoid of infrastructure development. Environmental degradation in these areas was extensive. The NAFTA would extend Maquiladora-type inducements throughout Mexico and thereby reduce the incentives for concentrating foreign investment along the narrow border region. It was a hope of the Mexican government that the NAFTA would spread out foreign direct investment, result in more balanced economic development, and avoid concentration of infrastructure stress in a small segment of the country.

Just as the United States considered it useful to limit NAFTA preferences for high value-added imports from Europe, Japan and Taiwan, so perhaps Mexico, with lower wage rates and a less developed social infrastructure, considered it useful to limit NAFTA preferences for mid- and low-tech goods from Thailand, India, Vietnam and the People's Republic of China. While Mexican import substitution policies had been a dismal failure, the NAFTA might constitute a workable intermediate path between the open market and import substitution.[26]

In Mexico the prospect of attaining closer political ties with the United States was not a positive selling point for the NAFTA. Mexico has prided itself on its political independence from the United States. The prospect that the NAFTA might threaten that independence was a prospect to be discounted. The Mexican government suggested that conclusion of the NAFTA would begin to put Mexico on an equal footing with the United States and Canada on the world economic stage. This suggestion was consistent with maintaining and even enhancing Mexican independence from the United States.

D. CANADA'S INTERESTS

Negotiation and conclusion of the Canada-United States Free Trade Agreement (CUSFTA) had engendered a major political battle in Canada in 1988.[27] When it decided to enter the NAFTA negotiations in 1991, Canada had in place a comprehensive free trade agreement with the United States and maintained negligible trade with Mexico. Canada's decision to enter the NAFTA negotiations was of a largely defensive nature. Canada could easily live without enhanced trade and investment opportunities with Mexico, but had reason to be

---

[26] Import substitution policy holds that domestic industries should be protected from imports by the erection of trade barriers. The theory is that developing industries require insulation from efficient competition during a transition period, following which the barriers may be removed.

[27] The relationship between the NAFTA and CUSFTA is discussed *infra*, Chapter Two.

concerned about future U.S. plans to extend a free trade zone throughout the Western Hemisphere. If it had chosen to stay on the sidelines during the NAFTA negotiations, Canada might have found itself left out of future hemispheric negotiations. Over the long term a policy of hemispheric isolation might have a significant adverse impact on the Canadian economy. Thus although the NAFTA was unlikely to have any significant short-term impact on Canada from either an economic or political perspective, it chose to participate in the arrangement largely to protect its long-term economic interests.

It is clear that the NAFTA negotiations were undertaken principally for economic reasons specific to the United States and Mexico. The consequences of this economic basis are manifest in the institutional structure of the NAFTA which is described and analyzed in Chapters Two and Six. The NAFTA institutional structure reflects very little of the political ambition or vision of the European Union. The institutions of the NAFTA by and large play the role of coordinating inter-governmental activity among the three Parties. These institutions do not in themselves have the power to make decisions which bind the Parties. The fundamental disparity between the NAFTA and European Union institutional structure illustrates that the motivating factors behind the formation of the RIA may significantly affect its structure.

APPENDIX I -- DETAILS CONCERNING THE APPROVAL PROCESS

I. TECHNICAL ASPECTS OF CONGRESSIONAL APPROVAL PROCESS

A. The NAFTA was principally negotiated by Bush Administration under fast-track authorization (19 USC §§2112, 2191). The President is obligated to consult with Congress during negotiations, in exchange for which Congress agrees to approve or reject the agreement and proposed implementing legislation without amendment. In fast-track legislation Congress reserves the right to modify the fast-track rules.

B. President Bush notified Congress of his intention to enter into the NAFTA on September 18, 1992, making December 17 the 90th day following, and per the fast-track statute the first day on which agreement could be signed (19 USC §2112(e)(1)).

C. Congressional approval is required in a maximum of 90 legislative days following signing and submission, per 19 USC §2191(e)(2), because Congress considered NAFTA implementing legislation as a revenue bill rather than as a trade agreement bill. For a trade agreement, there is a maximum 60 legislative day approval period (19 USC §2191(e)(1)). Under the revenue provision, House Committees first have 45 days to consider a bill, then full House approval must follow within 15 days. The bill is then sent to Senate Committees for 15 days, and full Senate approval must follow in an additional 15 days.

D. Congressional vote requirement is majority of a quorum in both houses (51 Senate, 218 House, of total 535 assures approval). This differs from the Senate "advice and consent" procedure which would require the affirmative vote of two-thirds of the Senators present.

II. PRESIDENT CLINTON CAUTIOUSLY SUPPORTED THE NAFTA THROUGHOUT CAMPAIGN

A. Candidate-Clinton detailed his position on the NAFTA in a speech of October 4, 1992 at North Carolina State University. He set forth three principal reservations to the agreement as negotiated by Bush Administration -- regarding the environment, labor and safeguards against import surges. Clinton recommended resolving concerns without reopening the main agreement, *i.e.*

through parallel track negotiations and agreements.

1. Environment - Clinton proposed establishing a trilateral commission with substantial authority to prevent and clean up pollution, to have investigative and enforcement authority.

    a. Under Bush three environmental chiefs had already agreed to establish a commission, but had not finalized a plan and the charter was vague. The proposal appeared to contemplate a purely advisory commission.

    b. A parallel environmental agreement was a virtual certainty because Congress has pushed on environmental issues from the outset and Vice-Presidential candidate Gore is an environmentalist. Creation of a body with power to mandate harmonization of environmental laws was unlikely because of Mexican concerns. A critical issue was funding. Congress had balked at funding President Bush's U.S.-Mexico border clean-up plan. Congressman Gephart proposed an environmental tariff/tax.

2. Labor - Clinton proposed a trilateral commission with "extensive powers to educate, train, develop minimum standards and have dispute settlement powers and remedies." The harmonization issue surfaced again. A major issue was where funding for worker retraining would come from.

    a. Bush proposed a $2 billion per year for five years ($10 billion) worker adjustment assistance program (Advanced Skills Through Education and Training (ASETS)) - skills training plus extension of unemployment benefits). A May 3, 1991 Memorandum of Understanding had been signed for cooperation between Mexico and the U.S. - providing for consultation on a variety of labor issues, *e.g.* health and safety, training.

3. Import surges - Clinton called for strengthened authority to take action against unanticipated surges in imports. Chapter Eight of the NAFTA text already permitted emergency safeguard action, after (for U.S.) International Trade Commission proceedings and findings.

    a. This was a technical issue, and unless Clinton chose, unlikely to create difficulty in Congress.

Chapter Two

THE BASIC STRUCTURE OF THE NAFTA

The NAFTA was not designed with the ultimate goal of political and social integration on the North American continent, but rather as a means of promoting economic growth in its constituent countries. If the NAFTA process some day results in a deeper integration of North America, it will not be because the NAFTA was initiated with that vision. The NAFTA institutions are designed to coordinate the activities of the Parties and not to make decisions on their behalf. This arrangement reflects the fundamental conceptual basis of the NAFTA as a means of promoting trade and investment.

I. THE NAFTA AND OTHER AGREEMENTS

The NAFTA[1] largely superseded the Canada-United States Free Trade Agreement (CUSFTA), but it did not expressly terminate or suspend the CUSFTA. The NAFTA provides at Article 103 that it prevails to the extent of inconsistencies with other agreements to which the Parties are party.[2] There is an exception to this general rule in the case of certain specified agreements relating to the environment, such as the Basel Convention on the Transboundary

---

[1] Canada-Mexico-United States: North American Free Trade Agreement [done Dec. 8-17, 1992], 32 I.L.M. 289 & 605, entered into force Jan. 1, 1994 [hereinafter NAFTA].

[2] Article 103 of the NAFTA provides:

1. The Parties affirm their existing rights and obligations with respect to each other under the *General Agreement on Tariffs and Trade* and other agreements to which such Parties are party.

2. In the event of any inconsistency between this Agreement and such other agreements, this Agreement shall prevail to the extent of the inconsistency, except as otherwise provided in this Agreement.

24   *Chapter Two*

Movement of Hazardous Waste.[3] Since the NAFTA in general prevails over inconsistent agreements, to the extent that the NAFTA and CUSFTA concerned the same subject matter, the NAFTA would govern. Various provisions of the CUSFTA are incorporated by reference in the NAFTA.[4] U.S. legislation implementing the NAFTA contemplated that the United States and Canada would agree to suspend the CUSFTA as a result of entry into force of the NAFTA.[5]

The CUSFTA was suspended upon entry into force of the NAFTA pursuant to an Exchange of Notes between the Canadian and U.S. governments.[6] The suspension will remain in effect for such time as the two countries remain Parties to the NAFTA.[7] Pursuant to an Exchange of Letters between Canada and the United States regarding suspension of the CUSFTA, antidumping and countervailing duty (AD/CVD) final determinations published prior to entry into force of the NAFTA remain subject to dispute resolution proceedings under the relevant CUSFTA AD/CVD dispute settlement provisions.[8] Pending disputes (and pending consultations that may result in dispute settlement proceedings) regarding interpretation and application of the CUSFTA, that would have been subject to general CUSFTA dispute settlement proceedings, will be subject to equivalent dispute settlement proceedings under the NAFTA.[9] This will not affect the application of CUSFTA substantive rules in any such proceedings.[10]

In Article 103 of the NAFTA, the Parties affirm their existing rights and obligations to each other under the GATT, but provide that the NAFTA prevails

---

[3] *Id.* art. 104.

[4] *See, e.g., id.* Annex 302.2 (Tariff Elimination).

[5] NAFTA Implementation Act, § 107.

[6] Note No. 134 of the Embassy of Canada to the Department of State of the United States of December 30, 1993 and Note No. 464 of the Embassy of the United States to the Department of External Affairs and International Trade of Canada of December 30, 1993 with reference to entry into force of the NAFTA and suspension of the Free Trade Agreement between Canada and the United States (in author's files).

[7] *Id.*

[8] Letter of Minister for International Trade (Canada), R. MacLaren, to U.S. Trade Representative, M. Kantor, of December 30, 1993 (in author's files)(confirmed by U.S. reply). Domestic implementation procedures adopted by each government in connection with such proceedings will continue to apply. *Id. See* Chapter Six *infra* for description of the separate antidumping and countervailing duty (AD/CVD) dispute resolution procedures under the NAFTA. These are substantially similar to the also separate CUSFTA AD/CVD procedures.

[9] *Id. See* Chapter Six *infra* regarding the general dispute settlement procedures of the NAFTA.

[10] The Letter of MacLaren, *supra* note 8, refers to the "interpretation and application of the substantive rights and obligations of the [CUS]FTA" as being subject to NAFTA dispute settlement procedures. This implies that CUSFTA substantive rules remain applicable.

over the GATT to the extent of inconsistencies between the two agreements.[11] As discussed in Chapter Four, the Parties expressly disavow at least one provision of the GATT relating to the adoption of measures necessary to protect human, animal and plant life and health (as it relates to sanitary and phytosanitary measures), in favor of different NAFTA rules on this subject matter.[12]

The fact that the NAFTA took priority over the GATT was of course significant from the standpoint both of defining the general relationship between the NAFTA and the GATT and establishing applicable norms in the dispute settlement process. The GATT establishes "working parties" to review the compliance by regional integration arrangements (RIAs) with GATT rules governing their formation.[13] A GATT Working Party reviewed the CUSFTA. A number of CUSFTA Working Party members were quite concerned with the potential implications of an equivalent hierarchy of norms established between the United States and Canada in the CUSFTA, both from the perspective of general policy and with respect to concern over the implications for dispute settlement.[14] The NAFTA is a more detailed agreement than the GATT and has a wider scope of coverage (for example, in the area of investment measures). It is tempting to conclude that the drafters of the NAFTA chose to give it priority over the GATT because its rules would be more easily applied in concrete situations. Nevertheless, even if the GATT is viewed as a broader constitutional charter, it would not have been extraordinary from a juridical perspective to have subjected the more narrow NAFTA rules to the GATT's overriding discipline. It therefore seems that the hierarchy of norms established by the NAFTA reflected a political bias favoring more direct regional concerns over more diffuse global concerns.[15]

---

[11] *See* the text of Article 103, *supra* note 2, which in para. 2 refers to "such other agreements" in para. 1, which para. 1 refers to the GATT.

[12] *See* Chapter Four *infra*, text accompanying notes 53-54.

[13] The working party review procedure is described in Chapter Three.

[14] Report of the Working Party on the Free-Trade Agreement between Canada and the United States, GATT doc. L/6927, adopted by GATT Council Nov. 12, 1991 [hereinafter Working Party Report], *e.g.*, at paras. 19-31, 93-94. The legal relationship between the CUSFTA and GATT was "[t]he foremost concern of many members of the Working Party" (*id.* at para. 93).

[15] It is an interesting question whether the Parties to the NAFTA may have breached the GATT by having agreed in NAFTA Article 103 to give that agreement priority over the GATT. GATT dispute settlement panels have held that laws which merely permit a violation of GATT rules are not GATT inconsistent, and that a GATT claim will not be considered until an action in breach of the GATT has been taken. *See, e.g.*, United States - Restrictions on Imports of Tuna: Report of the Panel, GATT Doc. DS21/R (Sept. 3, 1991), at paras. 5.20-5.21. These decisions have referred to the discretion reserved in legislation which may be invoked in breach of the GATT. NAFTA

Article 103 expressly establishes the NAFTA's priority over existing agreements between the Parties, including the GATT. The question arises whether the NAFTA prevails over the new WTO Agreement, which agreement is the subject of the next Chapter. Establishing the legal priority of the substantive rules of the NAFTA and those of the new WTO is a matter of considerable complexity. A number of contextual factors are involved in defining this relationship, and it may be some years before an authoritative definition of the relationship emerges, whether through action taken by the NAFTA Parties to expressly establish the relationship,[16] or through an accumulation of dispute settlement panel opinions that may establish a common law of interpretation. A discussion of the contextual factors will be better understood after the structure and rules of the WTO and the NAFTA have been more thoroughly described, and so a more detailed consideration of this relationship is found in Chapter Six, Part II (regarding dispute settlement). However, the situation in general terms may be described as follows.

The basic charter of the GATT is the General Agreement on Tariffs and Trade. The General Agreement, as amended, along with its accumulated formal understandings and interpretations, will become an integral part of the new WTO. However, in order to facilitate the transition between the GATT and WTO, the General Agreement incorporated in the WTO will be referred to as

---

Article 103 is not a discretionary provision. It is mandatory as between the Parties. However, to the extent the Parties have agreed to give priority to NAFTA rules as between themselves, the Parties may be obligated to refrain from bringing claims against each other in the GATT on the basis of GATT rules which conflict with NAFTA rules. This may exclude one substantial avenue of potential controversy. In addition, consistent with Article 30 of the Vienna Convention on the Law of Treaties, the Parties should interpret the NAFTA priority rule so as not to require them to apply NAFTA rules to third countries in the event of a conflict with GATT rules concerning the same subject matter. Article 30 of the Vienna Convention on the Law of Treaties provides that when a state enters into a successive/later-in-time treaty which does not include all parties to a prior treaty concerning the same subject matter, the prior treaty continues to govern as between that state and states which are not parties to the later treaty. Vienna Convention on the Law of Treaties, May 23, 1969, 1155 U.N.T.S. 331 (entered into force Jan. 27, 1980; not in force for the United States), U.N. Doc. A/Conf. 39 (1969), *reprinted in* 63 Am.J. Int'l L. 875 (1969). Although the United States has not ratified the Vienna Convention, the U.S. Department of State as well as the courts have indicated that they consider it for the most part to restate the customary international law of treaties. *See* Stefan A. Riesenfeld and Frederick M. Abbott, *The Scope of U.S. Senate Control Over the Conclusion and Operation of Treaties*, 67 CHI-KENT L. REV. 571, 574 (1991); *reprinted in* PARLIAMENTARY PARTICIPATION IN THE MAKING AND OPERATION OF TREATIES: A COMPARATIVE STUDY 261 (Stefan A. Riesenfeld and Frederick M. Abbott eds., 1994). If NAFTA rules are not given priority *vis-à-vis* non-Party countries that are parties to the GATT, the potential for conflict will be reduced. Nevertheless, as discussed in Chapter Six, the possibility will remain for dispute settlement panels of the NAFTA and WTO/GATT to reach conflicting conclusions with respect to the NAFTA Parties concerning the same subject matter, and thereby potentially to create political difficulties within the Parties.

[16] Through, for example, an exchange of diplomatic correspondence.

the "GATT 1994," and the old General Agreement will be referred to as the "GATT 1947." The GATT 1994 is "legally distinct" from the GATT 1947. Some countries may choose to remain parties only to the GATT 1947, at least for an interim period, and become parties neither to the WTO or the GATT 1994. Canada, Mexico and the United States are all expected to become parties to the WTO (and GATT 1994).

The parties to the WTO Agreement have agreed to follow the prior customs and practices of the GATT 1947, and only parties to the GATT 1947 may become "original Members" of the WTO (*i.e.*, they are not required to negotiate separate accession agreements). Neither the legal distinction between the GATT 1947 and the GATT 1994, nor the formation of the WTO, is intended to signal a break in the continuity of the GATT organization or its rules. Thus, from a contextual standpoint, the GATT 1994 is a continuous extension of the GATT 1947. The GATT 1994 is a successor agreement to the GATT 1947 that, in a narrow technical sense, may supersede the prior agreement. However, in light of the basis for the technical distinction between the agreements, that technical succession should probably not be understood to cause the GATT 1994 to be considered a new and different agreement than the GATT 1947 for NAFTA Article 103 purposes.

If the foregoing hypothesis is correct, there nevertheless remain important and difficult questions. Although the GATT 1994 and GATT 1947 are largely coextensive, the WTO as a whole contains agreements in addition to the GATT 1994. Some of these agreements take the place of existing GATT agreements negotiated in the Tokyo Round. The relationship between these new WTO agreements and the old Tokyo Round agreements may be evaluated on roughly the same basis as the GATT 1994 is evaluated in respect to the GATT 1947. Other new WTO agreements are more or less extensions of Tokyo Round agreements, or codifications of GATT practice, and are in somewhat more of a grey area than those that strictly take the place of the Tokyo Round agreements. Finally, some new WTO agreements concern subject matter areas (such as trade in services and protection of intellectual property) not previously regulated by the GATT. These agreements would be considered part of a GATT continuum only under a rather broad interpretative view of the GATT.

Therefore, as a preliminary conclusion it may be suggested that the rules of the NAFTA will continue to prevail over GATT 1994 rules, as well as WTO rules that take the place of Tokyo Round agreement rules. However, there are grey areas with respect to WTO rules that are not continuous extensions of GATT 1994 and Tokyo Round rules. These may not be subject to a general rule of priority, and evaluations may need to be made on a case by case basis. It may be quite some time before questions of NAFTA-WTO/GATT priority may be answered definitively.

II. THE PRINCIPLE INSTITUTIONS

The NAFTA establishes a Free Trade Commission (Commission) composed of cabinet level representatives of the Parties (or their designees).[17] The Commission generally acts by consensus, but may agree (by consensus) to act otherwise than by consensus.[18] The functions of the Commission are to supervise the implementation, oversee the elaboration, and assist in the resolution of disputes under the agreement, as well as to supervise the work of the various committees and working groups established under the agreement.[19] The Commission does not have authority to bind the Parties by legislative or regulatory measures. The Commission is obligated to meet at least once per year.[20]

Pursuant to Article 2001 of the NAFTA, the Commission shall "consider any other matter that may affect the operation of this Agreement"[21] and "take such other action in the exercise of its functions as the Parties may agree."[22] It is important to note that the Commission's power with respect to "any other matter" is a power to "consider," and not a power to act. "Action" other than as provided for in the text must be agreed upon by the Parties. This is an important limitation on the power of the Commission to self-expand its authority. Article 2204 concerning accession by third countries provides that the terms of accession will be negotiated by the Commission.[23] Nevertheless, accession agreements still must be approved in accordance with the applicable legal procedures of each Party.[24]

The Commission undertakes to establish and oversee a Secretariat, the functions of which are to provide assistance to the Commission, and provide administrative assistance to dispute settlement panels, committees and working

---

[17] NAFTA, art. 2001(1) & (4).
[18] *Id.* art. 2001(4).
[19] *Id.* art. 2001(2).
[20] *Id.* art. 2001(5).
[21] *Id.* art. 2001(2)(e).
[22] *Id.* art. 2001(3)(c).
[23] *Id.* art. 2204(1).
[24] *Id.*

groups.[25] The Secretariat is an administrative institution which is in continuous operation.[26] It is comprised of national sections, each with its own nationally-appointed Secretary.[27] There is no single Secretary-General or comparable official. Each Party funds the operations of its national Secretariat section.[28] The NAFTA establishes a number of working groups and committees, discussed in Chapter Six, to assist in monitoring and facilitating the cooperative implementation of various sectors of the agreement. The NAFTA dispute settlement mechanism, also discussed in Chapter Six, involves the appointment of arbitrators on a case-by-case basis. The NAFTA does not establish a permanent juridical organ comparable to the European Court of Justice. The NAFTA establishes no parliamentary assembly.

The NAFTA Parties are also party to two Supplemental Agreements. These are the North American Agreement on Environmental Cooperation (NAAEC) and North American Agreement on Labor Cooperation (NAALC).[29] The NAAEC establishes a Commission composed of a Council, Secretariat and Joint Public Advisory Committee. The NAAEC Council is composed of cabinet level representatives of the Parties. The NAALC establishes a Commission for Labor Cooperation composed of a Council and Secretariat. The Council is composed of the Labor Ministers of the Parties. The Parties participate equally in the funding of the NAAEC and NAALC Commissions.

The role of the NAAEC Council is to promote cooperation on environmental issues, make recommendations regarding environmental matters and oversee the activities of the NAAEC Secretariat. The NAAEC Council oversees the NAAEC dispute settlement process pursuant to which a panel of private arbitrators determines whether a Party has persistently failed to enforce its environmental laws. This procedure is discussed in detail in Chapter Six. The NAALC Council performs a role comparable to that of the NAAEC Council. The NAALC and its role are also discussed in detail in Chapter Six. In connection with, but not technically part of, the NAFTA, the United States and Mexico entered into an Agreement Concerning the Establishment of a Border Environment Commission and a North American Development Bank

---

[25] *Id.* art. 2002.

[26] *Id.* art. 2002(2).

[27] *Id.*

[28] *Id.*

[29] Canada-Mexico-United States: North American Agreement on Environmental Cooperation [done Sept. 8-14, 1993], 32 I.L.M. 1480 (1993) and Canada-Mexico-United States: North American Agreement on Labor Cooperation [done Sept. 8-14, 1993], 32 I.L.M. 1499 (1993), each entered into force Jan. 1, 1994.

(NADBANK).[30] The capital of the NADBANK will be subscribed to in equal proportions by the United States and Mexico, and it will provide funding for border environmental projects and worker adjustment assistance programs in the United States and Mexico.[31]

III. THE EXTERNAL PERSONALITY OF THE NAFTA

The NAFTA does not expressly confer on the arrangement an international personality. The NAFTA does not expressly grant to its principal institutions the authority to enter into treaties or otherwise to contract in their own names.[32] The fact that the NAFTA does not expressly create an international personality for the arrangement does not preclude such a legal status from developing.[33] However, the situation may be contrasted by way of illustration with that of the European Union. The Treaty on European Union both expressly confers a legal personality on the organization[34] and grants it the power to enter into treaties.[35] The European Union is generally understood to have an international personality.[36]

The NAFTA does not provide for the formulation and conduct of a coordinated external policy. Each Party therefore remains free to conduct its own external trade policy, provided of course that such policy is consistent with its obligations under the agreement. This is an extremely important institutional feature of the NAFTA and one which can fairly confidently be predicted to cause difficulties between its Parties. One might already sense some

---

[30] Mexico-United States: Agreement Concerning the Establishment of a Border Environment Cooperation Commission and a North American Development Bank [done Nov. 16-18, 1993], 32 I.L.M. 1545 (1993), entered into force Jan. 1, 1994

[31] *See, e.g.,* NAFTA Implementation Act, §§ 541-44.

[32] The Parties may confer additional authority on the Commission. It is to be expected that authority will be conferred by the Parties on the Commission and its Secretariat to act in their own names at least in so far as is necessary to conduct routine business.

[33] It may be recalled that the United Nations Organization was recognized by the International Court of Justice to have a legal personality on the international plane on the basis of various provisions in the U.N. Charter which did not expressly confer such a personality. *See* Reparation for Injuries Suffered in the Service of the United Nations, ICJ Advisory Opinion, 1949 I.C.J. 174 (Apr. 11).

[34] Article 210 provides that "The Community shall have legal personality." *See generally,* Eric Stein, *External Relations of the European Community: Structure and Process, in* COLLECTED COURSES OF THE ACADEMY OF EUROPEAN LAW, BK. 1, 115-88, 128-30 (1991).

[35] *See, e.g.,* arts. 113, 114, 228, 238, 229-31 & 237; *see* Stein, *id.* at 132-33.

[36] *See* Stein, *id.* at 129.

dissatisfaction in the U.S. Congress with Mexico's rapid and independent conclusion of free trade agreements with other Latin American countries as the NAFTA entered into force. This action may be perceived to diminish the control which the United States has over the future structure of Western Hemispheric integration and to dilute to some extent the benefits which the United States may obtain from the NAFTA.

The absence in the NAFTA of an express mechanism for the formulation and implementation of a common external policy is a major departure from the structure of the European Union. This departure is important from the standpoint of determining the relationship between the NAFTA and the World Trade Organization. The European Union formulates and conducts a common commercial policy pursuant to Article 113 of the Treaty on European Union.[37] The Council and Commission have exclusive control over the external commercial policy of the EU Member States. The precise boundaries of the common commercial policy are not always easy to determine and there continue to be conflicts between the EU executive authorities and the Member States concerning allocation of competences. Nevertheless, the existence of a mechanism which channels EU external commercial policy into a single voice greatly facilitates its participation qua European Union in the WTO.

As will be discussed in the next Chapter, the European Communities/Union is a party to the WTO Agreement, represents the Member States in the WTO and may vote collectively on behalf of the Member States. There are significant outstanding issues concerning the legal relationship between the EU and its Member States and the other Members of the WTO within the WTO framework. These issues arise out of the lack of full elaboration of the internal EU allocation of competences to its various authorities, and uncertainties concerning the flow of rights and obligations between third countries, on the one hand, and the EU and/or its several Member States, on the other hand.[38] Such issues may be a more or less the inevitable byproduct of the transformation of a group of independent states into a collectively acting regional organization.

The absence of express provisions in the NAFTA establishing a common external commercial policy by no means precludes the Parties from formulating and implementing such a common external policy. The representatives of the Parties to the Commission can certainly discuss mutual interests and agree on

---

[37] *See generally*, Stein, *supra* note 34; and Frederick M. Abbott, *Crosscurrents in European Union External Commercial Relations: The Controversy over the Germany-United States Treaty of Friendship*, 54 ZAöRV __ (1994 forthcoming).

[38] *See generally*, THE EUROPEAN COMMUNITY AND GATT (Meinhard Hilf et al. eds., 1986); Abbott, *Crosscurrents, id.*

a coordinated program of action to be carried out by the Parties. It seems likely that such coordination will take place, the real issue being one of the degree of coordination. There are, however, at least as respects the United States, constitutional limitations with respect to executive action in the field of international commerce which will influence the development of coordinated NAFTA external commercial relations.[39] Article I, section 8 of the U.S. Constitution allocates to Congress the power to regulate commerce with foreign nations. This provision is generally construed to give the Congress primary authority in the field of foreign commercial relations, and the President acts in the external commercial field under broad or specific delegation of authority from the Congress. Therefore, the U.S. representative to the NAFTA Commission could not agree to implement a coordinated program of action unless that agreement was within an appropriate delegation of authority from the Congress. Recall also that the NAFTA expressly gives only to the Parties the authority to expand the powers of the Commission to act. The Commission, at least in theory, may not self-expand its authority to *act* in the field of external commercial relations.

The NAFTA Parties may choose to coordinate their activities with respect to the WTO. Such a coordination must certainly begin as the Parties prepare to present the NAFTA to the WTO/GATT working party formed to review it.[40] The future course of NAFTA intra-WTO politics may prove quite interesting as the Parties pursue both their collective and independent interests. Mexico, for example, is now both an emerging developing country (just admitted to the OECD), and yet party to a close cooperative arrangement with two highly industrialized countries. Issues confronting the WTO are frequently framed in the context of competing North-South, or industrialized-developing country, interests. Mexico may be forced to choose between its First and Third World affiliations in WTO debates. It may be that Mexico's position straddling the North and South will give it the opportunity play an important role as conciliator.

---

[39] *See, e.g.*, Stefan A. Riesenfeld and Frederick M. Abbott, *The Scope of U.S. Senate Control Over the Conclusion and Operation of Treaties*, 67 CHI-KENT L. REV. 571, 637-41 (1991), reprinted in PARLIAMENTARY PARTICIPATION IN THE MAKING AND OPERATION OF TREATIES: A COMPARATIVE STUDY 261 (Stefan A. Riesenfeld and Frederick M. Abbott eds., 1994).

[40] After the WTO comes into force, a second working party in addition to the GATT Article XXIV working party might be formed pursuant to the terms of the GATS agreement. *See* discussion of GATS Article V review procedure, *infra* Chapter Three. Of course there has yet to evolve a WTO practice regarding whether a single RIA with both trade in goods and trade in services components will be subject to a joint GATT/GATS or separate GATT and GATS review processes.

IV. TRADE AND INVESTMENT PROVISIONS

The NAFTA establishes detailed rules governing trade, investment and related matters. It establishes a regulatory framework and dispute settlement procedures. These rules and procedures are decribed and analyzed in detail in Chapters Four, Five and Six. A principal objective of this book is to situate the NAFTA in the framework of the new World Trade Organization. The next Chapter is devoted to a description and analysis of the new WTO and its rules regarding regional integration arrangements (RIAs), so that the detailed provisions of the NAFTA can be understood in this context.

Chapter Three

REGIONAL INTEGRATION ARRANGEMENTS IN THE WTO FRAMEWORK

The World Trade Organization (WTO) succeeds the General Agreement on Tariffs and Trade (GATT) as the international organization principally responsible for the global regulation of trade. The WTO is the result of the Uruguay Round of GATT negotiations which began in 1986 and culminated with approval of a Final Act on December 15, 1993.[1] The agreements embodied in the Final Act were signed by the GATT Contracting Parties and European Communities/Union [hereinafter European Union or EU] on April 15, 1994.[2] The Agreement Establishing the WTO (WTO Agreement) was targeted to enter into force on January 1, 1995.[3]

The WTO Agreement formally constitutes the WTO as an international

---

[1] Final Act Embodying the Results of the Uruguay Round of Multilateral Trade Negotiations, GATT Doc. MTN/FA, 15 Dec. 1993, Special Distribution. Selected portions of this document are published at General Agreement on Tariffs and Trade - Multilateral Trade Negotiations (The Uruguay Round): Final Act Embodying the Results of the Uruguay Round of Trade Negotiations, Dec. 15, 1993, 33 I.L.M. 1 (1993) [hereinafter Final Act]. Due to the late date at which it was agreed to change the name of the new organization from the Multilateral Trade Organization (MTO) to the World Trade Organization, the December 15 document refers throughout to the MTO. All references herein are to the December 15 text and refer to the WTO. The text of the Final Act signed at Marrakesh on April 15, 1994 is found at General Agreement on Tariffs and Trade: Final Act Embodying the Results of the Uruguay Round of Multilateral Trade Negotiations, 1994 BDIEL AD LEXIS 58. *See generally, First Report of the Committee on International Trade Law (ITLC)*, International Law Association, Buenos Aires Conf., Aug. 14-20, 1994 (F.M. Abbott and E.-U. Petersmann, Rapporteurs), and Proceedings of the ILA 66th Conf., Meeting of the ITLC, Reports by John H. Jackson and Frederick M. Abbott, Aug. 16, 1994. As of October 31, 1994, U.S. ratification of the WTO Agreement had not been approved by the U.S. Congress.

[2] The WTO Agreement was signed by the European Communities. However, the organs of the Communities generally refer to the entity which they administer as the European Union, and that convention is adopted in this book. Regarding terminology, *see* European Commission Delegation, Office of Press and Public Affairs, *Post-Maastricht: EC Now Named European Union*, EUR. UNION NEWS, Dec. 13, 1993 (No. 61/93).

[3] January 1, 1995 was established as the target date for entry into force of the agreement. *See* Peter Sutherland, *The World Trade Organization and the Future of the Multilateral Trading System*, GATT PRESS COMMUNIQUÉ, GATT/1634, May 30, 1994, at 2/3.

organization.[4] The WTO Agreement includes among its integral parts applicable to all Members the General Agreement on Tariffs and Trade, and its related interpretative decisions and understandings (collectively referred to as the GATT 1994).[5] The integral agreements applicable to all Members (referred to as the Multilateral Trade Agreements or MTAs) also include the General Agreement on Trade in Services (GATS) and the Agreement on Trade-Related Aspects of Intellectual Property Rights (TRIPS Agreement).[6] The GATS and TRIPS Agreement incorporate important new areas of coverage into the framework of multilateral trade regulation. The WTO Agreement also incorporates an Understanding on Dispute Settlement which works significant changes to the GATT 1947 dispute settlement procedure. These changes are intended to enhance the binding character of WTO dispute settlement.[7] The Uruguay Round negotiations and the new WTO are the subject of an extensive literature.[8]

At the highest level of generality, the WTO establishes the basic framework of the liberal global trading system. It has as its overarching goal the progressive elimination of barriers to the trade of goods and services with a view to encouraging an optimal allocation of global resources. It seeks to accomplish this goal by the establishment of certain fundamental rules, principally; the Most Favored Nation principle, which generally requires that each Member treat all other Members on an equivalent basis, and; the National Treatment principle, which generally prohibits domestic discrimination against imported products, and covered foreign services and service providers.

As the global trading system has become an increasingly complex affair, the necessity of refining general principles into specific rules has become apparent. The lengthy and highly contentious Uruguay Round negotiations testify to the

---

[4] WTO Agreement, art. VIII.

[5] WTO Agreement, art. II:2 and Annex 1A. The original General Agreement on Tariffs and Trade will henceforth be referred to as the GATT 1947. *Id.* art. II:4. *See* Chapter Six, *infra*, regarding legal relationship between GATT 1947 and GATT 1994.

[6] *Id.* Annexes 1B and 1C.

[7] *See* Frederick M. Abbott, *The NAFTA Dispute Settlement System as Prototype for Regional Integration Arrangements*, 4 Y.B. INT'L ENVTL. L. 3, 12, 18-19 (Günther Handl ed., 1994).

[8] *See, e.g.*, JOHN H. JACKSON, THE WORLD TRADING SYSTEM (1989); THE NEW GATT ROUND OF MULTILATERAL TRADE NEGOTIATIONS (Ernst-Ulrich Petersmann & Meinhard Hilf eds., 1988); ROBERT HUDEC, ENFORCING INTERNATIONAL TRADE LAW 357 (1993); and articles on specific topics, *e.g.*, Frederick M. Abbott, *Protecting First World Assets in the Third World: Intellectual Property Negotiations in the GATT Multilateral Framework*, 22 VAND. J. TRANSNAT'L L. 689 (1989); Raymond J. Krommenacker, *Multilateral Services Negotiations: From Interest Lateralism to Reasoned Multilateralism in the Context of Servicization of the Economy*, *id*. THE NEW GATT ROUND, at 455. A negotiating history of the Uruguay Round is reported in I-III THE GATT URUGUAY ROUND: A NEGOTIATING HISTORY (Terence P. Stewart ed., 1993) [hereinafter URUGUAY ROUND: A NEGOTIATING HISTORY].

difficulty in reducing general principles to specific norms. The complete package of WTO agreements provide a lengthy, complex and not always entirely clear set of rules for the conduct of global trade. In this Chapter an attempt is made to describe and analyze the regulation of RIAs within this new framework.

I. RIAs IN THE WTO - TRADE IN GOODS

A. ARTICLE XXIV

The GATT 1947 was tolerant of the formation of RIAs.[9] The GATT 1994 retains that historical tolerance. While an Understanding on the Interpretation of Article XXIV of the GATT 1994 was adopted as a part of the Uruguay Round Final Act,[10] this understanding by and large addresses technical issues that have surfaced in the application of Article XXIV and does not alter the fundamental approach of the GATT to customs unions and free trade areas.

Provided that the members of a prospective RIA notify WTO Members[11] and agree to eliminate tariffs and other restrictive regulations of commerce on "substantially all the trade" in products originating in their territories within a reasonable length of time,[12] they are permitted under Article XXIV of the GATT 1994 to ignore that agreement's Most Favored Nation treatment principle and to grant each other tariff preferences which need not be extended to non-

---

[9] On the specific subject of the GATT RIA exemption, *see* Frederick M. Abbott, *GATT and the European Community: A Formula for Peaceful Coexistence*, 12 MICH. J. INT'L L. 1 (1990); Frederick M. Abbott, *Integration without Institutions, The NAFTA Mutation of the EC Model and the Future of the GATT Regime*, 40 AM. J. COMP. L. 917 (1992); Thomas Cottier, *Die Bedeutung des GATT im Prozess der europäischen Integration*, in EG-RECHT UND SCHWEIZERISCHE RECHTSORDNUNG (O.Jacot-Guillarmod et al. eds., 1990); Kenneth W. Dam, *Regional Economic Arrangements and the GATT: The Legacy of a Misconception*, 30 U. CHI. L. REV. 615 (1963); ROBERT E. HUDEC, THE GATT LEGAL SYSTEM AND WORLD TRADE DIPLOMACY 211-26 (2d ed. 1990); JOHN H. JACKSON, THE WORLD TRADING SYSTEM 141-43 (1989); JOHN H. JACKSON, WORLD TRADE AND THE LAW OF GATT 575-623 (1969) [hereinafter LAW OF GATT]; John H. Jackson, *Reflections on the Implications of the NAFTA for the World Trading System*, 30 COLUM. J. TRANSNAT'L L. 501 (1993).

[10] General Agreement on Tariffs and Trade - Multilateral Trade Negotiations (The Uruguay Round) Agreements on Trade in Goods: Understanding on the Interpretation of Article XXIV of the General Agreement on Tariffs and Trade 1994 [Dec. 15, 1993], 33 I.L.M. 34 (1994) [hereinafter Understanding on Article XXIV].

[11] General Agreement on Tariffs and Trade, *opened for signature* Oct. 30, 1947, 61 Stat. A3, T.I.A.S. No. 1700, 55 U.N.T.S. 187 to be incorporated by WTO Agreement as GATT 1994 [hereinafter GATT 1994 or GATT]. GATT, art. XXIV:7.

[12] *Id.* art. XXIV:5(c) & 8.

RIA members[13] (as well as, in the case of a "customs union" (CU), to form a common tariff wall).[14] The incidence of tariffs and other regulations of commerce affecting non-members of a CU shall not "on the whole" be higher or more restrictive than those which were applicable to them prior to the formation of the CU.[15] Tariffs and other regulations of commerce affecting non-members of a free trade area ("FTA") "shall be no higher or more restrictive" than those existing in the same constituent countries prior to its formation.[16] One survey of Article XXIV working party reports found that constituent countries have contended that from fifty to ninety-five percent trade coverage meets the requirement for RIA elimination of tariffs on "substantially all the trade".[17]

Article XXIV limits not only the raising of individual country (in the case of the FTA) or aggregate (in the case of the CU) tariffs in respect to non-members, but also limits the adoption of more restrictive "other regulations of commerce" in respect to non-members.[18] The meaning of this limitation has become an important subject of debate in respect to changes in rules of origin in the NAFTA context and is discussed further in Chapter Four.

Article XXIV specifies only that tariffs must be substantially eliminated on "products originating in" the constituent territories of an RIA.[19] There is no requirement that goods imported from outside the RIA will benefit from preferential tariff treatment once they have entered the territory of the RIA. The intra-RIA tariff treatment of such goods will be defined by the RIA members. The Treaty on European Union accords to imported goods free circulation within the territory of the EU once the applicable tariff has been paid on goods first entering a Member State.[20] However, the EU might have required that

---

[13] *Id.* art. XXIV:5.

[14] *Id.* art. XXIV:8(a)(ii).

[15] *Id.* art. XXIV:5(a).

[16] *Id.* art. XXIV:5(b).

[17] II URUGUAY ROUND: A NEGOTIATING HISTORY, at 1836.

[18] GATT, art. XXIV:5.

[19] *Id.* art. XXIV:8.

[20] Treaty on European Union, Feb. 7, 1992, arts. 9 & 10, 31 I.L.M. 253 (signed in Maastricht)[hereinafter Union Treaty]. The Union Treaty provides:

Article 9.1. The Community shall be based upon a customs union which shall cover all trade in goods and which shall involve the prohibition between Member States of customs duties on imports and exports and of all charges having equivalent effect, and the adoption of a common customs tariff in their relations with third countries.

Article 9.2. [This provision, *inter alia*,] shall apply to products originating in Member

additional tariffs be paid upon third country goods in the subsequent crossing of Member State borders without violating the terms of Article XXIV. The NAFTA, as will be detailed in Chapter Four, does not accord free circulation to imported goods after tariffs have been paid upon entry into the first Party. The NAFTA establishes strict rules of origin intended to prevent imported third country goods from obtaining preferential tariff treatment within the NAFTA territory. However, the NAFTA attempts to relieve imported goods from the imposition of a tariff in excess of the maximum single tariff of any of the Parties in its duty drawback rules.[21]

An "interim agreement" leading to the formation of a free trade area or customs union must include a plan for its formation within a "reasonable length of time."[22] Since the parties forming customs unions or FTAs typically phase in their preferential tariff reductions over a transition period, the typical CU or FTA will technically be considered an "interim agreement" during this period. The WTO Understanding regarding Article XXIV provides that the aforementioned "reasonable length of time" should "exceed ten years only in exceptional cases"; and that "where Members believe that ten years would be insufficient they shall provide a full explanation to the Council for Trade in Goods of the need for a longer period."[23] However, since Article XXIV requires only that constituent countries eliminate tariffs on "substantially all" the trade between them, it seems reasonable to conclude that an insubstantial portion of inter-constituent tariffs could be eliminated over a longer than ten year period without the provision of a special justification.

One of the principle objectives of the WTO Understanding with regard to Article XXIV is to resolve ambiguity concerning application of the requirement that a customs union's tariffs not "on the whole" be higher than "the general incidence of the duties and regulations of commerce" in the constituent territories prior to its formation.[24] It was not clear from the text of Article

---

States and to products coming from third countries which are in free circulation in Member States.

Article 10.1. Products coming from a third county shall be considered to be in free circulation in a Member State if the import formalities have been complied with and any customs duties or charges having equivalent effect which are payable have been levied in that Member State . . . .

[21] *See* Chapter Four, *infra* text accompanying note 43.
[22] GATT, art. XXIV:5(c).
[23] Understanding on Article XXIV, para. 3.
[24] GATT, art. XXIV:5(a); Understanding on Article XXIV, para. 2.

XXIV what tariff rates would be used to calculate the general incidence of duties since countries bind their duties in GATT schedules but often apply duties which are lower than their bound duties.[25] The Understanding specifies that "applied rates of duty" will be used in the calculation.[26] In addition, Article XXIV does not specify a method for determining the relative weight to be given tariffs applicable to different products. How is it to be determined whether the CU's lowering of duties with respect to one constituent country's imports of oranges will adequately compensate for the raising of duties with respect to another constituent country's imports of apples? The Understanding to Article XXIV establishes a mechanism for making such determinations.[27] The Understanding also permits countries adversely affected by increases in tariff rates, and which have been unable to obtain adequate compensatory adjustments, to withdraw concessions in accordance with other applicable provisions of the GATT 1994.[28]

B. WORKING PARTY REVIEW

Article XXIV provides that the parties to an RIA will notify the Members of the details of their arrangement and that the Members may make recommendations regarding it.[29] The parties to the RIA should not proceed if they are not prepared to modify it in accordance with the recommendations of the Members. As a matter of GATT custom, notifications with respect to RIAs are assigned to "working parties" which prepare reports for consideration by the Members. The GATT Members have never acted to oppose the implementation of an RIA (i.e. an Article XXIV waiver of the general MFN obligation has never been refused).[30] According to the GATT Secretariat, the Members have never made

---

[25] *See* Dam, *supra* note 9.

[26] Understanding on Article XXIV, para. 2.

[27] The Understanding specifies the use of weighted average tariff rates and customs duties collected, based on import statistics of a representative period. However, the technical aspects of the calculation are not specified in the Understanding, which provides that:

> The MTO [WTO] Secretariat shall compute the weighted average tariff rates and customs duties collected in accordance with the methodology used in the assessment of tariff offers in the Uruguay round. *Id.*

[28] *Id.* paras. 4-6.

[29] GATT, art. XXIV:7.

[30] *See* JACKSON, THE WORLD TRADING SYSTEM, *supra* note 9, at 141. The article XXIV

a formal recommendation to the parties to a customs union or free trade area on the basis of Article XXIV procedures.[31]

It is generally recognized that the GATT process for reviewing RIAs is inadequate.[32] Frieder Roessler, Director of the Legal Affairs Division of the GATT Secretariat, has called for the creation of "a review body that could act independently of the initiative of individual contracting parties."[33] Roessler's proposal for an independent review body is intended to address the GATT custom of action by consensus. Under the present system, the parties to an RIA effectively control the outcome of their own review. Roessler has also suggested submitting RIAs to scrutiny under the GATT Trade Policy Review Mechanism.[34]

The WTO Understanding with respect to Article XXIV does not significantly change the system for GATT review of RIAs. However, the Understanding provides that notifications with respect to formation of an RIA "shall be examined by a working party," thereby eliminating the requirement that a Member request the establishment of a working party for each RIA. Also, the Understanding requests periodic reports from RIAs to the Council for Trade in Goods, based on a 1971 Decision of the Members which calls for reports on preferential regional agreements to be made every two years.[35]

The Report of the Working Party on the Free-Trade Agreement between Canada and the United States[36] illustrates the difficulties encountered in the GATT concerning review of RIAs. Although the Report is largely supportive of the Canada-United States FTA (CUSFTA), there nevertheless are a number

---

"waiver" process involves a clearance by inaction as opposed to an affirmative act of approval. Pursuant to Article XXIV:7, a prospective RIA is notified to the Members which study the plan and, if they find it objectionable, make recommendations to the prospective RIA members which are obliged to modify their proposal in order to take advantage of the waiver.

[31] *Article XXIV of the General Agreement, Note by the Secretariat,* GATT Doc. MTN.GNG/NG7/W/13, Aug. 11, 1987, at 10, *cited in* II URUGUAY ROUND: A NEGOTIATING HISTORY, at 1836-37. The author was advised by the GATT Secretariat that in 1994 the first consensus approval of an RIA was reached by a Working Party in respect to the integration arrangement established by the Czech Republic and Slovakia.

[32] *See, e.g.,* Report of the European Parliament External Economic Relations Committee, *infra* Chapter Seven, at 126-27; Japan and India submissions regarding Article XXIV, *cited in* II URUGUAY ROUND: A NEGOTIATING HISTORY, at 1840-41, ns. 97-98.

[33] Frieder Roessler, *The Relationship Between Regional Integration Agreements and the Multilateral Trade Order, in* REGIONAL INTEGRATION AND THE GLOBAL TRADING SYSTEM 311, 323 (Kym Anderson & Richard Blackhurst eds., 1993).

[34] *Id.*

[35] Understanding on Article XXIV, para. 11.

[36] Adopted by the GATT Council, Nov. 12, 1991, *reprinted in* 4 WORLD TRADE MATERIALS 5 (1992).

of serious reservations expressed by various members of the Working Party. For example, the suggestion was made that the CUSFTA rules of origin be examined in the context of whether those rules were more restrictive than those that pertained to third countries prior to formation of the FTA.[37] Reservations were also expressed with respect to the consistency of agricultural snapback provisions with the requirement that duties be eliminated after a reasonable period of time.[38] Considerable concern was expressed with the provisions giving the CUSFTA precedence over the GATT as between Canada and the United States.[39] Yet despite the misgivings, the Working Group was unable to "reach agreed conclusions as to the consistency of the Agreement with the General Agreement" and "considered that it should limit itself to reporting to the Council the views expressed by its members during its discussions."[40]

The WTO/GATT 1994 mechanism for review of RIAs is not designed to permit public choice/social welfare determinations by WTO Members with respect to a prospective RIA. Its criteria are limited to fairly narrow economic considerations, *i.e.* whether or not the RIA members will eliminate substantially all duties and other restrictive regulations of commerce between the constituent territories. Having accepted that RIAs may exist within the WTO framework, the WTO leaves to the constituent members of the RIA wide discretion over the manner in which to put an integration plan into operation.

C. RIAs and WTO Rules

The working party review by no means represents the limit of WTO involvement with respect to the RIA. In the first instance, the individual members of the RIA remain as full Members of the WTO, unless they and the WTO might eventually decide to accept the RIA as a substitute Member. A complete substitution has not taken place to date, although the European Communities/Union will achieve a special concurrent form of membership with its Member States in the new WTO Agreement arrangement.[41] Under the new

---

[37] *Id.* at para. 37.

[38] *Id.* at para. 52. A "snapback" is a provision that permits a trade restriction to be reinstated under specified conditions.

[39] *Id.* at para. 93.

[40] *Id.* at para. 98.

[41] In April of 1994 it was reported by a representative of the European Commission at the Annual Meeting of the American Society of International Law in Washington, D.C., that the Commission had initiated litigation in the European Court of Justice to sort out competences with respect to the

arrangement with respect to the EU, the EU is party to the WTO Agreement (including the various Annexes) and may act on behalf of the Member States.[42] The Member States are also parties to the WTO Agreement. If the EU votes, its vote will be counted as the number of votes equal to the number of Member States.[43] The Member States may also vote individually, in which case the EU will not have a vote.[44] The mechanism for deciding whether the EU or the Member States will vote is an internal EU matter. Outside the special EU context, RIAs are not themselves Members of the WTO and so must be regulated vicariously through their constituent Member States.[45] The WTO Understanding on Interpretation of Article XXIV seeks to make clear that Members will undertake this responsibility by providing that each "shall take reasonable measures as may be available to it to ensure such observance [of the provisions of GATT 1994] by regional and local governments within its territory."[46]

1. Most Favored Nation and National Treatment Derogations

a. The MFN Principle. Article XXIV permits discriminatory preferences with respect to "duties and other regulations of commerce" maintained in each of the constituent territories of an RIA. Though Article XXIV is decidedly vague, this reference appears to be directed at permitting only derogations from the GATT

WTO. The author was subsequently advised that the Commission had asked the ECJ to declare that the Member States were not competent to ratify the WTO Agreement and that the Union was exclusively competent to ratify it. A political compromise was said to be under negotiation. The allocation of competences among the Union and its Member States in respect to the common commercial policy involves a number of complex issues. *See generally,* Frederick M. Abbott, *Crosscurrents in European Union External Commercial Relations: The Controversy over the Germany-United States Treaty of Friendship,* 54 ZaöRV __ (1994 forthcoming) and THE EUROPEAN COMMUNITY AND GATT (Meinhard Hilf et al. eds., 1986). *See* note 2, *supra,* regarding European Communities as legal party to agreement.

[42] Agreement Establishing the World Trade Organization, Dec. 15, 1993, art. XIV:1, 33 I.L.M. 22 (1993) [hereinafter WTO Agreement].
[43] WTO Agreement, *id.* art. IX:1.
[44] *Id.*
[45] GATT, art. XXIV: 1 & 2 permit customs territories to be treated as Members under certain circumstances, but these provisions are not generally applicable to customs unions and free trade areas unless special accession arrangements are made.
[46] Understanding on Article XXIV, para. 13. The Understanding also makes clear that the WTO dispute settlement mechanism may be invoked in regard to the actions of regional authorities, and that Member States will be responsible for taking reasonable steps to ensure observance of dispute settlement rulings involving regional authorities. *Id.* para. 14.

1994 MFN principle, specifically as it requires each WTO Member that grants a tariff benefit to any country to extend immediately and unconditionally the same benefit to all WTO Members.[47] Under this narrow construction, preferential arrangements under Article XXIV are limited to the discriminatory reduction or elimination of intra-RIA tariffs and should not extend to the discriminatory reduction or elimination of non-tariff barriers such as internal sales taxes (*e.g.*, the removal or reduction of taxes only in favor of regionally-produced goods). The latter type of preferential treatment would involve derogation both from the GATT 1994 MFN principle (regarding equivalency of treatment for all WTO Members) and from the GATT 1994 National Treatment principle.

b. The National Treatment Principle. The National Treatment principle is a fundamental tenet of the WTO/GATT. Each Member agrees to treat goods from each other Member on a level comparable to those produced in its own territory for the purposes of internal sale.[48] Article XXIV does not expressly address deviations from the National Treatment principle and there is no good reason to conclude that the drafters of the GATT 1947 and GATT 1994 intended that RIAs be permitted to grant internal preferences to locally produced goods. However, on a purely semantic level, a case for an interpretation of Article XXIV which permits derogation from the National Treatment principle can be made,[49] though such interpretation is by no means widely accepted.[50] The EU

---

[47] Dam and Jackson both refer to article XXIV as providing an exception to the MFN principle in the context of its application to tariffs. *See, e.g.,* Dam, *supra* note 9, at 616; JACKSON, *supra* note 30, at 141. Hudec's discussion of article XXIV is couched in terms of "discrimination," but also focuses on the historic use of article XXIV to justify preferential tariff arrangements (including the EC's controversial variable levies). HUDEC, THE GATT LEGAL SYSTEM, *supra* note 9.

When Dam wrote his analysis of article XXIV in 1963, tariff barriers and quotas were considered the most problematic barriers to international trade. Dam wrote:

> While many internal policies and practices both in importing and exporting countries may create other kinds of divergences between prices paid by consumers and costs incurred by producers -- monopolies, cartels and local direct and indirect taxes, for example -- the primary international barriers to optimization of allocation of world resources are tariffs and quantitative restrictions.

Dam, *supra* note 9, at 624.

[48] GATT, art. III.

[49] Since the article XXIV waiver refers explicitly to "other regulations of commerce," it might be construed to refer to the National Treatment principle involving, for example, tax regulations. In his 1969 treatise, Jackson reported one instance in which the EC argued that article XXIV:5(a) of the General Agreement permitted it to impose common quotas for balance of payments purposes when the individual Member States of the EC could not each justify a quota because of the

has from time to time adopted and been challenged for adopting regional internal discriminations with respect to locally produced goods.[51]

II. RIAs AND TRADE IN SERVICES

The regulation of trade in services is a more complex matter than the regulation of trade in goods. Because services are routinely provided by persons "at the site," they are generally not subject to border measures such as tariffs (although

---

reference to "other regulations." Most members of the GATT group studying the question objected to this interpretation, arguing, according to Jackson, "that this term ['regulations'] ... was meant to apply to such things as customs procedures, grading and marketing requirements, and similar routine controls." LAW OF GATT, *supra* note 9, at 616-17.

Another semantic approach to the suggestion that the Article XXIV waiver applies to National Treatment would note that Article I:1 of the General Agreement, in addressing the matters as to which MFN treatment must be extended (*e.g.*, "customs duties and charges"), requires that "all matters referred to in paragraphs 2 and 4 of Article III" be extended on an unconditional MFN basis. Article III establishes the National Treatment principle, and paragraphs 2 and 4 refer to internal taxes and all other regulations affecting internal sale, respectively. It might therefore be argued that an RIA exemption from the MFN principle includes at least a limited exemption from the National Treatment principle, since the MFN provision of the General Agreement operates to extend National Treatment on an MFN basis. However, this argument is not persuasive since, among other reasons, Article XXIV does not expressly refer to exemption from Article I:1, but instead to the preferential elimination of duties and other regulations of commerce.

[50] This is not to say that there is absolutely no scholarly support for the proposition that Article XXIV permits derogations from provisions of the GATT other than the MFN principle as it applies to tariffs and related charges and regulations. Perhaps some support for a more expansive view of the Article XXIV waiver can be gleaned from this passage by Petersmann in which he states:

> Some of these 'prohibitive' rules [of the GATT] (including rules prescribing non-discrimination and national treatment) are subject to exceptions which reserve a margin of discretion (*e.g.*, Art. XII: balance of payments restrictions; Art. XXI: security exceptions; Art. XXIV: free-trade areas and customs unions); hence, the invocation of such an exception clause may have the effect of suspending the direct applicability of the prohibitive rule or of reducing its directly applicable content to a certain normative core.

Ernst-Ulrich Petersmann, *The EEC as a GATT Member - Legal Conflicts between GATT Law and European Community Law, in* THE EUROPEAN COMMUNITY AND GATT 49 (Meinhard Hilf et al. eds., 1986).

[51] Petersmann, *id.* at 49-50, discusses a number of GATT dispute settlement proceedings involving claims that the EU violated "prohibitive" GATT rules, including the National Treatment principle. In a case involving a complaint by the United States regarding an alleged violation of Article III (national treatment), the European Court of Justice declared the complained-of discriminatory internal regulations null and void prior to a GATT Council ruling that the EU had violated Article III. When Portugal acceded to the EU in 1986, the United States imposed increased duties on EU products alleging, *inter alia*, the regulations reserving parts of Portugal's agricultural imports to Member States violated the EU's GATT obligations. *See* Judith H. Bello & Alan F. Holmer, *Significant Recent Developments in Section 301 Unfair Trade Cases*, 21 INT'L L. 211, 216-218 (1987). The parties eventually reached a settlement in this matter.

there are border measures affecting services, such as employee visa requirements). External service providers are typically regulated (and discriminated against) both on a national and RIA level by internal regulations such as licensing requirements which establish, either expressly or through their operational effect, different standards of treatment for local (or "national") and foreign (or non-RIA member country) service providers. The trade regulation of "foreign" service providers, then, occurs not necessarily (or even generally) at an RIA's external border, but rather internally where rules and regulations may be either expressly or operationally discriminatory.[52] A local service provider licensing requirement, in order to discriminate against a foreign service provider, need not expressly preclude the foreign service provider from operating locally if such licensing requirement provides, for example, that the provider must possess certain local academic credentials which cannot reasonably be obtained by a person seeking to enter the market (and which are not a reasonable requirement for the license). Insurance and banking enterprises might be discriminatorily impaired from providing services across borders as a result of disparate capital or reserve requirements which are arbitrary or unjustified. Thus, trade restrictions based on nationality may be disguised in the form of licensing or other regulatory requirements which do not expressly contain reference to nationality. To the extent that such regulatory requirements are arbitrary or unjustified, they are the equivalent, from a trade regulation standpoint, of denial of National Treatment.

A GATT Panel Report involving a claim by the EU against the United States, arising out of the discriminatory impact of section 337 of the Tariff Act of 1930, makes clear that compliance with the National Treatment principle is

---

[52] If foreign services (and service providers) were regulated/dutied by individual countries or RIAs only when they literally crossed borders, much foreign or external trade would go unregulated because it would in fact be provided locally. In the services context, if differential treatment is to be applied to domestic and foreign providers, it will to some extent be based (expressly or by operational effect) on the nationality of the service provider, and any such differential will involve the National Treatment principle.

To illustrate, an accounting firm in the United States can provide its services to a manufacturing entity in France in a number of ways. For example, it may respond to trans-Atlantic telephone calls, or it may open an office in France. If it establishes an office in France, the French and the EU can either treat the French office just like any French national's office and therefore not discriminate, or they can impose regulations on the office based on its American (or foreign) character. If they choose to treat the office like any French national's office, they have applied the National Treatment principle. If they choose to have special and differential licensing requirements for the office that create an unjustifiable obstacle to the provision of services by the U.S. firm, they have derogated from the National Treatment principle.

not to be confined by reference to the language of rules or regulations. An inquiry into the application (or potential application) of the rules or regulations is appropriate.[53] An analysis of legal rules should not be confined to instances of their application, but should take into account their "potential impact" as well.[54] This conclusion applies both to individual trading countries and RIAs.[55]

Because of the disparate ways in which trade in goods and trade in services are regulated, the new WTO General Agreement on Trade in Services includes an important provision regarding RIA services liberalization measures which is significantly different than GATT 1994 Article XXIV and its treatment of RIA trade in goods.

A. THE GENERAL AGREEMENT ON TRADE IN SERVICES

The new WTO General Agreement on Trade in Services (GATS) establishes a

---

[53] *United States - Section 337 of the Tariff Act of 1930, Report by the Panel*, GATT Doc. L/6439, at 52, para 5.11 (Jan. 16 1989), adopted by GATT Council, Nov. 7, 1989), *reprinted in* 2 WORLD TRADE MATERIALS 5 (1990) [hereinafter GATT Section 337 Panel Report].

[54] *Id.* at 53, para. 5.13.

[55] In an article published in 1990, I suggested a mechanism by which CUs and FTAs would be permitted to adopt service discriminations in favor of regional-national providers only when "necessary" to the formation or maintenance of the CU or FTA, and only for a limited time. "Necessary" in this regard would mean indispensable. See Abbott, *GATT and the European Community*, *supra* note 9, at 29-38. In fact, there are a number of existing GATT provisions in which the concept of necessity plays an important or controlling role -- *e.g.*, Article XI and Article XX -- and the meaning of the concept of necessity has recently been the subject of three important GATT panel reports.

In the GATT Section 337 Panel Report, the panel considered the meaning of "necessary" in the context of whether certain measures taken pursuant to a GATT exemption for the adoption of measures "necessary" for the protection of intellectual property rights under article XX(d) were justified. The panel said:

> a contracting party cannot justify a measure inconsistent with other GATT provisions as "necessary" in terms of Article XX(d) if an alternative measure which it could reasonably be expected to employ and which is not inconsistent with other GATT provisions is available to it. By the same token, in cases where a measure consistent with other GATT provisions is not reasonably available, a contracting party is bound to use, among the measures reasonably available to it, that which entails the least degree of inconsistency with other GATT provisions (*id.* at para. 5.26).

See also, the *Thai Cigarette* report and Report of the Panel, *United States - Restrictions on Imports of Tuna*, GATT Doc. DS21/R, Sept. 3, 1991, action to bring before Council deferred, *reprinted in* 3 WORLD TRADE MATERIALS 20 (1992), which evaluates whether certain U.S. legislation restricting imports of tuna to protect dolphins is "necessary" within the meaning of GATT article XX(b). *See* Frederick M. Abbott, *International Trade Rules, World Market Conditions and Environmental Effects*, 2 Y.B. INT'L ENVTL. L. 227, 230 (Günther Handl ed., 1992).

generally applicable set of rules with respect to Member services measures, and separate rules with respect to sectors in which Members have made market access commitments. The most important general commitment of each Member is to provide most favored nation treatment to other Members in regard to all services sectors,[56] provided, however, that Members are permitted to maintain measures inconsistent with the MFN requirement if such measures are listed in a GATS annex.[57] Other generally applicable rules include those relating to transparency (including notification),[58] domestic regulation procedures, recognition and emergency safeguards.[59] The general MFN provision establishes that each Member must treat the service providers of each other Member in an equivalent manner, but it does not require that each Member treat any (and all) other Member's service providers on the same basis as it treats its own. Members are entitled to maintain internal services regimes that discriminate against foreign service providers.

Non-discriminatory access to the internal services market of a Member is only provided by means of a specific market access commitment of the Member in a particular sector. Each Member maintains a schedule of market access commitments which sets out with respect to sectors in which commitments are made:

(a) terms, limitations and conditions on market access;
(b) conditions and qualifications of national treatment;
(c) undertakings relating to additional commitments;
(d) where appropriate the time-frame for implementation of such commitments; and
(e) date of entry into force of such commitments.[60]

Members agree to provide treatment no less favorable than that set out in their schedules, and with respect to each sector agree to eliminate a listed set of discriminatory restrictions.[61] Members may elect to eliminate discrimination with respect to some forms of service supply and not others;[62] although the financial services annex, for example, imposes specific requirements regarding

---

[56] General Agreement on Tariffs and Trade - Multilateral Trade Negotiations (The Uruguay Round): General Agreement on Trade in Services, Dec. 15, 1993, 33 I.L.M. 48 (1993) [hereinafter GATS] art. II:1.

[57] *Id.* at art. II:2.

[58] "Transparency" generally refers to the accessibility and clarity of trade-related measures.

[59] *Id.* arts. III, VI, VII & X.

[60] *Id.* art. XX:1.

[61] *Id.* art. XVI.

[62] *Cf.* art. XVI, n. 9.

modes of supply.[63] Each Member commits to according national treatment to service suppliers of other Members in respect of covered sectors, but this is subject to conditions and qualifications set out in the granting Member's schedule of market access commitments.[64] Thus with respect to each covered sector each Member commits both to providing the minimum standard of treatment set forth in its schedule and to providing treatment no less favorable than that accorded its own nationals, subject to specified qualifications.

B. GATS AND ECONOMIC INTEGRATION - ARTICLE V

1. Substantive Standards

As discussed earlier, GATT 1994 Article XXIV permits the Members of an RIA to avoid application of the MFN principle with respect to trade in goods. Thus the Members of an RIA may grant tariff preferences to each other without extending those preferences to third countries. The GATT Article XXIV waiver does not address trade in services. Since the nature of the regional integration arrangement is to establish preferences in favor of regional enterprises, the issue naturally arises whether RIAs may also establish preferences in favor of regional service providers under the new GATS regime.[65]

Consider, first, the way in which RIAs operate with respect to services. Before an RIA is formed, each of its constituent countries maintains its own rules applicable to service providers. Such rules may discriminate in favor of local (national) service providers. An RIA might begin the integration process by requiring each constituent country to provide MFN treatment to service providers of all constituent countries, without requiring that service providers of all constituent countries be accorded national treatment. This might result in a three tier system in which each RIA constituent country afforded its best treatment to local providers, its second best treatment to other RIA constituent country providers, and its third tier of treatment to service providers from outside the RIA. In such a circumstance, the failure of an RIA constituent member to provide MFN treatment to non-RIA member service providers would

---

[63] The Financial Services Annex requires that a right of establishment be included within the market access commitment. See note 77 *infra*.

[64] GATS, Art. XVII. This may involve either formally identical or operationally equivalent treatment. *Id.* at paras. 2 & 3.

[65] This is a question which the author addressed at some length in Abbott, *GATT and the European Community*, *supra* note 9, at 16-17 (1990).

be significant because it would place the non-RIA members' providers on a third tier below RIA constituent (but non-local) members.

However, in order to facilitate intra-regional trade, the RIA is likely to require each constituent country to treat the service providers of other constituent countries on the same basis as its own, *i.e.* to extend national treatment to them.[66] This is generally the case, for example, with respect to the services regimes of the EU and NAFTA. In such cases the distinction between MFN treatment and national treatment will collapse. The constituent countries will agree to provide national treatment to service providers of each other's territory. An RIA member will not likely treat service providers of other RIA members more favorably than it treats its own service providers, so that most favored nation treatment and national treatment will have the same meaning. Because the distinction between MFN and national treatment collapses, if an RIA member in this context chooses to discriminate against third country service providers, the discrimination will encompass both denial of MFN treatment and denial of national treatment.[67]

If an RIA achieves the status of a unitary entity from a trade standpoint, that is, if the individual identities of the constituent states merge into a single RIA personality, then the importance of conceptually distinguishing between MFN and national treatment reemerges. If the unitary RIA adopts services regulations applicable throughout its territory, this will in essence become the national treatment of the RIA. At this point, a service provider from outside the RIA that enjoys MFN treatment will be treated as well as any other service provider from outside the RIA. However, that service provider will not be assured of treatment equivalent to that of service providers from within the RIA unless it receives national treatment. If it is accorded national treatment, then MFN treatment will be superfluous, except in the unlikely case that the RIA chooses to treat at least some third country service providers more favorably than services providers established within its territory.

The new GATS provision permitting special and differential treatment of

---

[66] It is to be expected that each constituent country also will be required to treat all constituent countries within the RIA at least as well as well as any non-constituent country, *i.e.* that MFN treatment with respect to services will also be extended. MFN coverage in this context is likely to be superfluous, however, since it seems unlikely that an RIA member would decide to give a third country's service providers treatment more favorable than that it gives to its own nationals.

[67] If MFN treatment is denied without denying national treatment, then third country service providers will enjoy the same treatment as local service providers, which will likely be the most favorable accorded to anyone. Likewise, if national treatment is denied, but MFN treatment is accorded, then third country service providers will be treated as well as service providers from elsewhere within the RIA, and therefore still enjoy national treatment.

RIA services sectors avoids these conceptual difficulties. Rather than referring to an RIA exemption from providing national or MFN treatment, it "does not prevent Members from being a party to or entering into an agreement liberalizing trade in services between or among the parties to such an agreement," provided that certain conditions are met.[68] First, the liberalizing agreements must have "substantial sectoral coverage"[69] and provide for the "absence or elimination of substantially all discrimination," within the meaning of GATS Article XVII concerning national treatment, with respect to the covered sectors, either immediately or on the basis of a "reasonable time frame."[70] The parties to the liberalizing agreement "shall not in respect of any Member outside the agreement raise the overall level of barriers to trade in services within the respective sectors or sub-sectors compared to the level applicable prior to such an agreement."[71] Third country service providers which are established within the RIA territory (meeting an "engaged in substantive business operations in the territory" test) must receive the preferential treatment established under the agreement.[72]

GATS Article V seems intended to establish objective criteria for the approval of a preferential services arrangement within the overall GATS structure, though, as with Article XXIV of the GATT 1994 with respect to trade in goods, the objective nature of the criteria is perhaps illusory. For example, substantial sectoral coverage might refer to a limited number of sectors.[73] The requirement that "substantially all discrimination" be eliminated in the covered sectors or subsectors is cross-referenced to GATS Article XVII that defines National Treatment for GATS purposes. Article XVII permits a Member to derogate from strict National Treatment of other Members' nationals in respect

---

[68] GATS, art. V:1.

[69] The following interpretative note is appended to "substantial sectoral coverage": "This condition is understood in terms of number of sectors, volume of trade affected and modes of supply. In order to meet this condition, agreements should not provide for the *a priori* exclusion of any mode of supply." *Id.* art. V:1(a), n. 1.

[70] *Id.* art. V:1.

[71] *Id.* art. V:4. The Dunkel Draft GATS proposal permitted discrimination against third country service providers not established within the territory of the parties prior to the agreement if the agreement did not provide for "common treatment to third countries with respect to the sector or sub-sector concerned." *Draft Final Act Embodying the Results of the Uruguay Round of Multilateral Trade Negotiations,* GATT Doc. MTN.TNC/W/FA, Dec. 20, 1991, Annex II, art. V:6(b)(ii) [hereinafter Dunkel Draft]. This provision was eliminated in the final text.

[72] *Id.* art. VI.

[73] While the interpretative note, *see supra* note 69, indicates that "substantial" refers, *inter alia*, to the number of sectors, this is one of three expressly enumerated factors, and would not appear to preclude a finding that an agreement covering two sectors satisfies the requirement.

to sectors in which market access commitments are made, to the extent of "any conditions and qualifications" set out in its schedule of market access commitments. This raises the question whether parties to an agreement liberalizing trade in services among themselves may condition or qualify their intra-RIA liberalization commitments to the extent of any such conditions or qualifications set out in constituent member GATS market access schedules. Answering this question will require resolution of an Article V textual ambiguity. The condition that the "overall level" of services barriers not be raised over pre-agreement levels has a solid ring, but services barriers have proven exceedingly difficult to quantify,[74] and determining the overall level of barriers may prove difficult. Finally, because Article V, perhaps unavoidably, does not specify what kinds of liberalizing (*i.e.* discriminatory) arrangements the parties may reach, there is a considerably greater element of subjectivity to the potential application of this provision than may be immediately apparent.

a. The Established Enterprise Exception. The Dunkel Draft of GATS Article V permitted member parties to a services liberalization agreement to discriminate against newly established third country owned enterprises, provided that the members to the liberalizing agreement treated third country service providers from different countries on different bases.[75] The final GATS Article V requires that established entities receive the favorable treatment provided for by the liberalization agreement regardless of the country of ownership (which must, however, be a GATS Member).[76] This provision is of paramount importance in evaluating the potential discriminatory impact of GATS Article V. Although the GATS may not assure third country service providers of establishment

---

[74] *See* Abbott, *GATT and the European Community, supra* note 9, at 26-27.

[75] Dunkel Draft, art. V:6(b)(ii). This provision was rather ambiguous. Since it was deleted in the final agreement, this ambiguity will not be explored here. *See* Abbott, *Integration without Institutions*, *supra* note 9, at 925.

[76] GATS, art. V:6, provides:

A service supplier of any other Member that is a juridical person constituted under the laws of a party to an agreement referred to in paragraph 1 shall be entitled to treatment granted under such agreement, provided that it engages in substantive business operations in the territory of the parties to such agreement.

The engaged in substantive business operations requirement is typical of various tests in the commercial environment with respect to determining the treatment of a business as a resident entity and is unlikely to lead to appreciable interpretative difficulties. *See* discussion in Frederick M. Abbott, *NAFTA and the Future of United States-European Community Trade Relations: The Consequences of Asymmetry in an Emerging Era of Regionalism,* 16 HASTINGS INT'L & COMP. L. REV. 489, 515 (1993).

rights,[77] such rights are often accorded by bilateral commercial treaties, and may be part of GATS market access commitments. If third country service providers are guaranteed equal treatment by the expedient of establishment in an RIA, then this effectively precludes RIA discrimination in many circumstances. It may well be that the right to escape discrimination by establishment will benefit more highly capitalized business enterprises to a greater extent than less well capitalized enterprises since maintaining incorporated foreign entities which engage in substantive business can be an expensive undertaking.

b. The Review Procedure. The relationship of the review process established with respect to GATS Article V and the process established under GATT 1994 Article XXIV is quite interesting. In the first place, the invocation of GATS Article V is not limited to parties to an existing RIA which has undergone the Article XXIV review process.[78] The fact that parties to a services liberalization agreement are parties to "a wider process of economic integration or trade liberalization" may be taken into account when the extent of sectoral elimination of services barriers is evaluated.[79] It is possible that an RIA (perhaps a "services union" or "regional services arrangement") might be created solely on the basis of a more liberalized internal services regime.

Parties to a new services liberalizing agreement (or any enlargement or significant modification thereto) must notify the agreement to the new Council

---

[77] In most cases the grant of such rights is optional. However, the Financial Services Annex requires that such rights be granted as part of a market access commitment. Article XVI:1 of GATS provides:

> With respect to market access through the modes of supply specified in Article I, each Member shall accord services and services suppliers of any Member treatment no less favourable than that provided for under the terms, limitations and conditions agreed and specified in its schedule.

A footnote to this paragraph states that if a Member has agreed to permit the supply of service through the establishment of a commercial presence, then it will allow related transfers of capital into its territory. This footnote by inference confirms that a member may choose *not* to permit the supply of a service through the granting of establishment rights.

Note, however, that with respect to the Financial Services sector, each Member making a market access commitment in that sector will generally be obligated to permit financial service suppliers of other Members to establish a commercial presence in their territory. *See* General Agreement on Tariffs and Trade - Multilateral Trade Negotiations (the Uruguay Round): Ministerial Decisions and Declarations, Dec. 15, 1993, Understanding on Commitments in Financial Services, 33 I.L.M. 136, 145, 147, para. 5 (1994).

[78] GATS, art. V:1 & 2.

[79] *Id.* art. V:2.

on Trade in Services.[80] They are to make information available to the Council as requested by it. The Council may establish, but is not obligated to establish, a working party to examine the agreement or modification and report to the Council on consistency with GATS Article V.[81] Parties whose arrangements are to be implemented over a reasonable time frame must report to the Council periodically on its implementation, and the Council may establish a working party to examine such reports.[82] Based upon any of the foregoing working party reports, "the Council may make recommendations to the parties as it deems appropriate."[83] Oddly enough, and it contrast to Article XXIV, the provisions of GATS Article V which provide for review by the Council for Trade in Services do not expressly prohibit the parties to a liberalization agreement from implementing it over the contrary recommendation of the Council.[84] This interesting lacuna is perhaps considered to be filled by the GATS provisions with respect to dispute settlement, which generally permit adversely affected Members of GATS to bring complaints to the WTO Dispute Settlement Body. In view of the fact that GATT Members appear never to have made a formal recommendation to the parties to a CU or FTA under the Article XXIV review procedure, and that GATT Members have never denied an Article XXIV waiver to a prospective RIA, the fact that Council on Services recommendations technically may not obstruct the implementation of a services liberalization agreement seems of minor practical consequence. Perhaps this demonstrates that the Members of the WTO consider the potential adverse effects of services liberalization agreements a less serious threat than tariff-based discriminatory RIA regimes.

The ability of the WTO to keep RIA service liberalization agreements within tolerable limits will be a major test of the organization. The consistency of the NAFTA services regime with Article V of GATS is considered in Chapter Five.

III. THE INTERFACE OF RIA AND WTO REGULATORY SYSTEMS

The rule system of the WTO is principally addressed to individual countries generally referred to in the agreement as "Members". The GATT 1994 carries

---

[80] *Id*. art. V:7(a).
[81] *Id*.
[82] *Id*. art. V:7(b).
[83] *Id*. art. V:7(c).
[84] *Compare* GATT, art. XXIV:7(b).

forward the existing text of the GATT General Agreement (GATT 1947) and accompany interpretative understandings and related decisions (as the GATT 1994).[85] The GATT 1994 agreement is principally applicable to trade in goods. The fundamental rules of international trade embodied in the GATT 1994 are well known, including: (1) the most favored nation treatment principle; (2) the national treatment principle; (3) tariffs as the accepted means of trade protection; (4) prohibition of quotas; (5) reciprocity, and; (6) special and differential treatment for developing countries.[86] Of course, there are also rules relating to dumping and subsidization, safeguard measures and dispute settlement. All of these general rules of the GATT 1994 are at least indirectly applicable to RIAs through the responsibility of their constituent member countries. This constituent member responsibility, as discussed above in section I.C of this chapter, is confirmed in the Understanding regarding Article XXIV.

Since its inception, the GATT has undergone a continual process of refining its rules. The principal set of refinements was adopted at the conclusion of the Tokyo Round in 1979 in the form principally of a series of codes applicable only to the parties which accepted them (primarily the OECD countries). These codes covered dumping and subsidies, government procurement, technical standards, customs valuation and a number of other areas. Among the major goals of the GATT Uruguay Round was to further refine these codes or agreements, as well as to extend their application to a far wider group of parties. In the latter regard the Uruguay Round succeeded beyond expectations by extending the coverage of almost all of these supplementary agreements to all Members of the WTO.

As with the GATT 1994, the obligation of RIAs to comply with the rules of the supplementary agreements (referred to as "Multilateral Trade Agreements")[hereinafter MTAs], is principally based on the obligations of the constituent Members of the RIA.[87] However, the application of MTA rules to RIAs may become more direct as the RIA assumes control over constituent member regulatory activities. The regional bodies of the European Union, for

---

[85] WTO Agreement, art. XIV:1.

[86] *See* OLIVIER LONG, LAW AND ITS LIMITATIONS IN THE GATT MULTILATERAL TRADING SYSTEM (1987). Obviously this is but a summary recitation of the fundamental principles. The GATT library in Geneva is filled with treatises concerning the various provisions and intricacies of the GATT.

[87] The Agreement on Technical Barriers to Trade, Final Act, *supra* note 1, at MTN/FA II-AIA-6, specifically requires Members to take reasonable measures to assure that regional systems comply with provisions regarding conformity assessment. TBT Agreement, art. 9.2. It also requires that Members rely on regional conformity assessment systems only to the extent they are compatible with relevant provisions of the TBT Agreement. *Id.* art 9.3.

example, have assumed significant control over regulatory structures within the Member States of the EU. Moreover, in the particular case of the EU, the RIA is a Member of the WTO and should be understood to have accepted direct responsibility for compliance with both GATT 1994 and MTA rules. The Member States of the EU will also be parties to the WTO, and so share responsibility with the RIA governmental bodies for compliance with the rules.

At present, the EU situation is unique within the WTO structure as the EU is the only RIA which as an international person is accorded membership in the WTO. The NAFTA does not have an international legal personality, at least insofar as such a personality might be expressly established by its charter. In addition, unlike the EU, the NAFTA does not have central regional institutions with authority to exercise regulatory control within its constituent country parties.[88] To the extent that the NAFTA regional bodies may assume responsibility for regulatory matters, they will be obliged to observe the provisions of the WTO agreement by virtue of the responsibility of the constituent countries.

The mechanism for determining the hierarchy of norms between the RIA and the WTO is of great importance. The European Court of Justice has held that the EU is bound by the GATT,[89] but it has never overturned a Union regulation on the ground that such regulation is incompatible with GATT rules.[90]

In Article 103 of the NAFTA, the Parties affirm their existing GATT rights and obligations to each other,[91] but provide that:

> In the event of any inconsistency between this Agreement and other such agreements [including the GATT], this Agreement shall prevail to the extent of the inconsistency, except as otherwise provided in this Agreement.[92]

As discussed in Chapters Two and Six, the extent to which the Article 103 rule of priority applies to the WTO and GATT 1994 remains to be authoritatively determined. The potential conflict between WTO and NAFTA rules is manifestly of concern with respect to the compatible and complementary operation of the two rule systems. These concerns are explored in Chapter Six,

---

[88] *See* discussion of NAFTA institutional structure, *supra* Chapter Two and *infra* Chapter Six.

[89] International Fruit Co. v. Produktschap voor Groenten en Fruit, 1972 E.C.R. 1219.

[90] *See* Ernst-Ulrich Petersmann, *National Constitutions and International Economic Law*, in NATIONAL CONSTITUTIONS AND INTERNATIONAL ECONOMIC LAW (Meinhard Hilf & Ernst-Ulrich Petersmann eds., 1993), at 3, 20-22. A case in which the Court has been asked to do so by a Member State (the German challenge in the Banana case) is before it in mid-1994.

[91] NAFTA, art. 103(1).

[92] *Id.* art. 103(2).

infra. In Chapter Four, the extent to which the regulatory rules of the NAFTA may be inconsistent with the rules of the WTO is examined.

IV. RIAS AND TRADE-RELATED INVESTMENT MEASURES (TRIMS)

An Agreement on Trade-Related Investment Measures (TRIMS) is an MTA accepted by all Members of the WTO. The TRIMS agreement affirms the applicability of Articles III and XI of the GATT 1994 to Members. It breaks new ground principally by reference to an illustrative list of practices that are inconsistent with these provisions.[93] The illustrative list refers to local content requirements, export balancing requirements and exchange control restrictions.[94] Members are required to notify the WTO Council on Goods of any measures inconsistent with the TRIMS Agreement and to phase such measures out during a transitional period.[95] The transition period is two years for developed Members, five years for developing Members and seven years for least developed Members.[96] There is no provision of the TRIMS Agreement directed specifically to RIAs. Therefore, it is generally (*i.e.* except in the case of the EU) the responsibility of the individual constituent members of the RIA to assure that inconsistent measures are eliminated. The TRIMS Agreement is noteworthy with respect to NAFTA because it requires the elimination by Mexico of various local content and export balancing requirements which might have been maintained with respect to non-NAFTA Parties.[97]

V. THE INTERFACE OF RIA AND WTO DISPUTE RESOLUTION SYSTEMS

Article XXIII of GATT 1947 established a mechanism for the settlement of disputes between Contracting Parties. This broad provision was supplemented by customary practice which eventually was codified in an Understanding with

---

[93] WTO Agreement on Trade-Related Investment Measures, art. 2 and Annex.
[94] *Id.* Annex.
[95] *Id.* art. 5.
[96] *Id.* art. 5(2).
[97] *But see, infra* Chapter Seven, discussion of new Mexican Law on Foreign Investment which may have the effect of eliminating these restrictive provisions as to all foreign investors.

Chapter Three

respect to Dispute Settlement.[98] The WTO Agreement includes a new Understanding on Rules and Procedures Governing the Settlement of Disputes which substantially modifies prior GATT customs and rules with respect to the structure of the dispute settlement institution (principally by addition of a standing appellate body), the procedure by which the decisions of dispute settlement panels are adopted (moving from a consensual to quasi-automatic adoption procedure), and enhancing surveillance of implementation of decisions by WTO Members.[99]

Of course, each WTO Member maintains its own judicial system that performs dispute settlement functions, and national courts may interpret and apply the WTO Agreement to the extent it is either considered directly applicable or is transformed into national law by legislative act. It is certainly possible that a national court might interpret the WTO Agreement differently than the WTO Dispute Settlement Body (DSB); though, in respect to the same dispute, the decision of the DSB should be considered to authoritatively interpret the WTO charter since it is the DSB which is empowered by the charter to interpret and apply the agreement.[100] National courts also interpret and apply the domestic trade law of the country in which they operate, and that trade law may or may not be consistent with WTO law.

RIAs may also establish their own mechanisms for resolving disputes concerning interpretation of their charter document or its application by the constituent countries. Both the European Union and the NAFTA establish dispute settlement bodies, although the European Court of Justice and NAFTA arbitration panels differ markedly in the scope of their powers of review and the enforceability of their decisions. In the course of performing their functions, regional dispute settlement institutions may interpret and apply the WTO Agreement. It is possible that the decision of a regional dispute settlement institution with respect to interpretation of the WTO Agreement would differ from the interpretation of the WTO Dispute Settlement Body; but, as is the case with respect to national courts, the DSB's interpretation should be considered

---

[98] 1979 Understanding on Dispute Settlement, BISD 265/210, *reprinted in*, and *see generally* PIERRE PESCATORE ET AL., HANDBOOK OF GATT DISPUTE SETTLEMENT (1992).

[99] Understanding on Rules and Procedures Governing the Settlement of Disputes, Dec. 15, 1993, 33 I.L.M. 114 (1994).

[100] The GATT dispute settlement panel in the U.S. Section 337 case ruled that U.S. legislation was inconsistent with GATT law after a U.S. federal appellate court had held that the legislation did not violate the national treatment principle, although in that case the national treatment clause which the court interpreted was found in a bilateral trade treaty between the United States and the Netherlands. GATT Section 337 Panel Report, note 53, *supra*.

authoritative.[101]

The potential conflict between decisions of regional dispute settlement institutions and the WTO DSB with respect to interpretation of the WTO Agreement is perhaps of relatively minor consequence since it seems clear that the WTO ultimately is responsible for interpreting its own rules. The conflict which may arise when a regional dispute settlement institution applies RIA rules and the WTO DSB applies WTO rules with respect to the same dispute or subject matter may be more serious because both decisions will likely be most authoritative within the sphere of competence of the respective dispute settlement institution. A national government may find itself asked or directed to comply with two different decisions arising out of the same subject matter. This raises a number of concerns.

Both the WTO DSB and a regional dispute settlement body may find their authority eroded if a decision is ignored. The national government may be subject to sanction (*e.g.*, withdrawal of trade concessions) by the organization whose rules it disobeys. Interest groups may find that one dispute settlement decision is more compatible with their position than the other, and seek to manipulate the national political process to support the favored position. This may give rise to political pressure to more generally disapply the rules of the non-favored organization, and ultimately undermine the vitality of one or the other system.

There is no solution to the potential conflict between WTO and RIA dispute settlement decisions on the immediate horizon. This problem deserves systematic attention by WTO Members and RIA constituent countries.[102] The NAFTA dispute settlement mechanism and its interface with the WTO DSB is described and analyzed in Chapter Six.

---

[101] This is not intended to suggest that the ruling of the dispute settlement institution of an RIA or a national court with respect to interpretation of the WTO Agreement would not be applied within the relevant territory because the WTO DSB's decision is more authoritative. WTO DSB decisions are not directly applicable within the territory of a WTO Member. DSB decisions are addressed to Members, which are responsible for choosing the mechanism by which to comply with the decisions. Understanding on Rules and Procedures Governing the Settlement of Disputes, 31 I.L.M. 124 (1993), *e.g.*, para. 19.1.

[102] The dispute settlement interface problem is discussed by this author in Frederick M. Abbott, *The NAFTA Environmental Dispute Settlement System as Prototype for Regional Integration Arrangements*, 4 Y.B. INT'L ENVTL. L. 3 (Günther Handl ed., 1994).

VI. CONCLUSION

The place of RIAs in the WTO system is not very well defined. In light of the growing importance of RIAs within the world trading system it is necessary to begin to more carefully define the relationship between regional structures and the global structure. A fundamental difficulty in this regard is that the structures and functions of RIAs are dissimilar. It may be that no single set of rules will act as an adequate interface between RIAs and the WTO. It may be that a solution will lie in establishing an RIA accession procedure to the WTO that will be designed at least in part to define the relationship between the RIA and the WTO. This might be much like the present procedure by which individual countries accede to the GATT with separate protocols of accession. To some extent this has already taken place with respect to the European Union which is now to be considered a formal member of the WTO. However, even with respect to the EU, the relationship remains an uneasy one because of lingering internal EU-Member States differences concerning external competences. The relationship of NAFTA to the WTO is problematic, and efforts must begin to better define this relationship.

Chapter Four

THE NAFTA TRADE IN GOODS PROVISIONS

As detailed in Chapter Three, the constituent countries of an FTA must eliminate tariffs and other restrictive regulations of commerce on substantially all trade in products originating in their territory within a reasonable time to meet the requirements of Article XXIV of the GATT 1994. Tariffs and other regulations of commerce applicable to non-constituent countries must be no higher or more restrictive than those existing in the constituent countries prior to formation of the FTA. In this chapter the provisions of the NAFTA regarding trade in goods are examined for their conformity with these requirements, as well as with other relevant rules of the WTO.

I. TARIFF ELIMINATION

In broad principle the NAFTA rules for the elimination of tariffs are fairly straightforward.[1] The NAFTA provides for the progressive elimination of tariffs on trade in goods of Canadian, Mexican or United States origin ("originating goods") as defined by the agreement.[2] Tariffs on originating goods are eliminated immediately or over a five-, ten-, or fifteen-year period.[3] A tariff reduction schedule for each country is made part of the agreement. The

---

[1] The tariff elimination schedules are rather more complicated than the broad principles might suggest. In a number of cases tariff reductions are not to be taken in straight lines. The commencement of reductions is also staggered. For details, *see* USITC, Potential Impact on the U.S. Economy and Selected Industries of the North American Free-Trade Agreement, USITC Publication 2596, Jan. 1993 [hereinafter ITC 1993 Report], Appendix F, note 1, and sectoral reports generally. The tariff schedules and related provisions of the NAFTA are voluminous and complex. The staff of the ITC in cooperation with various federal agencies compiled this Report at the request of the Committee on Ways and Means of the U.S. House of Representatives. The Report also includes analysis of the potential effects of the tariff reductions on the U.S. economy.

[2] "Originating" is defined as "qualifying under the rules of origin set out in Chapter Four (*Rules of Origin*)." NAFTA, art. 201(1).

[3] *Id.* Annex 302.2(1).

tariff reductions scheduled by the Canada-United States Free Trade Agreement (CUSFTA) generally are extended to Mexico.[4]

A detailed survey of the tariff elimination effects of the NAFTA has been compiled by the U.S. International Trade Commission.[5] The staged reductions of tariffs between the United States and Mexico stated in terms of percentage of imports affected (based on 1990 trade data) are summarized as follows:[6]

Category	U.S. Imports from Mexico	U.S. Exports to Mexico
Total trade (million dollars)	28,892.9	14,245.5
A (free on implementation)	53.8	31.0
B (free within 5 years)	8.5	17.4
C (free within 10 years)	23.1	31.8
C+ (free within 15 years)	.7	1.4
D (currently free)	13.9	17.9
Other	(less than 0.05)	.5

This chart indicates that all U.S. tariffs on imports from Mexico will be eliminated by the NAFTA and that 99.5 percent of Mexican tariffs on goods from the United States will be eliminated by the NAFTA.[7] The tariff elimination program with respect to Canada is comparable.[8] All but .7 percent of U.S. tariffs applicable to Mexico will be eliminated within 10 years and all but 1.9 percent (including the .5 percent not identified as scheduled for elimination) of Mexican tariffs applicable to the United States will be similarly eliminated. A substantial percentage of the goods as to which a 15 year

---

[4] NAFTA, *e.g.*, art. 302.2(4).

[5] ITC 1993 Report.

[6] ITC 1993 Report, combining Table 1-1 and Table at ix.

[7] The ITC 1993 Report indicates, at 1-1, that all tariffs between the United States and Mexico will be eliminated, and the discrepancy between this statement and the various figures printed elsewhere in the Report do not appear to be explained. From an Article XXIV standpoint the discrepancy is insignificant.

[8] In general the tariff reduction schedules of each party apply to the other two Parties to the agreement. There are some sectors, such as agriculture, where special provisions are made on a bilateral basis. *See*, *e.g.*, ITC 1993 Report, at Part IV, regarding U.S.-Mexico bilateral agriculture tariff and tariff rate quota provisions.

elimination period applies are in the agricultural sector.[9] This may be at least partly explained by the fact that non-tariff barriers in the agricultural sector are tarifficated by the NAFTA and may be substantially higher (particularly when applied as tariff rate quotas [TRQs]) than tariffs on industrial products at the outset of the transition period.[10] A longer adjustment period for the agricultural sector may therefore be justified by the greater scope of the adjustment. It has been noted that "in virtually every free trade agreement the EC has concluded to date, the agricultural sector has been completely or partially excluded."[11]

As with respect to the CUSFTA, there are limited agricultural snapback provisions included in the NAFTA.[12] Pursuant to the NAFTA provisions, TRQs at the prevailing MFN rate could be applied by the United States (only seasonally) to seven categories of seasonal fruits and vegetables, and by Mexico to 17 categories of goods, including live swine, certain pork products, certain potato products, fresh apples, and coffee extract, with respect to over-quota imports.[13] In addition, the NAFTA permits emergency safeguard actions within a ten year transition period (or fifteen years for goods as to which the fifteen year elimination period applies) pursuant to which tariffs may revert to the lesser of pre-agreement MFN rates or then existing MFN rates, for a period generally not to exceed three years.[14] The NAFTA also requires that Parties which undertake a safeguard action under Article XIX of the GATT exclude imports of NAFTA Parties from that action, unless imports from a Party account for a substantial share of total imports and contribute importantly to the serious injury.[15]

Several members of the GATT Working Party regarding the CUSFTA

---

[9] ITC 1993 Report, Table F-1, showing 4.2 percent of U.S. tariffs and 7.4 percent of Mexican tariffs on agricultural products subject to 15 year elimination.

[10] *See* ITC 1993 Report, Part IV for data. The conclusion is this author's. A "tariff rate quota (TRQ)" refers to a tariff that increases after a set quantity of goods have entered the importing country. Because the expectation is that imports will be curtailed once the higher tariff rate becomes applicable, the tariff is analogized to a "quota".

[11] II URUGUAY ROUND: A NEGOTIATING HISTORY, at 1837 and n. 83 accompanying.

[12] NAFTA, art. 703.3; ITC 1993 Report, at 21-2.

[13] *Id.* Quota levels are progressively raised, so that the quantity of goods not subject to snapback is progressively increasing.

[14] NAFTA, Chapter Eight.

[15] *Id.*, art. 802. The NAFTA Parties also reached an Understanding with respect to Chapter Eight concerning Emergency Action. This Understanding principally acts to establish a Working Group on Emergency Action to provide a forum for consultations and make recommendations to the Commission. Canada-Mexico-United States: Understanding between the Parties to the North American Free Trade Agreement concerning Chapter Eight -- Emergency Action [done Sept. 14, 1993], 32 I.L.M. 1519 (1993).

expressed concern that certain of its agricultural snapback provisions might be considered to extend the time period for elimination of tariffs beyond a reasonable time.[16] The CUSFTA snapback provisions extend for twenty years, as opposed to the NAFTA's fifteen. In light of the broad scope of tariff reductions prescribed by the NAFTA, and the fact that the overwhelming majority of such reductions will take place over a ten year period, the very limited fifteen year agricultural snapbacks could not reasonably be considered to obstruct the conclusion that the NAFTA will eliminate substantially all tariffs between its Parties in a reasonable period of time.

Several members of the CUSFTA Working Party also expressed concern with a CUSFTA provision exempting country parties from global safeguard actions in a manner similar to the NAFTA provision.[17] The issue in this instance did not concern whether the CUSFTA parties were eliminating tariffs within a reasonable period of time, but rather whether discriminatory application of safeguard measures is inconsistent with GATT Article XIX. The WTO Agreement on Safeguards seeks to clarify that safeguard measures should be applied in a non-discriminatory manner, to the extent practicable.[18] Despite critical comments from some CUSFTA Working Party members, others noted that the idea of the FTA is to eliminate trade barriers between constituent countries to the FTA, and that the application of global safeguard measures as between them may be inconsistent with this objective. The Working Party did not reach a consensus concerning the relationship between GATT Articles XIX and XXIV. The WTO Safeguards Agreement includes in a footnote the following statement:

> Nothing in this Agreement prejudges the interpretation of the relationship between Article XIX and Article XXIV:8 of GATT 1994.[19]

It does indeed seem that the application of global safeguard measures as between constituent countries of an FTA would be inconsistent with their Article XXIV obligation to eliminate inter-constituent tariffs and other restrictive regulations of commerce. In light of the failure of the Uruguay Round to resolve the issue of the relationship between Articles XIX and XXIV, it seems rather

---

[16] Report of the Working Party on the Free-Trade Agreement between Canada and the United States, GATT doc. L/6927, adopted by GATT Council Nov. 12, 1991 [hereinafter Working Party Report], at para. 32.

[17] *See* text at note 15 *supra* and Working Party Report, para. 63.

[18] *See* WTO Agreement on Safeguards, Final Act, *supra* Chapter Three, note 1, at MTN/FA II-AIA-14, paras. 5 & 9.

[19] WTO Agreement on Safeguards, n. 1.

II. RULES OF ORIGIN

Article XXIV does not require that the constituent countries of an FTA permit goods which are not regionally produced to enjoy preferential tariff treatment once having entered a constituent country of the FTA. The NAFTA Parties in fact reserve preferential tariff treatment to goods originating within the NAFTA territory, applying an extremely complex set of rules to determine when products from outside the region may have achieved regionally-produced status and are therefore entitled to preferential tariff treatment.[20]

Typically, to qualify as an originating good, the good must be "wholly obtained or produced entirely in the territory of one or more of the Parties,"[21] undergo a change in tariff classification (described in an annex) "as a result of production occurring entirely in the territory of one or more of the Parties," or, in situations in which a foreign-produced part(s) is included in a regionally-produced good and for technical reasons may not satisfy the change in tariff classification requirement, the regional value content of the whole good must exceed a set percentage.[22]

In addition to the generally applicable rules of origin, specific rules with respect to the automotive sector require the progressive increase over an eight year period to a 62.5 percent regional value content for automobiles and certain original parts.[23] This represents a significant change to the rules of origin of the CUSFTA which specified a fifty percent regional content to qualify for preferential treatment.[24] Although there is some ambiguity in the NAFTA text

---

[20] *See* Donald Harrison and Kenneth G. Weigel, *Customs Provisions and Rules of Origin Under the NAFTA*, 27 INT'L LAWYER 647 (1993).

[21] NAFTA, art. 401(a).

[22] *Id.* art. 401. The regional value of the good under the third test must not be less than 60% where the transaction value method is used or 50% where the net cost method is used. *Id.* art. 401(d).

[23] *Id.* art. 403(5).

[24] CUSFTA, Annex 301.2, section XVII. *See* GARY CLYDE HUFBAUER & JEFFREY J. SCHOTT, NAFTA, AN ASSESSMENT 40-42 (1993) [hereinafter HUFBAUER & SCHOTT, AN ASSESSMENT]. Hufbauer and Schott note that because the method of calculating North American content differs as between the NAFTA and the CUSFTA, the percentages are not directly comparable. They suggest that under some production circumstances the new rules could be less strict than the old rules.

on this point, it appears that the NAFTA rules of origin regarding automobiles supersede those of the CUSFTA as between the United States and Canada,[25] except with respect to certain pre-existing Auto Pact rules affecting particular U.S. manufacturers.[26] NAFTA rules of origin clearly govern all transit of automobiles and parts into and out of Mexico.

Specific rules of origin for the textile sector typically limit originating apparel products, to those products cut or sewn in the territory of one of the parties from material of regional origin.[27] There are other specific rules of origin for products such as computers.[28] For example, a personal computer in order to qualify as originating must include a motherboard of regional origin.[29]

The NAFTA parties included restrictive rules of origin in order to assure that the benefits of North American integration primarily accrued to Canadian, Mexican and U.S. producers.[30] Of course, it must be recognized that many North American producers are in fact owned by non-regional nationals and that the NAFTA trade in goods provisions do not discriminate on the basis of the nationality of the owner of a business.[31]

---

[25] The NAFTA does not expressly provide for termination of the CUSFTA. Various provisions of the CUSFTA are incorporated by reference in the NAFTA. The CUSFTA has been suspended. *See* Chapter Two *supra*.

[26] The ambiguity is highlighted in the ITC 1993 Report which suggests that:

> The impact of NAFTA's rules of origin is limited because existing rules of origin already applicable to trade among the NAFTA parties will continue to cover the bulk of automotive trade. A substantial volume of U.S. exports to Canada will continue to be governed by Auto Pact rules of origin. The C[US]FTA rules of origin apparently will continue to apply to Canadian exports to the United States. The NAFTA rules of origin will apply to imports into Mexico from both the United States and Canada, as well as U.S. exports to Canada that are not covered by the Auto Pact. *Id.* at 4-6 [footnote omitted].

However, the ITC 1993 Report seems to assume that because a provision substituting NAFTA for CUSFTA rules of origin in the automotive sector is contained in Appendix 300-A.1 concerning Canada (and therefore affecting imports from the United States) and does not also appear in Appendix 300-A.3 concerning the United States (and therefore governing imports from Canada), that the new NAFTA rules will only be applicable to U.S. exports to Canada (except where governed by auto pact rules). This interpretation is probably not warranted (*see, e.g.,* NAFTA notes, para. 11 reiterating substitution of rules of origin under Appendix 300-A.1). The suggestion of the ITC 1993 Report does not appear accepted by knowledgeable commentators. *See* HUFBAUER & SCHOTT, AN ASSESSMENT, *supra* note 24. *See also* note 38 *infra* regarding potential rule of origin election by certain automobile importers.

[27] *See, e.g., id.* at Annex 401.1, ch. 61, n.2. Only the fiber-comprising yarn may be imported, resulting in a so-called "yarn forward" rule. *See* ITC 1993 Report, at 8-2.

[28] NAFTA, Annex 401, chs. 84-85. *See also* ITC 1993 Report, at 5-2.

[29] ITC 1993 Report, at 5-3, n. 7, and references to NAFTA Annex 401 at notes 6 & 8.

[30] *See* ITC 1993 Report, at ix.

[31] *See, e.g.*, Report of European Parliament, discussed *infra* Chapter Seven.

The question has been raised whether the NAFTA rules of origin, insofar as they may be more restrictive than those of the CUSFTA, are inconsistent with the GATT.[32] This particularly relates to the increase in the percentage of an automobile which must be of regional origin in order to qualify for preferential treatment from 50 to 62.5 percent (at the end of the transition period). Article XXIV requires that an FTA constituent country's post-FTA duties and other regulations of commerce "shall not be higher or more restrictive than [its] corresponding duties and other regulations of commerce" prior to formation of the FTA. Perhaps constituent countries of an FTA are not permitted to adopt rules which make it more difficult for imported goods to qualify for preferential tariff treatment when some or all of those constituent countries are also constituents of a previously established FTA. Perhaps an increase in the regional content requirement might be considered to nullify or impair existing GATT benefits.

A passage from the Working Party Report with respect to the CUSFTA considers the foregoing issue, though obviously prior to the increase in regional content requirement included in the NAFTA. One member of the Working Party, on behalf of a group of countries, said:

> an increase in the percentage or frequent modification of rules of origin could have adverse effects on the trade of third parties and could give rise to disputes. In operating provisions of the FTA on rules of origin, parties should bear in mind the provisions of Article XXIV:4 and Article XXIV:5(b) which clearly stipulated that barriers to the trade of other contracting parties with free-trade areas should not be raised and that any new regulations of commerce shall not be more restrictive than those existing prior to the formation of free trade areas. The compatibility of the rules of origin in the FTA with the GATT should be examined in the light of these criteria. The representative of Canada said that the discussion of the question of whether rules of origin were one of "other regulations of commerce" in terms of Article XXIV:5(b) had not led to a solution in previous working parties on free trade agreements. Rules of origin for the FTA would operate so as not to have adverse effects on the trade of third parties.[33]

The NAFTA rules of origin regarding automobiles, in superseding the CUSFTA rules, do not raise tariffs as respects third country exporters to the region. Instead, they limit the circumstances under which third country

---

[32] The author's opinion on this question was solicited on a number of occasions in meetings with Japanese business officials.

[33] Working Party Report, at para. 37. The paragraph continues:

> It was important to note that the provisions on rules of origin in the FTA affected only bilateral trade between the parties. The same questioner, said that even if that were the case, it should be noted that the rules of origin in the context of the FTA had to be operated in such a manner as not to cause adverse effects on the trade of third parties, as provided in Article XXIV.

automotive goods may benefit from preferential tariff treatment. As such they would appear to be "regulations of commerce" and, at least as respects third country exporters to the region, they would appear to be more restrictive. Canada and the United States may point out that because of the addition of Mexico to the regional market now constituting the NAFTA, the opportunities for third country exporters to sell within the region are significantly enhanced. Thus, while the rules governing regional content may be more restrictive, the opportunities for selling regionally transformed goods will be increased. Market growth may offset the more restrictive elements of the new rules of origin. The fact that GATT Article XXIV working parties have not been able to agree on whether rules of origin are within the scope of "regulations of commerce" may presage a similar outcome with respect to NAFTA.[34]

The suggestion that the new rules of origin nullify or impair GATT 1994 benefits should be considered in light of the fact that rules of origin for establishing tariff preferences are not the subject of GATT bindings or other agreed rules. Changes to these rules therefore perhaps should not be considered to nullify benefits of the GATT agreement.

The results of the Uruguay Round include a WTO Agreement on Rules of Origin. This Agreement is in general not applicable to rules relating to RIAs,[35] but incorporates a Common Declaration with regard to Preferential Rules of Origin which is applicable to the rules adopted by RIA members with respect to these entities.[36] This Declaration does *not* preclude RIA members from adopting changes to rules of origin which make it more difficult for third country exports to qualify for preferential treatment. It states:

> when introducing changes to their preferential rules of origin or new preferential rules of origin, they shall not apply such changes retroactively as defined in, and without prejudice to, their laws and regulations;[37]

The NAFTA does not mandate changes to CUSFTA rules of origin with retroactive effect.[38] The absence in the Declaration of a prohibition on adverse

---

[34] This may also demonstrate the wisdom of Frieder Roessler's observation that unless an independent body is called upon to review RIAs, changes to the substantive rules for evaluation are of relatively little consequence.

[35] WTO Agreement on Rules of Origin, Final Act, Chapter Three *supra*, note 1, at MTN/FA II-AIA-II, art. 1(1).

[36] *Id*. Annex II.

[37] *Id*. para. 3(e).

[38] HUFBAUER & SCHOTT, AN ASSESSMENT, at 41, n. 11. Note, however, that as a means to resolve a dispute between the United States and Canada concerning the application of CUSFTA rules of origin to Honda automobiles assembled in Canada, automobile manufacturers are permitted

changes to rules of origin appears to make the case of third countries which might seek to challenge the NAFTA changes to CUSFTA rules much more difficult since it appears to demonstrate the absence of a consensus against such changes. Whether the absence of a prohibition in the Declaration should be considered to definitively interpret Article XXIV:5, is an interesting and difficult legal question. In light of the apparent lack of consensus on the rules of origin issue, the answer to the question may not be terribly important from a pragmatic WTO perspective. A working party formed to review an RIA incorporating rules of origin changes would be unlikely to reach a consensus recommending a modification of these rules.

III. DUTY DRAWBACKS

A very important component of the NAFTA from the standpoint of third country exporters to the region are changes mandated with respect to duty drawback and remission rules. This refers to refunds or remissions of duties generally contingent on the reexportation of the goods as to which the duty was paid (or was otherwise due upon importation). Much of bilateral U.S.-Mexico trade is conducted under a duty remission program known as the Maquiladora system under which U.S. manufacturers are able to ship components to Mexico for assembly and reexport to the United States without payment of Mexican duties (and with generally favorable tariff treatment by the United States).[39] Mexican duty drawback and remission programs are not limited to U.S. exporters.[40] In order to limit the use of Mexico by third countries as an export platform for the NAFTA region, the NAFTA establishes significant limitations on duty drawback and remission programs.

The CUSFTA had provided for the total elimination of duty drawback and remission programs as between Canada and the United States.[41] Under the CUSFTA, once drawbacks and remissions had been eliminated, a third country export may have been subject to payment of tariffs upon entry to both the

---

by NAFTA implementing legislation in the United States to elect either NAFTA or CUSFTA rules for goods whose entry has not been finally liquidated. NAFTA Implementation Act, § 202(a)(7).

[39] *See* ITC 1993 Report, at 3-3 to 3-5; GARY CLYDE HUFBAUER & JEFFREY J. SCHOTT, NORTH AMERICAN FREE TRADE, ISSUES AND RECOMMENDATIONS 91-105 (1992) [hereinafter HUFBAUER & SCHOTT, NORTH AMERICAN FREE TRADE]. U.S. duties are generally levied only upon the value of Mexican processing and of Mexican and third country components.

[40] HUFBAUER & SCHOTT, NORTH AMERICAN FREE TRADE, at 96.

[41] This was to take full effect as of January 1, 1994. The NAFTA provisions supersede the CUSFTA provisions and extend the date to January 1, 1996. ITC 1993 Report, at 3-4, n. 24.

country of initial importation and upon entry into the second CUSFTA country.[42] The NAFTA instead provides in effect that goods must pay the higher of the two possible customs duties to which they may have been subject either upon importation into the first NAFTA country or upon export to a second NAFTA country. Thus, assuming that Mexico's duties are higher than those of the United States, a third country exporter to Mexico must have effectively paid the Mexican rate of tariff when its goods enter the United States.[43] Since goods which originate in the NAFTA will not be subject to duty (after any applicable transition period), the limitations on the drawback or remission program do not disadvantage NAFTA-origin products, but operate only to disadvantage third country originating products.

Like its changes to rules of origin, NAFTA's placement of limitations on duty drawback or remission programs could be viewed as a restrictive regulation of commerce with respect to non-NAFTA Party exports to Mexico. The circumstances in which non-NAFTA Party goods can pass through Mexican territory without payment of tariffs are reduced. Non-NAFTA Party exports to Canada and the United States are not similarly affected since Canada and the United States previously agreed in the CUSFTA to eliminate drawback and remission programs. The rules of the WTO do not require Members to offer drawback or remission programs, and such programs do not involve the GATT binding of tariff rates. Third country exporters which benefitted from such programs nevertheless will be adversely affected by the new restrictions.

The CUSFTA provisions eliminating duty drawbacks and remissions were addressed in the Working Party Report:

> some members considered that the suppression of the drawback scheme might create a situation, in the language of article XXIV, more restrictive than prior to the FTA. Also this could create an unfavourable economic situation for those benefitting from the scheme. The representative of Canada said that a more fundamental question raised in this matter was whether the intent of Article XXIV was that any party entering into a free-trade area was bound itself never to increase M.f.n. rate of duty, the application of which had been

---

[42] *Cf.* Harrison and Weigel, *supra* note 20, at 650.

[43] The rule is that a duty waiver, reduction or refund that is contingent on the exportation of goods may not exceed the lesser of: (1) the total amount of the duties paid or owed on the initial importation of the third country goods into North America or (2) the total amount of duties paid on the goods' subsequent shipment to another NAFTA country. Thus, in the hypothetical in the text, the lesser amount would be the amount of U.S. duties. The Mexican government must collect at its own tariff rate, but could waive or refund the amount of U.S. duties upon reexport. The reexporter must then pay duties to the United States, thereby ultimately being subject to the full Mexican duty rate.

The limitations on drawbacks or remissions do not apply to goods which are reexported in the same condition, which enter in bond for transportation, or to raw sugar imported to the United States for refining and reexport to Canada or Mexico. ITC 1993 Report, at 3-4.

subject to exoneration in some way. One member said that this was not necessarily related to whether or not the customs duty had been bound. Changing the rules mid-stream could cause trade diversion.[44]

The issues raised by NAFTA-mandated changes to rules of origin and drawback schemes are analogous. In both situations the Parties to the NAFTA were not obliged to grant even limited preferential treatment to third country produced goods prior to the NAFTA, but had elected to do so. In both cases, third country exporters which had relied on the prior rules will be adversely affected by the change. The foregoing observation by the representative of Canada to the CUSFTA Working Party goes to the heart of the matter from a WTO standpoint. Does the WTO require that its Members in general refrain from changing their non-WTO mandated rules governing trade so as to preclude adverse effects on third country exporters? Is there some form of general estoppel principle at work in the WTO, or are Members only bound to: (a) follow express or customary WTO rules and (b) abide by their bound commitments? Is the intent of Article XXIV:5 to establish a general estoppel against rule changes or only to preclude parties from withdrawing bound commitments? These are not easy questions to answer and are unlikely to be conclusively answered by the NAFTA Working Party.

IV. CUSTOMS USER FEES

NAFTA provides for the eventual elimination of customs user fees with respect to regional goods, as had the CUSFTA.[45] This appears consistent with Article XXIV:8(b), which states that the constituent countries to an FTA shall eliminate duties and "other restrictive regulations of commerce" on trade between them. Article XXIV:5(b), provides that the constituent countries shall not apply more restrictive regulations of commerce to third countries as a consequence of forming the FTA.

The elimination of customs user fees on regionally-produced goods shipped between the NAFTA Parties will raise an interesting GATT/WTO issue if any of the Parties raise their customs user fees to offset the loss of revenues from intra-NAFTA shipments. Articles II:2(c) and VIII of the GATT permit countries to charge customs fees in the approximate cost of the customs services rendered. These provisions have been given a detailed interpretation by a GATT panel in

---

[44] Working Party Report, at. para. 42.
[45] NAFTA, art. 310 and Annex 310.1. *See* Harrison and Weigel, *supra* note 20, at 652.

a case involving U.S. customs user fees.[46] GATT Members are clearly entitled to collect service fees which are directly or sufficiently related to the processing of imports. If imports from a group of countries do not receive services, they should not be charged for them. Outside the FTA context, if the exclusion of some imports from service charges results in higher costs charged to other imports (because, e.g., fixed costs do not change significantly), it would appear appropriate that higher fees be charged on the other imports. The question arises with respect to an FTA whether the raising of fees on non-constituent imports because of the elimination of fees on constituent imports would constitute the application of higher or more restrictive regulations of commerce as to the non-FTA imports. In the CUSFTA Working Party Report, the representative of the United States took the position that the customs user fee applied by the U.S. was an "other regulation of commerce" covered by GATT Article XXIV:5(b).[47] Because Article XXIV:5(b) stipulates that the constituent countries of an FTA should not raise tariffs or other regulations of commerce, this suggests that the United States would agree that customs user fees should not be raised by a constituent country, even if its total fee revenues drop as a consequence of an FTA exemption.

V. GOVERNMENT PROCUREMENT

With respect to government procurement, the NAFTA will provide substantial market opening for regionally-originating goods by mandating national treatment by covered purchasing entities in covered sectors.[48] The NAFTA provides that the rules of origin generally applicable for conferring intra-regional preferences will apply with respect to government procurement.[49] The removal of restrictions on access to government purchasing entities would appear to be within the scope of eliminating restrictions of commerce on trade between

---

[46] United-States-Customs User Fee, Report by the Panel adopted on 2 February 1988 (L/6264), BISD 35S/245.

[47] Working Party Report, at para. 40. The U.S. representative also said that the U.S. customs user fee was not a "restrictive regulation of commerce" in the sense of GATT Article XXIV:8(b). Presumably the U.S. representative was suggesting that since fees are charged for services, they are neutral and not "restrictive." This position undercuts reliance on Article XXIV as the basis for the elimination of customs user fees in the NAFTA. However, the U.S. representative would likely argue that since Canadian and Mexican goods will not be dutied, they should not be subject to user fees, making reliance on Article XXIV as the basis for fee elimination unnecessary.

[48] *See, e.g.*, NAFTA, arts. 1001-1003 and related Annexes.

[49] *Id.* art. 1004.

constituent countries of the FTA and as such to be consistent with Article XXIV of the GATT, even if this results in preferential treatment of regionally produced goods. The parties to the WTO Government Procurement Agreement, which is a Plurilateral Agreement and not compulsory for WTO Members, is reported to have been extended to cover regional purchasing entities.[50] This would be of limited application with respect to the NAFTA since, unlike regional institutions of the EU, the NAFTA regional institutions will have very limited roles.[51]

VI. TECHNICAL STANDARDS AND SANITARY AND PHYTOSANITARY MEASURES (SPS)

The NAFTA establishes detailed rules with respect to technical standards and sanitary and phytosanitary measures (SPS).[52] SPS measures generally relate to agricultural products and therefore raise health and safety issues. The parties to the NAFTA expressly disapply Article XX(b) of the GATT as it may relate to SPS measures.[53] Article XX(b) permits WTO Members to adopt measures otherwise inconsistent with the GATT 1994 that are "necessary" to protect human, animal and plant life and health. Article XX(b) was a major focus of the GATT Tuna Panel Report that found, *inter alia,* that U.S. legislation protecting dolphin on the high seas, enforced by the imposition of an embargo on tuna imports, was not necessary to the protection of human or animal life in the United States.[54] The NAFTA's express disapplication of Article XX(b) is a signal that the Parties consider that greater flexibility is needed in the adoption of SPS measures than might be provided for by the GATT standard of necessity (at least insofar as that term may have been interpreted prior to conclusion of the new WTO SPS Agreement).

The dissatisfaction of environmental non-governmental organizations (NGOs) in the United States with the GATT Tuna Panel ruling was well known to the

---

[50] *See U.S., E.U. Agree to Open Markets in Public Procurement, Except Telecom,* 11 BNA INT'L TR. REPTR., Apr. 20, 1994, at 627.

[51] *See* discussion of NAFTA institutions, Chapters Two and Six.

[52] NAFTA, Chapter 7, Section B (Sanitary and Phytosanitary Measures) & Chapter Nine (Standards-Related Measures).

[53] NAFTA, art. 710.

[54] United States--Restrictions on Imports of Tuna, Report of the Panel, action to bring before the Council deferred, GATT Doc. DS21, Sept. 3, 1991, *reprinted in* 3 WORLD TRADE MATERIALS 5 (1991).

NAFTA drafters. Many members of the U.S. Congress had committed themselves to assuring a high level of environmental protection in the NAFTA, and the Congress would of course be voting to approve the NAFTA. There was therefore considerable pressure on the NAFTA drafters to improve upon what was perceived as a less than adequate performance by the GATT on environment-related issues. Changes made to the Dunkel Draft text of WTO SPS provisions immediately prior to the conclusion of the Uruguay Round did much to bring the NAFTA and WTO/GATT rule systems closer together. The final WTO SPS rules in fact come fairly close to approximating the NAFTA rules and at least to a certain extent disavow prior GATT rulings with respect to the standard of necessity.[55]

In the Technical Barriers to Trade Chapter of the NAFTA, the Parties do not expressly disapply GATT Article XX(b). In this chapter, in addition to establishing their own technical standards jurisprudence, the NAFTA Parties expressly "affirm with respect to each other their existing rights and obligations relating to standards-related measures under the GATT Agreement on Technical Barriers to Trade."[56] The answer to the question raised in Chapter Two, whether the NAFTA retains priority over the WTO and related agreements, becomes particularly important in respect to evaluating the relationship between NAFTA and WTO SPS and technical standards rules.[57] The extensive negotiating effort involved in the creation of NAFTA provisions in these areas weighs in favor of a determination that NAFTA rules are intended to take priority in these areas. However, the question may not yet be authoritatively answered.

The NAFTA's technical standards and SPS rules may provide greater leeway for deviations from international standards than WTO/GATT rules. The NAFTA allows adoption of measures more stringent than international standards, while prohibiting the adoption of measures creating an unnecessary obstacle to trade between the Parties.[58] The Parties are supposed to use relevant international standards as a basis for their measures, but there are fairly broad exceptions from this guideline. For example, a Party need not use international standards when those standards would not achieve "the level of protection that the Party

---

[55] For example, the necessary standard has generally been interpreted to require that a party apply measures that are the least trade restrictive possible. The new WTO SPS Agreement requires instead that such measures be not more trade restrictive than required.

[56] NAFTA, art. 903.

[57] NAFTA, art. 103. See Chapter Two, *supra* and Chapter Six, *infra*.

[58] See, e.g., NAFTA, arts. 712(1), 713(3), 904(2), 904(4) & 905(3).

considers appropriate" for fulfilling its legitimate objectives.[59] Perhaps of greatest importance, the NAFTA expressly places on the complaining party the burden of proof when challenging the scientific basis or risk assessment methodology used in establishing a technical[60] or SPS measure.[61] Thus, with respect to SPS measures, NAFTA Article 723(6) provides that the "Parties confirm that a Party asserting that a sanitary or phytosanitary measure of another Party is inconsistent with this Section shall have the burden of establishing the inconsistency."

As noted above, the WTO Agreement on SPS is significantly more favorable to adopting and maintaining high levels of environmental protection than was the Dunkel Draft version of the SPS Agreement.[62] Nevertheless, the WTO SPS Agreement still establishes a strong presumption in favor of measures consistent

---

[59] *Id.* art. 905(1).

[60] *Id.* art. 914(4).

[61] *Id.* art. 723(6).

[62] Two subtle but important changes were made to the prior Dunkel Draft SPS Agreement in the Final Act Agreement on the Application of Sanitary and Phytosanitary Measures. Final Act, *supra* Chapter Three, note 1, at MTN/FA II-AIA-4 [hereinafter SPS Agreement]. First, in respect to para. 11 which permits members to introduce higher levels of SPS protection than would be achieved by application of international standards, based on scientific justification or risk assessment procedure, an interpretative footnote was added. It provides:

> For purposes of paragraph 11, there is scientific justification if, on the basis of examination and evaluation of available scientific information in accordance with the relevant provisions of this Agreement, a Member determines that the relevant international standards, guidelines or recommendations are not sufficient to achieve *its appropriate level of protection.* [Emphasis added]

The highlighted language appears intended to clarify that each Member is entitled to make a unilateral determination regarding what is the appropriate level of protection, and that the question of scientific justification is aimed only at whether specific measures are justifiable in achieving this level of protection.

The second important change in the SPS Agreement is to para. 21, which in the Dunkel Draft provided that in adopting measures, parties would use the "least restrictive to trade." The Final Act version states instead that "Members shall ensure that such measures are *not more trade restrictive than required* to achieve their appropriate level of protection" [Emphasis added]. An interpretative footnote is also added to para. 21, providing:

> For purposes of paragraph 21, a measure is not more trade restrictive than required unless there is another measure, reasonably available taking into account technical and economic feasibility, that achieves the appropriate level of protection and is significantly less restrictive to trade.

The foregoing changes suggest that while the NAFTA remains to a certain extent more favorable than the WTO to adopting and maintaining more stringent than international SPS standards, the Final Act reduced the gap between the two systems with respect to the environment.

with international standards,[63] and requires at least implicitly that measures deviating from those standards be justified by the party adopting them. The WTO SPS Agreement requires that SPS measures taken by the Members are "necessary for the protection of human, animal or plant life or health"[64] and that such measures be applied "only to the extent necessary" for such protection.[65] GATT dispute settlement panels interpreting the GATT Article XX "necessary" measures exception to the General Agreement appear to have consistently placed the burden of proof for justifying an exceptional measure on the Member that has adopted the measure.[66]

Although GATT/WTO dispute settlement panels interpreting the SPS Agreement will not be obligated to follow the practice of panels interpreting the Article XX exception, the use of the word "necessary" to indicate the level of justification required for an SPS measure suggests a conscious decision to invoke prior analogous practice under Article XX. The requirement that SPS measures be scientifically or otherwise justified likewise suggests that the party adopting the measure must demonstrate the justification.[67] The placement of the burden of proof in disputes concerning environment-related measures is quite significant because the scientific basis for such measures is often indeterminate.

The NAFTA parties have agreed with respect to the application of technical standards and SPS measures that goods produced in any Party will receive treatment at least as favorable as that received by goods from any third country (Most Favored Nation or MFN treatment).[68] This provision has significant implications with respect to dispute resolution and will be discussed in Chapter Six, *infra*.

There was little discussion of technical standards and SPS measures in the

---

[63] Measures consistent with international standards "shall be deemed to be necessary to protect human, animal or plant life or health, and presumed to be consistent with the relevant provisions of this Agreement and the GATT 1994." SPS Agreement, para. 10.

[64] *Id.* para. 5.

[65] *Id.* para. 6.

[66] *See, e.g.*, Canada--Administration of the Foreign Investment Review Act, Report of the Panel adopted Feb. 7, 1985, BISD 30S/140, at para. 5.20; United States--Section 337 of the Tariff Act of 1930, Report of the Panel adopted Nov. 7, 1989, BISD 36S/345, at para. 5.27; Thailand--Restrictions on Importation of and Internal Taxes on Cigarettes, Report of the Panel adopted Nov. 7, 1990, BISD 37S/200, at paras. 74-75; United States--Restrictions on Imports of Tuna, Report of the Panel, action to bring before the Council deferred, GATT Doc. DS21, Sept. 3, 1991, *reprinted in* 3 WORLD TRADE MATERIALS 5, at para. 5.22. (1991).

[67] *See* SPS Agreement, para. 11.

[68] *See, e.g.*, NAFTA, art. 904(3)(b), regarding technical standards, which is a pure form of MFN treatment and article 712(4), regarding SPS measures, which permits discrimination on the limited basis of differing conditions.

CUSFTA Working Party report.[69] The heightened sensitivity of the WTO to environment-related issues in the wake of the Tuna Panel controversy will probably result in greater attention to technical standards and SPS measures by the NAFTA Working Party. The NAFTA rules may permit its constituent countries in some cases to maintain measures that would be disallowed by the WTO. However, as a customary matter the WTO/GATT does not act against legislative measures which permit, but do not mandate, WTO/GATT-inconsistent action. Since the NAFTA technical standards and SPS provisions do not require the parties to adopt WTO-inconsistent measures, there does not appear to be a basis for objection by the Working Party. It is clear, on the other hand, that attention must be focused on means to coordinate the environment-related activities of the WTO and NAFTA, as well as other regional groups. This is further discussed in Chapter Six, *infra*.

VII. CONCLUSION

The conclusion is inescapable that the NAFTA qualifies for treatment as an interim agreement leading to the formation within a reasonable time of a free trade area under the terms of Article XXIV of GATT 1994. Nevertheless, the foregoing analysis should make apparent that Article XXIV deals with the interface of RIAs and the WTO in a rather incomplete way.

---

[69] Working Party Report, at para. 58. The principal question was whether third country participation in standards harmonizing activities was provided for. It is not provided for either in the CUSFTA or NAFTA, but as noted by the representative from Canada, "countries could make their views known through normal channels."

Chapter Five

THE NAFTA PROVISIONS REGARDING SERVICES, INVESTMENT AND INTELLECTUAL PROPERTY

In this chapter the NAFTA provisions regarding trade in services are described and analyzed in the context of the new WTO rules governing services liberalization agreements among parties to RIAs. The NAFTA services provisions have, by any reasonable construction of the terms, "substantial sectoral coverage" as required by General Agreement on Trade in Services (GATS) Article V.[1] Likewise, it is quite clear that the NAFTA services provisions do not, in respect to Members outside the agreement, "raise the overall level of barriers to trade in services within the respective sectors or sub-sectors compared to the level applicable prior to such an agreement,"[2] because the NAFTA does not require its constituent countries to maintain or raise barriers with respect to third country service providers. Though, finally, it also seems certain that the NAFTA services provisions must be construed as eliminating "substantially all discrimination ... in the sectors covered ... on the basis of a reasonable time-frame,"[3] consideration of this GATS Article V requirement demonstrates some of the interpretative difficulties inherent in it.

This chapter also examines NAFTA provisions with respect to intellectual property rights protection, and considers the implications of comparable WTO TRIPS provisions for the NAFTA rules. The new WTO trade-related aspects of investment measures (TRIMS) provisions are briefly discussed in the context of the NAFTA services and investment regime.

---

[1] GATS, art. V:1(a).
[2] *Id.* art. V:4.
[3] *Id.* art. V:1(b).

Chapter Five

I. TRADE IN SERVICES

The scope of NAFTA liberalization measures in respect to trade in services is far more extensive than the scope of GATS liberalization measures. To begin with, the NAFTA services agreement is of the "negative listing" type, whereas the GATS is principally of the "positive listing" type. That is, NAFTA liberalizing measures generally extend to all services sectors, with specific exceptions carved out by the Parties in various annexes. The GATS contains certain modest liberalizing provisions applicable to all services sectors of its Members, but reserves the important market access commitments of its Members to those affirmatively listed in annexes.

A. THE GENERAL FRAMEWORK OF NAFTA SERVICES MEASURES

The NAFTA acts to generally liberalize trade in services between Canada, Mexico and the United States by extending the rights of national and most favored nation treatment to the service providers of each Party.[4] Service providers of the Parties are not required to establish a presence within the territories of one another in order to enjoy the right to provide services.[5] The Parties are entitled to maintain existing discriminatory measures that are set forth in an annex to the agreement, though many of these measures are subject to liberalization commitments,[6] as well as to adopt and maintain discriminatory measures as described in another annex.[7] The Parties have each reserved their basic telephone services sector (but not their value added sector) from present and future liberalization commitments.[8] A separate chapter of the NAFTA deals with telecommunications services and establishes the rules regarding enhanced or value-added services.[9] Air and maritime transport services are generally excluded from the scope of the agreement.[10] Financial services are dealt with in a chapter of the agreement separate from the general services framework,[11]

---

[4] NAFTA, art. 1202 & 1203.
[5] *Id.* art. 1205.
[6] *Id.* art. 1206(1) & Annex I.
[7] *Id.* art. 1206(4) & Annex II.
[8] *Id.* Annex II.
[9] NAFTA, Chapter Thirteen.
[10] *Id.* art. 1201(2)(b).
[11] Services are generally covered in Chapter Twelve. Financial Services are covered in Chapter

and a separate chapter addresses issues connected with liberalization of the telecommunications services market.[12] While there are limitations on the commitments of the Parties with respect to financial services (at least on a temporary basis),[13] the guiding principles of the financial services chapter nevertheless are national and most favored treatment.[14] The specific services liberalization commitments of the parties are discussed in subsection C below.

The NAFTA provides liberal treatment to service providers of non-Party countries through the mechanism of an establishment criterion. Pursuant to the services chapter, national treatment and MFN rights are extended by each Party to "service providers of another Party."[15] A service provider of a Party is defined as "a person of a Party that provides a service."[16] A "person of a Party" is defined by the NAFTA as "a national, or an enterprise of a Party."[17] An "enterprise" is generally defined by the NAFTA as a form of business organization organized under applicable law,[18] with branches specifically added to the definition for purposes of the services chapter (but *not* the financial services chapter).[19] An "enterprise of a Party" is defined by the services chapter as "an enterprise constituted or organized under the laws and regulations of a Party, including a branch."[20] Therefore, a business organization which is established in the territory of a NAFTA Party qualifies for the benefits of the services chapter regardless of the ultimate country of ownership of the organization.

There is, however, a provision which permits third-country-owned

---

Fourteen. *Id.*
[12] NAFTA, Chapter Thirteen.
[13] *See, e.g.,* NAFTA, art. 1412 & Annex VII. *See infra* text accompanying notes 45-50 regarding restrictions on financial services investments. There is provision for continuing consultation regarding future liberalization commitments. *See, e.g., id.* Annex 1405.4.
[14] *Id.* arts. 1407-08.
[15] *See, e.g.,* art. 1202-03.
[16] *Id.* art. 1213(2).
[17] *Id.* art. 201(1).
[18] Article 201, *id.*, defines "enterprise" as:

> any entity constituted or organized under applicable law, whether or not for profit, and whether privately-owned or governmentally-owned, including any corporation, trust, partnership, sole proprietorship, joint venture or other association.

[19] *Id.* art. 1213(2). At least on an interim basis, financial institutions may need to be incorporated in the territory of the party in which they are providing services to enjoy the benefits of the financial services chapter. *Id.* art. 1404(3)&(4).
[20] *Id.*

enterprises to be denied access to the privileges of the services chapter. Article 1211(2) provides:

> Subject to prior notification and consultation ... a Party may deny the benefits of this Chapter to a services provider of another Party where the Party establishes that such service is being provided by an enterprise of another Party that is owned or controlled by persons of a non-Party and that has *no substantial business activities in the territory of any Party*.[21] [emphasis added]

The financial services chapter of the NAFTA expressly incorporates Article 1211 of the services chapter regarding denial of benefits.[22] The NAFTA does not define "substantial business activities" and thus leaves an element of discretion to the Parties in potentially denying the benefits of the services chapter to foreign-owned enterprises.[23] However, as a practical matter it seems unlikely that the requirement of a substantial business presence will meaningfully hinder a non-Party-owned enterprise from conducting a services trade within the NAFTA because (a) in most cases establishment will not be in doubt and (b) the phrase "substantial business activities" conveys content familiar in at least broad context to commercial lawyers and is not especially susceptible to arbitrary interpretation and application.

The NAFTA provisions which generally afford non-discriminatory treatment to third country service providers based on an establishment requirement are consistent with a comparable provision in GATS Article V, discussed *supra*.

The NAFTA will enhance opportunities of regional enterprises with respect to the supply of services to the government market.[24] The rule pursuant to which the NAFTA parties are permitted to deny government procurement access to non-Party-owned enterprises is equivalent to that generally established in the services chapter. That is, a foreign-owned services enterprise may be denied government procurement-related benefits if it "has no substantial business

---

[21] Article 1211(3) places the burden of establishing that its action is in accordance with this provision on the Party denying the benefits. There also is in Article 1211(1) the possibility for a Party to deny benefits with respect to services provided by third-country-controlled enterprises when the Party does not maintain diplomatic relations with the third country, or when the third country has had prohibitory measures imposed against it. *Id.*

[22] *Id.* art. 1401(2).

[23] There are numerous potential legal analogies in U.S. domestic law to the "substantial business activities" requirement, particularly in the area of State tax and business regulation with respect to foreign enterprises doing or transacting business within the State. *See, e.g.*, Cal. Corp. Code § 191 (1993) and definition of "transact intrastate business" and annotations thereto, and Cal. Corp. Code § 2100 (1993). There is also analogy to the European Union's "continuous and effective link" test (*infra* Chapter Seven, note 61).

[24] *See* NAFTA art. 1002 & related Annexes.

activities in the territory of the Party under whose laws it is constituted."[25]

B. THE FRAMEWORK OF NAFTA INVESTMENT MEASURES

The NAFTA contains a separate chapter with respect to investment. The investment chapter confers the rights of national and most favored nation treatment to investors of another Party "with respect to the establishment, acquisition, expansion, management, conduct, operation, and sale or other disposition of investments."[26] The specific content of the obligation is set forth to include prohibition of minimum levels of local equity ownership,[27] and prohibition of the imposition of performance requirements.[28] These obligations are subject to present and prospective reservations by the Parties with respect to sectors and regulations set out in annexes to the agreement.[29] These annexes are the same as those which pertain to the services chapter.[30] Mexico has excluded investment, *inter alia*, in its petroleum sector.[31]

Investments in the financial services sector generally are governed by the financial services chapter.[32] The financial services chapter generally accords the rights of national and MFN treatment to investors of each Party,[33] including an express right of establishment,[34] and incorporates article 1211 on denial of benefits.[35] Exceptions are set forth in an annex. Specific rules applicable to investment in the financial services sector are discussed in subsection C below.

In addition to the separate rules of the financial services chapter, the NAFTA chapter on telecommunications services exempts the Parties from any

---

[25] *Id.* art. 1005(2). This is slightly different than the general provision on denial of benefits in the services chapter (art. 1211(2)) because, under the latter, substantial business activities in the territory of "any Party" (and not just the party in which the enterprise is established) avoid disqualification.

[26] *Id.* art. 1102.

[27] *Id.* art. 1102(4).

[28] *Id.* art. 1106.

[29] *Id.* art. 1108, Annexes I & II, & Annex IV (limited to MFN exception).

[30] *Id.* Annex II.

[31] *Id.* art. 1101 & Annex III.

[32] *Id.* art. 1101(3).

[33] *Id.* art. 1407-08.

[34] *Id.* art. 1404.

[35] *Id.* art. 1401(2).

84   *Chapter Five*

commitment with respect to investments in the basic voice telephone sector.[36]

C. A PRACTICAL PERSPECTIVE ON NAFTA SERVICES AND INVESTMENT MEASURES

The NAFTA provisions relating to services liberalization refer to legislative and administrative measures of the Parties and are difficult to penetrate in the absence of in-depth knowledge concerning the affected service industries. Following is a review of the effects of the NAFTA on several important and illustrative sectors.[37]

1. Telecommunications

As noted above, NAFTA excludes basic voice telephone services from the scope of each Party's services liberalization commitments, and exempts the Parties from commitments regarding investments in this sector.[38] The largest component of cross-border NAFTA telecommunications services trade is in the basic voice telephone sector, with payments flows representing the sharing of revenues on cross-border calls.[39] The NAFTA services, investment and telecommunications chapters combine to provide that service providers of the parties will have non-discriminatory access to providing value-added telecommunications services, will be entitled to invest in entities providing such services,[40] and will have access to public telecommunications transport networks on reasonable terms.[41]

There has customarily been a division between regulatory treatment of basic

---

[36] *Id.* art. 1301(3).

[37] This analysis relies in substantial measure on the ITC 1993 Report which incorporates interviews with industry and government officials concerning the prospective impact on affected sectors.

[38] NAFTA, art. 1301(3) & Annex II. *See* note 8, *supra*. *See* ITC 1993 Report, at 39-1 to 39-2. *See also*, HUFBAUER & SCHOTT, AN ASSESSMENT, at 74-75.

[39] ITC 1993 Report, at 39-1.

[40] Licensing requirements may remain in this sector, but the provisions of the investment and telecommunications chapters are intended to assure that such requirements are not used as a means to deny market access. *See* NAFTA, art. 1111, 1303 & Annex I of Mexico, Telecommunications (Enhanced or Value-Added Services). There is a brief transition period to 100% ownership in Mexican entities providing videotext or enhance packet switching services. *Id.* Annex of Mexico.

[41] *See, e.g.*, art. 1302.

and value-added telephone services.[42] This distinction is effectively maintained in the GATS Annex on Telecommunications which, like the NAFTA, exempts members from commitments to permit investment in or operation of basic voice telephone supply.[43] Basic voice telephone and value-added telecommunications services might either be considered separate services sectors, or both could be considered sub-sectors of a broader telecommunications sector. In either event, it seems clear that, as to the value-added telecommunications services sector, the NAFTA eliminates substantially all discrimination within a reasonable time frame and does not raise concern under GATS Article V.

2. Banking

NAFTA provides for the substantial elimination of restrictions on the establishment and operation of banking services between the Parties.[44] The financial services provisions generally permit investors to establish or acquire wholly-owned financial service entities in each other's territory, and to provide a wide range of customary banking and related financial services in those territories. The Parties are not obligated to permit operation through branches, and this will have a significant impact because bank subsidiaries are required to meet minimum capital reserve requirements. This may well limit the size of loans that NAFTA Party-owned foreign subsidiaries will provide locally.[45]

There are some restrictions in respect to the banking sector. Most importantly, during a 10 year transition period Mexico will limit the individual and aggregate market penetration of foreign banks, as stated in terms of the individual and aggregate total of authorized capital of such banks.[46] These restrictions will be removed at the end of the ten year transition period, although Mexico may impose an additional three year moratorium on aggregate foreign

---

[42] *See* Frederick M. Abbott, *GATT and the European Community: A Formula for Peaceful Coexistence*, 12 MICH.J.INT'L L. 1, 41 (1990).

[43] GATS Telecommunications Annex, at 2.3.

[44] This section focuses on banking services, although other financial services (including those relating to the purchase and sale of securities) are covered by the financial services chapter.

[45] *See* ITC 1993 Report, at 42-2 to 42-3. The restriction on branches is reported to be based on Canadian and Mexican dissatisfaction with existing U.S. restrictions on interstate branch banking. If the U.S. legislation is changed to permit interstate branch banking, all three countries may at least permit such banking based on the initial establishment of a local subsidiary. *See* HUFBAUER & SCHOTT, AN ASSESSMENT, at 62-63, n. 43.

[46] NAFTA, art. 1412(3) & Annex VII of Mexico, Section B, Establishment and Operation of Financial Institutions.

capital for the four years following the transition period, for a period not to exceed three years.[47] It would appear that the maximum duration of restrictions by Mexico for market penetration in its banking sector is 17 years. All of the Parties may limit participation in respect to certain public sector activities.[48] The United States maintains certain restrictions with respect to interstate banking.[49] Finally, although Canada expressly exempts U.S. and Mexican investors (defined in terms of nationality of ultimate ownership) from Canadian limitations on foreign ownership in its banking sector, it does not exempt third country investors from these restrictions.[50]

NAFTA provisions with respect to banking and related financial services raise some interesting questions with respect to interpretation of GATS Article V. First, does the removal of restrictions on cross-border subsidiary banking, but not branch banking, constitute the elimination of substantially all restrictions in the sense of GATS Article XVII regarding National Treatment? Even if the NAFTA Parties have not reserved branch banking restrictions in their GATS market access schedules,[51] it would seem that this question must be answered in the affirmative, on the grounds that requiring the operation of subsidiaries (as opposed to branches) can be justified on a public interest regulatory basis. That is, if subsidiaries are required to maintain adequate capital reserves locally, but branches are not, then the public is better protected under the subsidiary requirement. The principle that parties to a liberalizing agreement may maintain restrictive measures in the public interest is codified in Article V of GATS, which provides that parties are not obligated to eliminate restrictions permitted under Article XIV (*inter alia*) of GATS. Article XIV permits maintenance of measures necessary to maintain public order,[52] and to "deal with the effects of a default on services contracts."[53] The inability of a bank to repay its depositors would seem to fall into the category of default on a services contract.

The second interesting question relates to the time frame for the elimination

---

[47] Annex, *id.*, para. 9, the percentage being 25% as to commercial banks and 30% as to securities firms.

[48] NAFTA, art. 1401.3, *e.g.*, relating to statutory systems of social security. *See* ITC 1993 Report, at 42-2.

[49] *Id.* art. 1412 & Annex VII, Part A.

[50] *Id.* art. 1412(6) & Annex VII, Part E.

[51] If the NAFTA Parties maintain branch banking restrictions in their GATS market access schedules, they may be permitted to maintain these restrictions under an agreement between them to liberalize their banking sector, subject to resolution of the GATS Article V interpretative question, discussed *supra* Chapter Three, at 51-52.

[52] GATS, art. XIV(a).

[53] *Id.* art. XIV(c)(i).

of restrictions on access to the Mexican market. To begin with, unlike GATT Article XXIV as newly interpreted by the Understanding on Interpretation, Article V does not set out a presumption that 10 years is the general limit of a reasonable time frame. Given the express incorporation of such a limit regarding Article XXIV, it must be assumed that the GATS negotiators deliberately rejected the ten year presumption of timeliness. It should also be noted that Mexico has in general committed to a ten year elimination of its restrictions, and that the additional seven year maximum restriction period is itself an exception within the liberalization framework. It may be pointed out that the Mexican restrictions relate to investment capital and not services market share and it might be suggested that this is not a services liberalization restriction at all. However, since the provision of banking services by a subsidiary is defined to a large extent by its capital reserves, this may be an instance wherein an investment restriction is by operational effect a limitation on access to providing services.[54] Lastly, but by no means of minor import, is that Mexico is a relatively less developed country by OECD standards. GATS Article V expressly provides that developing countries who are parties to services liberalization agreements shall be accorded "flexibility" in meeting the conditions of eliminating substantially all discrimination in a reasonable time frame.[55] This express provision would appear to conclusively resolve in the NAFTA's favor the question whether the Mexican program for removal of banking restrictions meets the criteria of Article V.[56]

3. Transportation

Air transport services[57] and maritime transport services[58] generally are

---

[54] *See* Chapter Three, *supra*, text accompanying notes 52-55, regarding the distinction between measures which expressly discriminate against foreign service providers and measures which discriminate against foreign service providers in their operation. In the context of applying the National Treatment principle to trade in goods, GATT panels have held that discrimination through operational effect is prohibited just as express discrimination.

[55] GATS, art. V:3(a).

[56] NAFTA treatment of insurance services is similar to its treatment of banking services, including limitations on branch operations and transitional limitations on market share. However, with respect to insurance services Mexico may not extend the ten year transition period in the basis of aggregate capital holdings by foreigners. Annex VII of Mexico, Section B, Establishment and Operation of Financial Institutions, para. 9.

[57] NAFTA, art. 1201(2)(b).

[58] *Id., e.g.*, Annex I of Mexico, Water Transportation (regarding maritime transport), pursuant to which Mexico reserves domestic water transport to Mexican flag vessels; and Annex II of United

excluded from the scope of NAFTA transportation liberalization provisions.[59] Some modest liberalization measures are included with respect to access to the rail services market.[60] On the other hand, the NAFTA provides for substantial market liberalization with respect to truck and bus transportation services. Within six years of NAFTA's entry into force, trucks of each Party will be given access to the entire territory of the other Parties with respect to cross-border services.[61] The Parties, however, do not agree to permit each other's firms to provide domestic (intra-country) truck transport services.[62] Within three years the Parties generally will permit access of cross-border bus services (though not purely domestic services) to their full territories, although some provincial Canadian restrictions will remain.[63] There will be a phase-in of access to investment in bus and truck transport services, with reciprocal access to 100 percent ownership after ten years.[64]

The truck and bus services sub-sectors of the land transportation sector again present issues with respect to the relationship between domestic regulatory interests and the degree of liberalization. After a transition period, service providers of each Party may engage in the relatively unrestricted provision of cross-border services, but will be permitted to provide domestic services only by investing in local companies. Investors of the Parties will, however, be entitled to have 100 percent ownership interest in local service providers. There is therefor an establishment requirement with respect to the domestic/local provision of services. The provision of GATS Article V which says that a liberalizing agreement must have substantial sectoral coverage includes a footnote which states that this condition is understood, *inter alia*, in terms of "modes of supply."[65]

States, Water Transportation (broadly preserving U.S. maritime restrictions, including those relating to domestic transport).

[59] *See* ITC 1993 Report, at 40-1, n.1 and HUFBAUER & SCHOTT, AN ASSESSMENT, at 70.

[60] *See* ITC 1993 Report, at 40-3 regarding permission granted by Mexico to own and operate rail terminals, bring in locomotives, and market services; but reserving to Mexico the exclusive right to operate and control the system.

[61] *See* NAFTA, Annex I of United States and Mexico. Canada apparently will provide such access immediately since it appears only to reserve its domestic cabotage. *Id.* Annex I of Canada. *See* ITC 1993 Report, at 40-2.

[62] *See* NAFTA, Annex I of Canada, United States and Mexico; ITC 1993 Report, at 40-2.

[63] ITC 1993 Report, at 40-2.

[64] *See, e.g.,* NAFTA, Annex I of Mexico, Land Transportation; ITC 1993 Report, at 40-3 & ns. 15-16.

[65] *See* Chapter Three, *supra*. The footnote continues: "In order to meet this condition, agreements should not provide for the *a priori* exclusion of any mode of supply."

There is probably less of a public interest justification in requiring the local ownership of bus and truck companies than there is in requiring the local incorporation of bank subsidiaries. It would seem that most of the regulatory restrictions which are placed on local bus and truck owners could likewise be imposed on foreign bus and truck companies operating locally, and that liability concerns could be met by local insurance and bonding requirements. It may be that local ownership requirements with respect to bus and transport services do not serve a significant public interest.

Perhaps cross-border (international) transport services and intra-country (domestic) transport services are separate sub-sectors of the transportation market and should be considered separately. If it is concluded that cross-border services are adequately liberalized but domestic services are not, does this have any consequences under GATS Article V? Should the NAFTA GATS Working Party make a recommendation regarding domestic transport services? This depends upon how the requirement of eliminating "substantially all discrimination" is interpreted.[66] Even if a formalistic interpretation might suggest that restrictions on domestic transport as well as on cross-border transport should be eliminated, the adoption of such a strict interpretation would place an extraordinary burden on the practical capacity of RIAs to conform with the new GATS Article V rules. It is well to recall that the Treaty of Rome in 1958 mandated non-discrimination in the EU services market. More than three decades later, application to the EU Member States services sectors of strictly interpreted Treaty of Rome services provisions would present a picture of less than full compliance. If the NAFTA and other RIAs are to operate in a reasonably harmonious manner with the WTO, it may be necessary to take a practical perspective in the interpretation of the requirements of GATS Article V and its requirement of eliminating substantially all discrimination.

4. Construction and Engineering

The construction and engineering services sectors will by and large be governed by the general provisions of the NAFTA relating to services. The Parties to NAFTA have agreed to eliminate citizenship and permanent residency requirements (as set out in a schedule) that they maintain for the licensing or

---

[66] Recall that GATS Article V may be interpreted to permit Members to retain restrictions that are included as qualifications to their GATS market access schedules. See note 51, *supra*.

certification of professional service providers of the other Parties.[67] The United States and Canada do not maintain such restrictions for engineers and construction service providers at the federal level,[68] and Mexico has agreed to remove such restrictions within two years.[69] Mexico has agreed to phase-out ownership restrictions in the construction sector over a ten year period.[70] Mexico will retain restrictions regarding construction of roads.[71] NAFTA provides that the Parties will permit the temporary entry of professionals, though the United States appears to have reserved an annual numerical limitation with respect to Mexico.[72]

The parties appear to have substantially eliminated restrictions on access to their construction services markets within a reasonable time frame. However, it must be noted that because the NAFTA does not generally provide for the free movement of persons, construction services must be understood in the limited sense of a right to invest in enterprises and to provide professional and managerial services. Primary construction work remains to be performed by local employees. Second, because the NAFTA does not eliminate local licensing and certification requirements, there remain in general considerable obstacles to the cross-border provision of professional services. NAFTA encourages relevant bodies in the respective Parties to "develop mutually acceptable standards and criteria for licensing and certification of professional service providers and to provide recommendations on mutual recognition to the Commission."[73] It also provides specific guidance designed to lead to specific proposals in certain sectors.[74] However, there remains much work to be done before these provisions which encourage the approximation and mutual recognition of professional standards are translated into an open market for professional services providers.

---

[67] NAFTA, art. 1210(3).

[68] There are, however, a myriad of such restrictions on the State, provincial and local levels which Canada and the United States have agreed to eliminate over the two year period. *Id.*

[69] *Id.* and ITC 1993 Report at 41-1 to 41-2.

[70] NAFTA, Annex I of Mexico generally provides for a five year phase-in (31 I.L.M. at 724), though the ITC 1993 Report refers to a ten-year phase-in.

[71] *Id.*

[72] *See* the rather ambiguously phrased NAFTA, Appendix 1603.D.4, para. 1 of the United States.

[73] NAFTA, Annex 1210.5A(2).

[74] *See, e.g., id.* Appendix 1210.5B, Foreign Legal Consultants.

C. Concluding Observations

The NAFTA services liberalization measures clearly have substantial sectoral coverage and therefore meet the first criterion of GATS Article V. A review of specific sectors and sub-sectors of coverage reveals a fundamental interpretative problem with regard to the criteria that substantially all discrimination must be eliminated in the covered sectors and sub-sectors. This fundamental problem arises from the nature of regulation of services industries.

Article XXIV of the GATT 1994 which establishes the criteria for a free trade area with respect to trade in goods provides principally for the elimination of tariffs, and also for the elimination of other restrictive regulations of commerce. The elimination of tariffs is a straightforward matter. The federal government simply orders reductions in the tariffs applied to imported goods. Article V of GATS concerns a far more complex enterprise. The transnational liberalization of services markets is virtually assured of being a long term enterprise. The Treaty of Rome establishing the European Economic Community provided in 1958 for the creation of a liberalized inter-Member State services market, but in the mid-1980s when the Commission undertook to evaluate the situation in the Community it concluded that extensive work remained to be done and proposed the 1992 Plan. The liberalization of services markets may involve dismantling extensive regulatory structures cutting across not only the federal and sub-federal levels, but also among private groups.

In this context, it may be unrealistic to expect that any regional organization will in the first stage of services market integration be able to present an agreement which substantially eliminates all inter-country restrictions in the same sense that tariffs may be eliminated. It is perhaps for this reason that GATS Article V provides that services liberalization agreements should be understood in the overall context of regional integration, providing that:

> In evaluating whether the conditions under paragraph 1(b)[regarding elimination of substantially all discrimination] are met, consideration may be given to the relationship of the agreement to a wider process of economic integration or trade liberalization among the countries concerned.

From a realistic standpoint, the NAFTA obviously makes great strides toward liberalizing the internal services market. However, in some sectors there will remain local incorporation requirements (*e.g.*, local land transportation); the regulatory frameworks of the three countries may be approximated only by a very gradual process (*e.g.*, regarding professional services); and in some sectors or sub-sectors there are some elements of liberalization, but there is certainly not elimination of substantially all discrimination (*e.g.*, maritime port services and rail services).

The NAFTA parties have agreed to treat third country service providers as regional providers under essentially the same criteria as provided for in GATS Article V,[75] so that any discriminatory effects of the NAFTA generally will apply equally to all Members of the GATS.

The NAFTA GATS Article V Working Party may provide a service to the NAFTA Parties by pointing out some of the areas wherein additional liberalization measures may be useful. On the other hand, in light of the fairly extensive scope of NAFTA liberalization measures on the whole, a general objection to the NAFTA liberalizing measures would both be unwarranted and unfortunate. The NAFTA services liberalization measures are part of a broader NAFTA regime which will essentially eliminate all tariffs on goods originating in the NAFTA territory. The NAFTA services liberalization measures must be evaluated as a component of this wider process. In this "on the whole" context, the NAFTA services measures should be considered to meet the criteria of GATS Article V for eliminating substantially all discrimination over a reasonable time frame.

It finally should be noted with respect to the NAFTA's investment liberalization program, that Mexico will be required pursuant to the WTO TRIMS Agreement, described in Chapter Three, to eliminate its remaining local content and export balancing requirements within five years of entry into force of the WTO TRIMS Agreement. This should alleviate concerns that such measures may be eliminated *vis-à-vis* NAFTA-owned enterprises but not third country-owned enterprises.[76]

II. THE NAFTA INTELLECTUAL PROPERTY REGIME

The NAFTA chapter on Intellectual Property[77] is part of a broad global undertaking to incorporate intellectual property rights protection into regimes governing international trade.[78] This undertaking effectively commenced with

---

[75] The only apparent exception relates to a Canadian reservation which permits it to limit aggregate foreign penetration of its banking sector on the basis of nationality of ownership, but exempts U.S. and Mexican owned enterprises. *See* discussion *supra*.

[76] *See* discussion regarding new Mexican Foreign Investment Law, *infra* Chapter Seven, and Japanese concerns regarding Mexican restrictions, *infra* Chapter Eight.

[77] NAFTA, Chapter Seventeen.

[78] *See* Frederick M. Abbott, *Protecting First World Assets in the Third World: Intellectual Property Negotiations in the GATT Multilateral Framework*, 22 VAND. J. TRANSNAT'L L. 689

the 1986 GATT Uruguay Round mandate which authorized the initiation of negotiations concerning trade-related aspects of intellectual property rights (TRIPS). It culminated on a broad multilateral level with the approval in December 1993 of the WTO Agreement on Trade-Related Aspects of Intellectual Property Rights [hereinafter WTO TRIPS Agreement]. The NAFTA text was negotiated principally on the basis of the Dunkel Draft text of the TRIPS Agreement,[79] and it is comparable in almost all essential respects to the final WTO TRIPS Agreement text.[80] Both the NAFTA and WTO TRIPS texts establish substantive standards for the protection of patents, trademarks, copyrights and neighboring rights, industrial designs, integrated circuit layouts, trade secrets, and geographical indications of origin. Both texts also require that parties adopt and maintain effective civil and criminal enforcement mechanisms with respect to the substantive IPRs rules. The NAFTA and WTO TRIPS texts will for the most part result in the multilateral application of IPRs standards comparable to those presently in place in the OECD countries.

Mexico began several years ago to overhaul its intellectual property rights (IPRs) regime to begin to approximate it with industrialized country standards.[81] The impact of the NAFTA and TRIPS texts on Mexico will not therefore be terribly dramatic.[82] The principal effects appear to be that Mexico will broaden the scope of "pipeline" protection granted to pharmaceutical and agricultural products that may have not have been available prior to conclusion of the NAFTA,[83] provide IPRs protection for integrated circuit layouts,[84] and

---

(1989); and First Report of the Committee on International Trade Law (ITLC), International Law Association, Buenos Aires Conf., Aug. 14-20, 1994 (F.M. Abbott and E.-U. Petersmann, Rapporteurs), Part III (TRIPS) and citations therein.

[79] The Dunkel Draft refers to a draft text prepared by the GATT Secretariat in coordination with the various Uruguay Round negotiating groups and distributed to the parties in late 1991 in order to facilitate completion of the negotiations.

[80] An example of a U.S. industry-perspective commentary which, even in attempting to unfavorably compare the Dunkel Draft text to the NAFTA text, finds few meaningful distinctions, see Charles S. Levy & Stuart M. Weiner, *The NAFTA: A Watershed for Protection of Intellectual Property*, 27 INT'L LAWYER 671 (1993).

[81] See Mexico, Law on the Promotion and Protection of Industrial Property (of June 25, 1991), INDUSTRIAL PROPERTY, Oct. 1991, MEXICO - Text 1-001, at 1, and Gretchen A. Pemberton and Mariano Soni, Jr., *Mexico's 1991 Industrial Property Law*, 25 CORN. INT'L L.J. 103 (1992). See also ITC 1993 Report, at 1-9; HUFBAUER & SCHOTT, AN ASSESSMENT, at 85-90.

[82] See, e.g., Frank J. Garcia, *Protection of Intellectual Property Rights in the North American Free Trade Agreement: A Successful Case of Regional Trade Regulation*, 8 AM. U.J. INT'L L. & P. 817, 825-29, 831-33 (1993).

[83] NAFTA, art. 1709(4).

[84] Although Mexico is given a four year period to implement this protection. NAFTA, Art. 1710 & Annex 1710.9. See HUFBAUER AND SCHOTT, AN ASSESSMENT, at 89.

Chapter Five

expressly protect encrypted program-carrying satellite signals with civil and criminal measures.[85] Mexico has entered fairly broad reservations in the NAFTA with respect to its broadcast and film industries, requiring that a majority of time of each day's live broadcast programs feature Mexican nationals,[86] limiting non-national ownership in cable service providers to minority interests,[87] and requiring that thirty percent of per theater movie screen time be reserved for Mexican persons.[88]

It may be that the NAFTA IPRs negotiations were more significant from a U.S. standpoint with respect to Canada because during the course of the NAFTA negotiations Canada agreed to eliminate an exceptionally permissive compulsory licensing regime applicable to pharmaceuticals.[89] The NAFTA, on the other hand, carries forward Canada's protection of its cultural industries from the CUSFTA (making it applicable to all third countries).[90] The cultural exemption permits Canada to discriminate in terms of services, investment and copyright protection in favor of its nationals, though Canada apparently has little intention of invoking the exemption in practice.[91] The United States has reserved its right to withdraw comparable benefits if Canada invokes the exemption.[92]

The principal change to U.S. IPRs law mandated by the NAFTA relates to the date of invention for Canadian and Mexican patents. Under current U.S. patent law, the earliest date of invention for inventions made outside the United States is the date of initial filing of a patent application.[93] For inventions made in the United States the actual date of invention is used.[94] Thus U.S. law discriminates on the basis of the place where an invention is made. The NAFTA prohibits discrimination with respect to patents on the basis of the place of invention in the Parties. It resulted in an amendment to U.S. patent law with

---

[85] NAFTA, art. 1707. HUFBAUER AND SCHOTT, AN ASSESSMENT, at 85; Garcia, *supra* note 82, at 829.

[86] NAFTA, Annex I of Mexico, Communications, Entertainment Services (Broadcasting, Multipoint Distribution Systems (MDS) and Cable Television).

[87] *Id.* Annex I of Mexico, Communications Services (Cable Television).

[88] *Id.* Annex I of Mexico, Entertainment Services (Cinema).

[89] *See, e.g.,* HUFBAUER & SCHOTT, AN ASSESSMENT, at 88.

[90] NAFTA, Annex 2106.

[91] HUFBAUER & SCHOTT, AN ASSESSMENT, at 87, n. 16.

[92] CUSFTA, art. 2005(2) and *id.* at 87.

[93] Section 104 of the Patent Act. 35 U.S.C. § 104.

[94] 35 U.S.C. § 102.

respect to inventions made in Canada and Mexico.[95]

The WTO TRIPS Agreement contains a broad national treatment provision.[96] Therefore, the TRIPS Agreement requires the NAFTA parties to extend all of the IPRs benefits they have accorded to each other under the NAFTA to third countries. Bear in mind that the exemption in GATS Article V for services liberalizing agreements does not apply to IPRs agreements. In fact the European Union at one point in the Uruguay Round negotiations tabled a TRIPS proposal which would have permitted regional groups to adopt discriminatory IPRs regimes, though it subsequently explained that its proposal had been too broadly drafted and did not reflect its intention.[97] It must be noted that the WTO TRIPS Agreement contains a general most favored nation provision. However, this MFN provision exempts from the MFN obligation rights granted under preexisting international IPRs agreements (which includes the NAFTA).[98] Nevertheless, because the WTO TRIPS Agreement contains both national and MFN treatment provisions, non-Parties to the NAFTA should still be entitled to receive treatment from each Party at least as favorable as that which each Party accords to its own nationals.[99]

The NAFTA does in some cases provide for higher levels of protection than the WTO TRIPS Agreement. Because the TRIPS Agreement requires the extension of national treatment, and does not contain an exemption for RIAs, these benefits should be passed on to third countries. By failing to recognize this requirement, the NAFTA Parties could come into conflict with their WTO obligations, but there is no reason to believe that they will choose to do so.[100]

---

[95] *See* Japan 1994 ISC Report, *infra* Chapter Eight, note 17, at 318-320.

[96] WTO TRIPS Agreement, art. 3.

[97] *See* Abbott, *GATT and the European Community*, *supra* note 42, at 5, n. 9. The EU said that it had intended only to make sure that its regional exhaustion doctrine remained intact.

[98] Exempted are:

any advantage, favour, privilege or immunity accorded by a Member:
...
(d) deriving from international agreements related to the protection of intellectual property which entered into force prior to the entry into force of the Agreement Establishing the WTO, provided that such agreements ... do not constitute an arbitrary or unjustifiable discrimination against nationals of other Members. WTO TRIPS Agreement, art. 4.

[99] The MFN exemption should only be applicable to those cases in which the NAFTA Parties decided to provide better than national treatment to persons from other Parties. Thus, for example, if Mexico provided better IPRs protection pursuant to the NAFTA to nationals of the United States than it provided to its own nationals, then third country nationals would not be entitled to the level of protection afforded U.S. nationals. No such case has come to this author's attention.

[100] *But cf.* Japan 1994 ISC Report, *supra* note 93, for an expression of interest in the issue.

The Canadian and Mexican reservations protecting their cultural industries are troubling from the standpoint of IPRs rights holders who at least potentially face market access restrictions. The United States and the European Union fought an intense battle in the Uruguay Round negotiations regarding the permissibility of market access restrictions on audio-visual and related services and products. This battle was inconclusive. The WTO Agreement does not directly address the subject, and both sides reserved their positions. In view of this situation, the NAFTA reservations with respect to audio-visual services and products are unlikely to be considered inconsistent with the WTO Agreement.

Chapter Six

THE NAFTA REGULATORY FRAMEWORK AND DISPUTE SETTLEMENT PROCEDURES

The basic institutional structure of the NAFTA was described in Chapter Two. The principal institutional organ of the NAFTA is the Free Trade Commission (Commission) which serves generally to coordinate the activities of the Parties under the agreement. Coordination of more specific NAFTA-related activities is allocated to various subsidiary entities that are described in the first part of this chapter. Procedures for the settlement of disputes are necessary to the undertaking of any significant international enterprise. International dispute settlement can be structured in a variety of ways. The NAFTA employs a number of dispute settlement models, though none involving the establishment of a permanent judicial organ comparable to the European Court of Justice. Most of the NAFTA procedures are accessible only to the governments of the Parties, but some provide direct or indirect access to private parties. The NAFTA Supplemental Agreements with respect to the Environment and Labor establish novel dispute settlement procedures that can be used to address whether the Parties have persistently failed to enforce their laws. The various NAFTA dispute settlement procedures raise a host of interesting issues which are explored in this chapter. Of central importance is the potential for conflict between the NAFTA and WTO dispute settlement mechanisms, and the impact that such conflict might have on the WTO system.

I. THE NAFTA REGULATORY FRAMEWORK

The NAFTA establishes a variety of committees and working groups intended to facilitate implementation of the agreement and to coordinate efforts to make regulatory standards compatible.[1] For example, the NAFTA chapter on

---

[1] Pursuant to the text of the NAFTA, eight committees and six working groups are to be established. See NAFTA, Annex 2001.2. Pursuant to the Understanding concerning Emergency

technical standards provides for the establishment of a Committee on Standards-Related Measures.[2] This Committee is chartered, *inter alia*, to facilitate the process by which the Parties make compatible their standards-related measures and to provide a forum for consultation on issues relating to standards-related measures.[3] The Standards Committee's functions also include "[c]onsidering non-governmental, regional and multilateral developments regarding standards-related measures, including under the GATT."[4] The Standards Committee may establish and determine the scope and mandate of various subcommittees and working groups created by the technical standards chapter, including the Land Transportation, Telecommunications, Automotive and Labelling of Textiles and Apparel Standards Subcommittees.[5] The provisions establishing the Standards Committee and its various Subcommittees do not authorize those bodies to adopt measures on behalf of the Parties.[6] In fact, while the NAFTA provides that the Standards Committee will be comprised of representatives of the Parties, it does not establish rules for the taking of decisions by the Committee or the

---

Action, Chapter Four *supra*, note 15, an additional Working Group on Emergency Action is established. The NAFTA text, for example, provides for establishment of a Committee on Agricultural Trade to monitor and promote cooperation on the implementation of agriculture-related measures. *Id.* art. 706. A Committee on Sanitary and Phytosanitary Measures will be established to facilitate, *inter alia*, enhancement of food safety and improvement of sanitary and phytosanitary conditions, and to pursue the equivalence of sanitary and phytosanitary measures, to facilitate technical cooperation and consultations, including those involving dispute settlement. This committee may also establish and determine the mandate of working groups. *Id.* art. 722. A Committee on Standards-Related Measures is to be established to monitor and implement the technical standards provisions of the agreement, and to facilitate the attainment of standards compatibility and enforcement, as well as to facilitate consultations regarding disputes. *Id.* art. 913. This committee has the authority to establish and determine the scope and mandate of subcommittees and working groups, which may consult with experts and interest groups. The establishment of several specific subcommittees and working groups is mandated. *Id.* art. 913(4) and (5). A Working Group on Trade and Competition will be established to report and make recommendations on further work regarding issues relating to the relationship between trade and competition law. *Id.* art. 1504. An Advisory Committee will be established to study issues related to alternative private dispute settlement. *Id.* art. 2022(4). *See also* Committee on Trade in Goods (*id.* art. 316), Committee on Trade in Worn Clothing (*id.* Annex 300-B, sec. 9.1), Committee on Small Business (*id.* art. 1021), Financial Services Committee (*id.* art. 1412), Working Group on Rules of Origin (*id.* art 513), Working Group on Agricultural Subsidies (*id.* art. 705(6)), Mexico-United States and Mexico-Canada Working Groups on Agricultural Grading and Marketing Standards (*id.* Annex 703.2(A)(25) & (B)(13), and Temporary Entry Working Group (*id.* art. 1605).

[2] *Id.* art. 913.

[3] *Id.* art. 913 (2)(b)&(c).

[4] *Id.* art. 913(e).

[5] *See id.* Annexes 908.2, 913.5.a-1,913.5.a-2,913.5.a-3 & 913.5a-4.

[6] *But see* note 9 *infra* regarding the Automotive Standards Council which may adopt measures which the Parties are expected to implement. However, in this special case, each Party must consent to the measures which the Council recommends.

Subcommittees.[7] It is clear that the Parties themselves must act to adopt and implement standards-related measures.[8] The charters of the Committee and Subcommittees are framed in terms of development and/or implementation of "work programs." These work programs appear intended to result in specific recommendations from the Committee and Subcommittees to the Parties with respect to the means for making trade-related standards measures compatible.[9]

The NAFTA does not provide for third country representation to its regulation-related committees, subcommittees and working groups. Even though the NAFTA committees will not make decisions with binding effect, third country exporters and investors nevertheless may be concerned that a lack of input into the regulation formation process, and delayed access to the results of the committee recommendation process, will place them at a competitive disadvantage in comparison to NAFTA national enterprises. Business enterprises have long been concerned with the trade distorting effect of lack of access to the regulation formation process, whether on a regional, national or local level.[10]

The WTO Agreement on Technical Barriers to Trade addresses this concern by obligating Members to provide timely information with regard to technical regulations, standards and conformity assessment procedures adopted or proposed by regional organization bodies of which they are members or participants.[11] The European Union, as a special case, is subject to the same

---

[7] NAFTA, art. 913. *But see* note 9 *infra*, regarding Automotive Standards Council establishing a procedure.

[8] *See, e.g.* NAFTA, art. 906(2). This view of the technical standards chapter is reinforced by the NAFTA Implementation Act in the United States which states in regards to its chapter on standards-related measures:

...Nothing in this chapter shall be construed -
(1) to prohibit a federal agency from engaging in activity related to standards-related measures, including any such measure relating to safety, the protection of human, animal, or plant life or health, the environment or consumers; or
(2) to limit the authority of a federal agency to determine the level it considers appropriate of safety or of protection of human, animal, or plant life or health, the environment or consumers. NAFTA Implementation Act, § 471(a).

[9] Of some particular interest is the charter of the Automotive Standards Council. NAFTA, Annex 913.5a-3. Each Party must consent to any recommendation of the Council. However, once that recommendation has been agreed upon, the Parties agree to implement it within a reasonable time in accordance with the legal and procedural requirements and international obligations of each Party. Where the adoption of a law is required for a Party, the Party shall use its best efforts to secure the adoption of the law and shall implement any such law within a reasonable time. *Id.* para. 4.

[10] *See* Abbott, *GATT and the European Community*, *supra* Chapter Five, note 42, at 49-51.

[11] WTO TBT Agreement, Art. 10.1.

obligations as national governments with respect to the adoption of technical regulations and standards,[12] which obligations include publishing proposals for new regulations at a sufficiently early stage that comments can be provided by third parties prior to adoption.[13] The NAFTA Parties have expressly affirmed their obligations under the GATT Technical Barriers to Trade and other international agreements, and it is therefore reasonable to expect that the Parties will provide WTO-compatible access to their joint regulatory coordination efforts. The WTO-related obligations of the NAFTA Parties will arise both from their membership in regional bodies (which will oblige them to provide information concerning the activities of those bodies), as well as from their separate membership in the relevant WTO agreements.

II. THE DISPUTE SETTLEMENT MECHANISM OF THE MAIN AGREEMENT

The general mechanism for the settlement of disputes regarding interpretation and application of the NAFTA is contained in NAFTA Chapter Twenty. Pursuant to Article 2005(1) of the NAFTA, disputes between the Parties arising under both the NAFTA and GATT may be resolved at the discretion of the complaining Party pursuant to either the WTO/GATT or NAFTA dispute settlement procedure.[14] Article 2005(1) expressly refers to disputes under the GATT, agreements negotiated under the GATT, or GATT successor agreements, and thus avoids the ambiguity inherent in NAFTA Article 103 regarding NAFTA-GATT-WTO priority. If a third NAFTA Party requests dispute settlement under the NAFTA, a dispute will ordinarily be settled pursuant to the NAFTA.[15] Matters involving the relationship of the NAFTA to specified environmental agreements,[16] and matters involving sanitary and phytosanitary measures or standards measures relating to the environment, health, safety or conservation must be settled under the NAFTA procedure at the request of the respondent.[17]

---

[12] WTO TBT Agreement, Annex I, para. 6 which provides that the European Communities/Union will be treated as a central government body for purposes of the TBT Agreement.

[13] *Id.*, *e.g.*, art. 2.9.

[14] NAFTA, art. 2005(1).

[15] *Id.* art. 2005(2).

[16] *Id.* art. 2005(3).

[17] *Id.* art. 2005(4).

Following a consultation and conciliation period, at the request of a Party, an arbitral panel is established.[18] Five panelists are selected by the disputing Parties, generally from a roster of experts that the Parties will have agreed upon by consensus.[19] The panel receives written and oral testimony from the Parties, may request (subject to consent by the Parties) the input of outside experts, and renders a majority decision to the Parties that recommends actions to be taken by a Party whose measures have been found inconsistent with the NAFTA. Such a decision is not subject to appeal. A Party is expected to comply with a decision of an arbitral panel, preferably by reforming or removing an offending measure.[20] If a complained-against Party fails to comply satisfactorily with a panel decision, the complaining Party "may suspend the application to the Party complained against of benefits of equivalent effect until such time as they have reached agreement on a resolution of the dispute."[21] A panel cannot compel compliance with its recommendations.[22]

A separate dispute settlement mechanism is established for antidumping and countervailing duty (AD/CVD) matters.[23] The Parties may initiate claims based upon final AD/CVD determinations by national administrative authorities. In addition, private parties to adverse AD/CVD final determinations may require their governments to initiate claims under the NAFTA AD/CVD dispute settlement procedure.[24] Under this procedure, decisions of arbitral panels[25]

---

[18] *Id.* art. 2008(2). A third party may join as a complainant. *Id.* art. 2008(3). If the third party does not join as complainant, it is expected to refrain from initiating separate proceedings under NAFTA or GATT on substantially similar grounds. *Id.* art. 2008(4).

[19] *Id.* arts. 2009 & 2011.

[20] *Id.* art. 2018.

[21] *Id.* art. 2019(1).

[22] It is of cardinal significance to the institutional structure of the NAFTA that the Parties must agree on a resolution of a dispute after the panel renders its decision.

> 1. On receipt of the final report of a panel, the disputing Parties shall agree on the resolution of the dispute, which normally shall conform with the determinations and recommendation of the panel, and shall notify their Sections of the Secretariat of any agreed resolution of any dispute.
>
> 2. Whenever possible, such resolution shall be non-implementation or removal of a measure not conforming with this Agreement or causing nullification or impairment in the sense of Annex 2004 or, failing such resolution, compensation. *Id.* art. 2018.

[23] *Id.* Chapter Nineteen.

[24] If a person who would otherwise be entitled to judicial review of a final determination under the law of the importing country requests a Party to initiate a panel proceeding, the Party is obligated to initiate the proceeding. *Id.* art. 1904(5).

[25] The panels consider complaints regarding the compatibility with the NAFTA of amendments

with respect to appeals of AD/CVD final determinations are binding on the Parties as to the matter at issue.[26] The AD/CVD dispute settlement mechanism includes an appellate panel procedure which is limited to considering issues such as excess of power and arbitrator misconduct.[27] In addition, pursuant to the NAFTA investment chapter, the Parties agree to submit disputes with investors (including enterprises) of other Parties to binding third-party arbitration (*i.e.*, under the ICSID Convention or in accordance with UNCITRAL rules).[28] Thus, private party investors may have recourse against the NAFTA governments under the third party arbitration provisions.[29] The Parties are expected to provide for the recognition and enforcement of the arbitral awards resulting from this process.[30] Investors, for example, enterprises of Party, are not restrictively defined *(e.g.*, in accordance with the nationality of their ultimate ownership),[31] so that the investment arbitration process should be open to third country-owned enterprises established in the NAFTA territory.

A. Reconciling NAFTA and WTO Dispute Settlement Systems

Inherent in the NAFTA dispute settlement mechanism is the potential for conflict with the WTO dispute settlement mechanism. The new WTO dispute settlement mechanism substantially modifies the prior GATT mechanism by making the adoption of panel reports virtually automatic, by creating a standing appellate body and an appeals procedure, and by strengthening the rules intended to assure that WTO dispute settlement decisions are implemented by Members.[32] These changes in the WTO mechanism increase the likelihood of

---

to national AD/CVD laws (although the NAFTA does not itself establish specific substantive AD/CVD rules) and replace national judicial authorities with respect to appeals of final administrative determinations in AD/CVD actions. *Id., e.g.*, arts. 1903-04.

[26] *Id.* art. 1904.

[27] *Id.* art. 1904(13).

[28] *Id.* arts. 1115, et seq.

[29] *Id.* Chapter Eleven, Section B.

[30] *Id.* art. 1136(4).

[31] *See, e.g., id.* art. 1139.

[32] *See* WTO Understanding with respect to Dispute Settlement. This creates the Dispute Settlement Body (DSB) which is composed of all WTO Members. Under prior GATT rules, decisions of dispute settlement panels were adopted only by consensus of all parties, including the parties to a dispute. This gave the losing party the ability to block adoption of a panel report. Under the WTO DSU, a negative consensus is required to block adoption of a report, virtually assuring that reports will be adopted. However, decisions of panels of first instance are subject to review on questions of law to the standing Appellate Body, the decisions of which are also subject

conflict with NAFTA dispute settlement decisions because the NAFTA Parties will not be able to block the adoption of WTO panel reports and thereby prevent conflicts from reaching full fruition. Moreover, elements of the new WTO procedure designed to assure implementation of decisions will heighten the pressure on NAFTA Parties to implement WTO decisions which may conflict with NAFTA dispute settlement decisions or obligations, therefore heightening the potential for political tension between NAFTA and WTO interests.

The situation is particularly problematic in respect to environmental issues for two reasons. First, because only with respect to environmental issues may NAFTA Party respondents demand that a dispute be settled in the NAFTA forum and, second, because of the particular political sensitivity of environmental issues. Moreover, because the NAFTA requires that goods of the Parties receive MFN treatment with respect to the application of sanitary and phytosanitary measures and technical standards,[33] a WTO decision which obligated a Party to reduce its level of protection as to non-NAFTA Party goods would obligate that Party to reduce its level of protection as to NAFTA Party goods.

The experience under the CUSFTA which also permits recourse to CUSFTA and GATT dispute settlement is that claims between the United States and Canada have been brought in both forums.[34] CUSFTA panels have examined national anti-dumping laws for their consistency with GATT rules, although the CUSFTA does not itself establish substantive rules regarding dumping so that no conflict between CUSFTA rules and GATT rules was potentially at issue in these cases.[35] CUSFTA panels have stated that it is important to construe Canadian and U.S. antidumping law consistently with the GATT.[36] In no CUSFTA panel decision does it appear that a GATT rule has been given

---

to quasi-automatic adoption. The DSU establishes fairly strict timetables intended to govern the implementation of decisions, and makes clear the procedure for withdrawal of concessions based on failure to implement. *See* Frederick M. Abbott, *The NAFTA Environmental Dispute Settlement System as Prototype for Regional Integration Arrangements*, 4 Y.B. INT'L ENVTL. L. 3 (Günther Handl ed., 1994).

[33] *See* Chapter Four, *supra*.

[34] Through the middle of 1994 about twenty claims had been resolved by CUSFTA dispute settlement panels. Frieder Roessler noted that in 1991 alone, the United States and Canada were party to four disputes before GATT dispute settlement panels. Roessler, Chapter Three, *supra*, note 33, at 318.

[35] *See, e.g.,* In the matter of Replacement Parts for Self-Propelled Bituminous Paving Equipment from Canada, Panel Nos. USA-89-1904-03, Mar. 7, 1990 (1990 FTAPD LEXIS 3) and USA-90-1904-01, May 15, 1992 (1992 FTAPD LEXIS 2).

[36] *Id.*

priority over a CUSFTA rule.[37]

The WTO Dispute Settlement Understanding (DSU) generally provides that its mechanism for dispute settlement applies to disputes under WTO-related agreements.[38] The WTO DSU does not preclude WTO panels from considering relevant rules of other agreements, provided implicitly that such rules are invoked in the context of a WTO-agreement-related controversy.

Defining the relationship between the substantive rules of the NAFTA and those of the new WTO/GATT is a matter of considerable complexity. As noted in Chapter Two, Article 103 of the NAFTA provides that the NAFTA prevails over the GATT to the extent of any inconsistencies. The central issue is whether reference to the GATT in Article 103 of the NAFTA should be interpreted to encompass the GATT 1994 that, pursuant to the terms of the WTO Agreement, will enter into force along with the WTO Agreement.[39] The GATT 1994 includes the GATT General Agreement that has operated as the charter of the GATT since its formation, as amended, as well as the accumulated formal understandings and interpretations regarding that General Agreement.[40] The WTO expressly provides that the GATT 1994 is "legally distinct" from the GATT 1947.[41] Since the reference in NAFTA Article 103 to the GATT is a reference to the GATT in force on January 1, 1994,[42] that Article 103 reference might, on its face, be understood as a reference to the GATT 1947. In this very limited context, the rule of NAFTA Article 103 that the NAFTA prevails over the GATT might be understood not to survive entry into force of the WTO Agreement.

There are, however, a number of other important factors to take into account. First, the reason that the WTO Agreement provides that the GATT 1994 is "legally distinct" from the GATT 1947 is that it was foreseen that, at least for an interim period, some parties to the old GATT regime (the GATT 1947 regime) might not become Members of the WTO (and the GATT 1994). The GATT 1947 is left in place so that these parties would continue to have at

---

[37] In In the Matter of Pure Alloy and Magnesium from Canada (CVD), Panel No. USA-92-1904-03, Aug. 16, 1993 (1993 FTAPD LEXIS 7), the panel noted that certain GATT panel rulings that had not been formally adopted by the GATT were "nonbinding precedents for the GATT, let alone this panel."

[38] WTO Dispute Settlement Understanding, para. 1.1.

[39] The structure of the WTO is described *supra* Chapter Three.

[40] WTO Agreement, art. II:2 & Annex 1A.

[41] *Id*. art. II:4.

[42] That is the date the NAFTA entered into force. *See* NAFTA, art. 2203 and Chapter Two *supra*, note 1.

least a minimum rule-system in place. Some Members of the WTO may choose also to remain parties to the GATT 1947 so as to maintain existing relationships with non-WTO Members. Questions with respect to transition from the GATT 1947 to the WTO and GATT 1994 will be considered by a Preparatory Committee for the World Trade Organization (PCWTO).[43] The important point for present purposes is that the "legal distinc[tion]" between the GATT 1947 and GATT 1994 was not adopted so as to signal a break between the rules of the old GATT and the rules of the new GATT, but rather to facilitate a transition. In fact, the GATT parties that negotiated the WTO Agreement expressly stated that the new GATT (GATT 1994) was intended to continue the customs and practices of the old GATT (GATT 1947). Thus, "[e]xcept as otherwise provided ..., the WTO shall be guided by the decisions, procedures and customary practices followed by the Contracting Parties to GATT 1947 and the bodies established in the framework of the GATT 1947."[44]

The continuity between the GATT 1947 and the GATT 1994 is further reinforced by the fact that right to be an "original Member" in the WTO is limited to parties to the GATT 1947.[45] Countries that wish to become Members of the WTO and that are not parties to the GATT 1947 are required to enter into separate accession agreements with the WTO.[46] The WTO Agreement is open for acceptance only by "original Members."[47]

In light of these factors, it appears reasonable to conclude that if the GATT 1994 is technically considered the successor agreement to the GATT 1947 for parties such as the United States, Canada and Mexico,[48] it should not be considered a new and different GATT from that referred to in Article 103 of the NAFTA because of the context of the succession. The intent of the parties that negotiated the WTO Agreement, as expressed in that Agreement, is that the GATT 1994 will take the place of the GATT 1947 in a continuum in which the customs, practices and interpretations of the prior regime will survive. Thus, for

---

[43] See generally, *First Report of the Committee on International Trade Law (ITLC)*, International Law Association, Buenos Aires Conf., Aug. 14-20, 1994 (F. M. Abbott & E.-U. Petersmann, Rapporteurs). There are a myriad of complex legal issues regarding the transition from the GATT to the WTO that remain to be resolved.

[44] WTO Agreement, art. XVI:1. *See also*, art. IX:1 regarding continuation of the GATT 1947 practice of decision-making by consensus.

[45] *Id.* art. XI:1.

[46] *Id.* art. XII.

[47] *Id.* art. XIV:1.

[48] Even if these countries remain parties to the GATT 1947 during an interim period to facilitate their trade relations with third countries, as between themselves they will be governed by the WTO/GATT 1994 and the NAFTA.

purposes of Article 103 of the NAFTA, the GATT 1994 may well be considered to stand in the place of the GATT 1947, so that the NAFTA will continue to prevail over the GATT.

Assuming that the GATT 1994 is considered to take the place of the GATT 1947 for NAFTA Article 103 priority purposes, there nevertheless remain issues with respect to the relationship of NAFTA rules to WTO rules more generally.[49] Some WTO agreements, such as the Agreement on Technical Barriers to Trade (TBT), may be refinements of Tokyo Round agreements, *i.e.* the Technical Standards Code, and questions regarding the legal priority of these agreements may be analyzed on roughly the same basis as the GATT 1947 to the GATT 1994. That is, the later agreement is successor in a continuum to the earlier, and the rule of NAFTA priority may be applied. In respect to certain other WTO agreements, such as the Agreement on Sanitary and Phytosanitary Measures (SPS), the rules that are incorporated may largely reflect prior GATT custom, or may reflect clarifications or extensions of existing GATT rules. For example, the SPS Agreement may be viewed largely as an extension of the TBT Agreement into the area of agriculture, as well as a codification of GATT practice. WTO agreements that are not direct refinements of Tokyo Round agreements are, nevertheless, in somewhat more of a grey area than direct refinements to Tokyo Round agreements from the standpoint of priority.

Finally, there are WTO agreements, such as the General Agreement on Trade in Services (GATS) and the Agreement on Trade-Related Aspects of Intellectual Property Rights (TRIPS), that concern "new areas" of GATT coverage, and may appear to fall within the range of a "successor agreement in a continuum" to the GATT only if that expression is construed very broadly. In regards to these "new area" agreements, a stronger argument can be made that the rule of priority set forth in NAFTA Article 103 may not apply.

It is of considerable interest that Article 2005 of the NAFTA, concerning the forum for settlement of disputes, makes more direct reference than NAFTA Article 103 to the succession question. Article 2005(1) provides that "disputes regarding any matter arising under this Agreement and the *General Agreement on Tariffs and Trade*, any agreement negotiated thereunder, or any successor agreement (GATT), may be settled in either forum at the discretion of the complaining Party." For purposes of forum selection, the entire WTO Agreement is encompassed by the "any agreement negotiated thereunder" language, since the WTO Agreement was negotiated under GATT auspices as

---

[49] The various agreements incorporated in the WTO are discussed in Chapter Three, *supra*, and elsewhere herein.

a consequence of the Uruguay Round mandate. The situation is thus that disputes arising under the NAFTA and WTO may certainly be settled in the NAFTA dispute settlement forum (and must be settled there in the environmental context at the demand of a respondent). What rules NAFTA dispute settlement panels should apply is less clear.

It would in fact seem rather anomalous if NAFTA dispute settlement panels, whose default terms of reference are to interpret the NAFTA, would be assumed to apply WTO rules in sensitive areas such as that of environmental protection, particularly in light of the intense debate that preceded the adoption of the NAFTA rules. Nevertheless, for the time being at least, the answer to the question whether NAFTA rules prevail over WTO rules pursuant to Article 103 of the NAFTA is not a certain one. Because of the number of contextual factors involved in defining this relationship, it may be some years before an authoritative definition of the relationship emerges, whether through action taken by the NAFTA Parties to expressly establish the relationship, or through an accumulation of dispute settlement panel opinions that may establish a common law of interpretation.

It is apparent that NAFTA and WTO panels may develop different answers to the same questions arising under the same agreements, and different answers to the same questions arising under different agreements. The potential for conflict between regional dispute settlement decisions and WTO dispute settlement decisions does not arise uniquely in the NAFTA context. The same situation pertains as to the European Union and its European Court of Justice dispute settlement system, and the WTO. In the European Union system disputes between Member States regarding trade matters are resolved solely by the European Court of Justice.[50] As yet there is no formal mechanism for resolving dispute settlement conflicts beyond application by judges and arbitrators of the rules of international law which establish a hierarchy of norms. Such rules would seem to make clear that, at least as respects obligations to third country Members of the WTO, Parties to the NAFTA and EU Member States must give

---

[50] Since the common commercial policy is within the exclusive competence of the Union (Treaty on European Union, art. 113), issues arising among the Member States with respect to the external trade policy of the Union are within the exclusive jurisdiction of the ECJ (*id.* arts. 164 et seq.).

Might the EU Member States have better chosen to allow recourse to GATT dispute settlement to resolve differences among themselves in matters under the scope of the Union Treaty? Frieder Roessler has praised the NAFTA for preserving recourse by its parties to WTO dispute settlement. He views this as helpful to preserving WTO authority. Roessler intimates that the European Union is a special case because of the extent to which it approximates a single juridical entity for GATT purposes. *See* Roessler, *supra*, note 34, at 311-12, 318-20.

priority to WTO rules over regional rules.[51] Recourse to general rules of international law regarding the hierarchy of treaty norms is unlikely to provide clear answers to questions of the priority of NAFTA and WTO rules and decisions as among the NAFTA Parties. The general rules of international law concerning interpretation and the effect of successor agreements on prior agreements are sufficiently dependent on the intentions of the treaty parties that the relative weighting of contextual factors will strongly influence decisions.[52] Moreover, reliance on general rules of international law to resolve conflicts between multilateral and regional organizations may not be a sound idea in practice, because of the intensity of political friction likely to accompany an application of these norms.

The principal mechanism presently available in the WTO Agreement for reconciling conflicts between the WTO and other rule systems is the waiver mechanism by which the WTO Members may on a one-time or continuing basis permit certain members to avoid application of WTO norms. The grant by the WTO of a waiver to NAFTA and other RIAs to maintain inconsistent rules would not appear to be an attractive long term solution to the problem of conflicting rules for a number of reasons. Trading rules are most effective in promoting economic development when there is sufficient stability in expectations to allow private parties to rely on those rules. A case-by-case waiver system would not be likely to enhance stability in expectations. A blanket waiver system would be more conducive to stability than a case-by-case waiver system, but it would still embody substantial uncertainty for both the RIAs and other WTO Members. A waiver system may also appear to condone the adoption or maintenance of measures with discriminatory effects and thereby undermine fundamental WTO principles. Additionally, just as with the GATT code system which preceded the inclusive WTO system, there may develop a

---

[51] The Vienna Convention on the Law of Treaties provides that treaties adopted by a limited group of states do not supersede the obligations of members of that group to third countries under separate treaties. Vienna Convention, art. 30(4)(b). *See* Thomas Schoenbaum, *Free International Trade and Protection of the Environment: Irreconcilable Conflict?*, 86 A.J.I.L. 700 (1992).

[52] Under article 30(3) of the Vienna Convention on the Law of Treaties, as between parties to treaties concerning the same subject matter, if the earlier treaty is not terminated or suspended, the later in time treaty prevails, and the earlier treaty applies only to the extent its provisions are compatible with the later. Under article 59(1), a later in time treaty concluded between all parties to a prior treaty concerning the same subject matter is considered to terminate the prior treaty if that is either expressly provided for, it appears to be the intention of the parties, or if the provisions of the later treaty are so far incompatible with the earlier so as not to be capable of application at the same time. Under art. 59(2), the earlier treaty will be considered as only suspended if that appears to be the parties' intentions. Under art. 70(1), termination releases the parties from further obligations to perform, but does not affect matters prior to termination.

multi-tiered rule structure that would impede the efficient functioning of the multilateral trading system. Such a multi-tiered system presents special obstacles to the developing countries with less resources to adjust their production to varying sets of rules.

In the environmental area efforts are beginning to reconcile the competing RIA and WTO rule systems in the context of an ambitious WTO work program.[53] However, systematic attention to the RIA/WTO interface problem also is required on a broader basis. The need for such attention is recognized by trade law scholars and is the subject of current work programs.[54]

III. THE SUPPLEMENTAL AGREEMENT WITH RESPECT TO THE ENVIRONMENT

Each NAFTA Party adhered to the North American Agreement on Environmental Cooperation (NAAEC or Supplemental Agreement). The Supplemental Agreement principally obligates the parties to maintain high levels of environmental protection[55] and to implement and enforce their environmental laws[56] through the use of a variety of measures.[57] Under the

---

[53] *See* Abbott, NAFTA as Prototype, *supra* note 32.

[54] *See First Report of the ILA Committee on International Trade Law* (F.M. Abbott and E.-U. Petersmann, Rapporteurs), *supra* note 43.

[55] Canada-Mexico-United States: North American Agreement on Environmental Cooperation [done Sept. 8-14, 1993], 32 I.L.M. 1480 (1993), entered into force Jan. 1, 1994 [hereinafter Supplemental Agreement or NAAEC]. Article 3 of the Supplemental Agreement provides as follows:

> Recognizing the right of each Party to establish its own levels of domestic environmental protection and environmental development policies and priorities, and to adopt or modify accordingly its environmental laws and regulations, each Party shall ensure that its laws and regulations provide high levels of environmental protection and shall strive to continue to improve those laws and regulations.

[56] Article 5 of the Supplemental Agreement provides, in part:

> With the aim of achieving high levels of environmental protection and compliance with its environmental laws and regulations, each Party shall effectively enforce its environmental laws and regulations through appropriate governmental action, subject to Article 37, such as [followed by list of possible activities, including, *e.g.*, (j) initiating, in a timely manner, judicial, quasi-judicial or administrative proceedings to seek appropriate sanctions or remedies for violations of its environmental laws and regulations.

Article 37 provides:

> Nothing in this Agreement shall be construed to empower a Party's authorities to undertake

Supplemental Agreement, implementation and enforcement measures must permit private access to courts and administrative proceedings to compel compliance,[58] provide private remedies,[59] and be transparent.[60] The establishment of the NAAEC Commission for Environmental Cooperation is provided for in Part Three of the Supplemental Agreement. The Commission will be comprised of a Council, a Secretariat, and a Joint Public Advisory Committee.[61]

The Secretariat is established to support implementation of the Agreement and assist and advise the Council.[62] Private parties, including interest groups, have the right to initiate proceedings before the Secretariat, alleging that a Party is failing to effectively enforce its environmental law. Upon approval by two-thirds vote of the Council, the Secretariat will prepare a factual record regarding the matter. By a two-thirds vote, the Council may make the factual record public.

A principal role of the Council will be to oversee the conduct of arbitration proceedings brought by one or more Parties against another seeking to remedy "a persistent pattern of failure by the Party complained against to effectively enforce its environmental law."[63] The Supplemental Agreement establishes an

---

environmental law enforcement activities in the territory of another Party.

[57] *Id.*

[58] Article 6 of the Supplemental Agreement provides, *inter alia*:

2. Each Party shall ensure that persons with a legally recognized interest under its law in a particular matter have appropriate access to administrative, quasi-judicial or judicial proceedings for the enforcement of the Party's environmental laws and regulations.

[59] *Id.* art. 6(3).

[60] *See, e.g., id.* art. 7, concerning "Procedural Guarantees."

[61] *See* Supplemental Agreement, arts. 8-10 regarding the functions of the Council. The Joint Public Advisory Committee is intended to provide a consultation and recommendation function, including with respect to the preparation of factual records and the Secretariat's annual program. See *id.* arts. 16-18.

[62] *Id.* arts. 11-15.

[63] *See* Article 24 of the Supplemental Agreement. The alleged enforcement failure must relate:

... to a situation involving workplaces, firms, companies or sectors that produce goods or provide services:

(a) traded between the territories of the Parties; or

(b) that compete, in the territory of the Party complained against, with goods or services produced or provided by persons of another Party. *Id.*

elaborate (Byzantine) and lengthy procedure by which the Council, after a failed effort at conciliation,[64] may decide by a two-thirds vote[65] that a panel of five expert arbitrators should be selected and convened by the disputing Parties.[66] The panel will examine the allegations concerning a persistent pattern of failure to enforce and, upon finding such a pattern, the panel's recommendations "normally shall be that the Party complained against adopt and implement an action plan sufficient to remedy the pattern of non-enforcement."[67] The final reports of panels are to be made public.[68]

If the Parties are unable to agree on an action plan, and if the panel finds that the losing Party's proposed plan is inadequate, a plan may be imposed by the panel.[69] If Party is found by a panel to have failed to implement the approved action plan, then the panel shall impose a monetary penalty against that Party.[70] The procedure outlined in the Supplemental Agreement may well last up to two years before the panel finally assesses a monetary penalty.[71] The maximum amount of the potential monetary penalty is $20 million in the first year after the date of entry into force of the NAFTA, and thereafter .007 percent of the total trade between the Parties during the most recent year for which data is available.[72] Except as against Canada, the complaining Party(ies) may collect the assessment by suspending trade benefits under the NAFTA.[73] The monetary penalty may be assessed annually if failure to implement the

---

[64] *Id.* arts. 22-24.

[65] *Id.* art. 24(1).

[66] A third Party with a substantial interest in the matter may join by right as a complaining Party. *Id.* art. 24(2). Otherwise a third Party may attend hearings, and receive and make submissions to the panel. *Id.* art. 29. The panelists ordinarily are to be selected from a roster of forty-five candidates created by consensus. *Id.* arts. 25-28. Unless the disputing parties agree otherwise, the duties of the panel will be:

> To examine in light of the relevant provision of the Agreement, including those in Part Five [regarding Consultation and Resolution of Disputes], whether there has been a persistent pattern of failure by the Party complained against to effectively enforce its environmental law, and to make findings, determinations and recommendations in accordance with Article 31(2) [regarding contents of panel report]. *Id.* art. 28.

[67] *Id.* art. 31(2).

[68] *Id.* art. 32(3).

[69] *Id.* art. 34(4).

[70] *Id.* art. 34(5)(b) & Annex 34.

[71] This time period is derived by counting the maximum number of days allocated to each stage of the arbitration procedure, plus the minimum consultation and reconciliation time period.

[72] *Id.* Annex 34(1).

[73] *Id.* art. 36.

action plan continues.[74] A penalty against Canada may only be collected by Canadian court enforcement (although such enforcement is automatic).[75] The monetary penalty is to be paid into a fund "to be expended at the direction of the Council to improve or enhance the environment or environmental law enforcement in the Party complained against, consistent with its law."[76]

The NAFTA dispute settlement system established by the Supplementary Agreement is not redundant with the WTO dispute settlement system. The WTO makes no explicit provision outside the new TRIPS Agreement for assuring that countries either (a) maintain minimum national regulatory standards or (b) enforce these standards. The WTO-based rules directly applicable to the environment are that countries not adopt measures which are disguised barriers to trade (*e.g.*, under the Agreement on Technical Barriers to Trade) and that, to the extent regulatory standards are applied, they are applied in a non-discriminatory manner.[77] The Supplemental Agreement requires the NAFTA Parties to enforce their environmental laws and thus fills a lacuna in the WTO system.

---

[74] *Id*. art. 35(2).

[75] *Id*. art. 36; Annex 36A.

[76] *Id*. Annex 34(3). The NAFTA's mechanism to assure against underprotection of the environment includes two additional measures. First, the NAFTA provides that specified environmental agreements, such as the Basel Convention on Transboundary Waste, will take precedence over the provisions of the agreement. NAFTA, art. 104. Second, the investment chapter of the NAFTA provides that the country parties should not seek to attract or retain investments by waiving, offering to waive, derogating from, or offering to derogate from domestic health, safety or environmental measures. *Id*. art. 1114. Although there is some ambiguity on this point, it may be that only consultative mechanisms are available to challenge an alleged granting of or offer to grant a waiver of environmental standards for the purpose of attracting or retaining investments. Article 1114(2), NAFTA, provides, in relevant part:

> If a Party considers that another Party has offered such an encouragement [regarding waiver of environmental standards], it may request consultations with the other Party and the two Parties shall consult with a view to avoiding any such encouragement. NAFTA, art. 1114(2).

To the extent that disputes involving either of the foregoing rules are the subject of complaints (and are cognizable), these would ordinarily be resolved under the NAFTA's general arbitration mechanism. *See also*, Supplemental Agreement, art. 10(6)(b) regarding the role of the NAAEC Council in providing assistance in consultations.

[77] *See* Chapters Three and Four, *supra*.

IV. THE SUPPLEMENTAL AGREEMENT WITH RESPECT TO LABOR

The second Supplemental Agreement to the NAFTA is the North American Agreement on Labor Cooperation (NAALC).[78] The NAALC is structurally similar in most respects to the NAAEC. The NAALC establishes for the Parties a general obligation to maintain high labor standards.[79] The Parties are also obligated to promote compliance with and to effectively enforce their labor laws, and the NAALC sets out a variety of measures that would be considered appropriate to fulfill this obligation.[80] The NAALC requires the Parties to assure that private individuals with a legally recognized interest under their law have a right of access to administrative or judicial procedures to seek enforcement of labor laws,[81] and that appropriate procedural guarantees are provided.[82] The NAALC makes clear that each Party is entitled to adopt and maintain its own labor laws and standards,[83] although the agreement also contains an Annex which sets out basic labor principles which the Parties commit themselves to promote (but which do not constitute minimum standards).[84]

The NAALC establishes a Commission for Labor Cooperation, comprised of a Council and Secretariat.[85] The Council is composed of the Labor Ministers of each Party, and generally acts by consensus.[86] The Council will act to oversee the implementation of the NAALC and the work of the Secretariat,[87] as well as to promote cooperative activities between the Parties with respect to labor issues generally.[88] The Secretariat is the permanent administrative organ of the Council headed by an Executive Director (appointed on a rotating basis from among the Parties).[89] Each Party also agrees to establish a National Administrative Office (NAO) to provide a contact point for

---

[78] Canada-Mexico-United States: North American Agreement on Labor Cooperation [done Sept. 8-14, 1993], 32 I.L.M. 1499 (1993) [hereinafter NAALC or Labor Supplement].
[79] *Id.* art. 2.
[80] *Id.* art. 3 (*e.g.*, the timely initiation of enforcement proceedings).
[81] *Id.* art. 4.
[82] *Id.* art. 5.
[83] *Id.* arts. 2 & 42.
[84] *Id.* Annex 1.
[85] *Id.* Part Three.
[86] *Id.* art 9.
[87] *Id.* art. 10.
[88] *Id.* art. 11.
[89] *Id.* art. 12.

regional cooperation.[90] Each NAO will act to receive and publish public communications on labor law matters arising within the territory of another Party.[91]

A Party may demand that an Evaluation Committee of Experts (ECE) be convened to prepare a report concerning the labor enforcement practices of another Party.[92] The reports of such ECEs ordinarily will be made public.[93] The preparation of such a report is a prerequisite to a demand for the establishment of a dispute settlement panel.[94] A dispute settlement panel will be convened to consider allegations that a Party has persistently failed to enforce its labor standards.[95] Upon an adverse finding, a Party will ordinarily be expected to implement an action plan to remedy the failure.[96] If it fails to do so, then a panel may impose a monetary penalty against it.[97] If a Party fails to pay the award, then (except as against Canada) the other Party may suspend benefits under the NAFTA.[98] Only automatic court enforcement is available as against Canada.[99] A monetary penalty will be paid into a fund to be expended at the direction of the Council to improve or enhance the enforcement of labor law in the Party complained against.[100]

The principal difference between the NAALC and the NAAEC is that under the NAALC private parties do not have a right to petition the Secretariat for the preparation of a factual report as they do under the NAAEC.[101] However, labor groups in the United States have already filed complaints with the U.S. NAO alleging that companies in Mexico have failed to comply with Mexican labor standards, and perhaps the expectation of U.S. labor organizations is that the NAOs will be forced to initiate consultations and dispute settlement

---

[90] *Id.* arts. 15 & 16.
[91] *Id.* art. 16(3).
[92] *Id.* art. 23.
[93] *Id.* art. 26. The report will not be made public if the Council unanimously agrees.
[94] *Id.* art. 27.
[95] *Id., e.g.,* art. 33.
[96] *Id.* art. 38.
[97] The maximum potential monetary penalty is the same provided for under the NAAEC; that is $20 million in the first year after entry into force and thereafter .007 percent of the total trade in goods between the Parties. *Id.* Annex 39.
[98] *Id.* art. 41.
[99] *Id.* Annex 41A.
[100] *Id.* Annex 39(3).
[101] *See* discussion of NAAEC, *supra* text accompanying notes 52-53.

proceedings on the basis of such complaints.[102]

Like the NAAEC, the NAALC fills a gap in the WTO system by providing that the Parties will maintain high standards regarding the treatment of labor and by providing a mechanism pursuant to which the Parties may bring complaints for persistent failure to apply labor laws.

V. THIRD COUNTRY ACCESS

As a general proposition, the NAFTA makes its institutional procedures and guarantees available either to the Party governments or to nationals of the Parties. The Treaty on European Union similarly addresses itself to the Member States and to nationals of the Member States. This does not, however, foreclose to individuals from third countries access to judicial or institutional processes in the territories of the NAFTA Parties, just as it does not foreclose to individuals from third countries access to the courts and institutional processes of the EU.

As discussed in Chapter Five, juridical entities established by third country nationals in the NAFTA territories are assimilated to NAFTA nationals and thus will have the rights and obligations of NAFTA nationals, including rights of access to proceedings. This will not directly benefit individuals from third countries who do not establish legal entities, but is an important step in providing equivalent treatment. Many third countries which do business in the NAFTA maintain bilateral treaties of commerce with NAFTA Parties.[103] These treaties typically provide nationals of each country with guarantees of access to judicial and administrative proceedings. In addition, at least insofar as the United States is concerned, the courts are generally amenable to suits brought by citizens of foreign countries.[104]

---

[102] *See NAO Decides to Review Union Charges Against Honeywell, General Electric*, 11 BNA INT'L TR. REPTR. 657, Apr. 27, 1994.

[103] Typically Treaties of Friendship, Commerce and Navigation (FCN Treaties) or Bilateral Investment Treaties (BITs). *See, e.g.,* Frederick M. Abbott, *NAFTA and the Future of United States-European Community Trade Relations: The Consequences of Asymmetry in an Emerging Era of Regionalism,* 16 HASTINGS INT'L & COMP. L. REV. 489 (1993).

[104] *See, e.g.,* Article III of the U.S. Constitution which gives the federal courts jurisdiction over cases involving foreign citizens. Both U.S. citizens/resident aliens and foreign parties have access to federal courts for proceedings against the United States government (USG) under either 28 USC § 1346 (general civil action against USG); 28 USC §§ 1581, *et seq.* & 2631 *et seq.* (*see* definitions of "interested party" and "party-at-interest" 28 USC § 2631(k))(civil actions before Court of International Trade against USG based upon various trade laws), and; 28 USC § 1491 (United States Claims Court).

VI. SELF-EXECUTING EFFECT

The U.S. Congress has denied the NAFTA self-executing effect,[105] and in consequence neither U.S. nationals, NAFTA territory nationals or third country nationals can bring suit in the United States directly on the basis of the agreement. Claims must instead be brought on the basis of the NAFTA implementing legislation.[106] There are strong arguments in favor of permitting the NAFTA to retain a self-executing character (to the extent such a character would be determined by the courts). Self-execution would likely accelerate the integration process by increasing the diversity of claims which might be brought under the agreement. If the U.S. were to permit the NAFTA to be construed by the courts as self-executing, it would provide an example to other countries in the region and perhaps reduce the likelihood that their legislatures will erode treaty commitments through inconsistent national rules. As matters now stand, the NAFTA may not be directly relied upon by private parties in courts of the United States.

VII. CONCLUSION

The provisions of the WTO which permit the formation of regional arrangements, Article XXIV of GATT 1994 and Article V of GATS, do not address the institutional structures of these arrangements. As with respect to individual states, the basic philosophy is one of non-interference in the internal affairs of the regional arrangement. In this structural context, there is no inconsistency involving the NAFTA and the legal requirements of the WTO. There are, however, conflicts between the NAFTA norm system and the WTO norm system, and there is a potential for conflict between dispute settlement decisions of NAFTA arbitral panels and dispute settlement decisions of the WTO dispute settlement body. It seems doubtful that any party to either organization will have an interest in deliberately provoking a clash between the two systems, and it may be pointed out that the European Union and GATT have co-existed in a similar situation for more than three decades without a serious rupture in relations. The NAFTA, EU and WTO are each organizations that function adequately because the parties to each of them have an interest in

---

[105] NAFTA Implementation Act, § 102.

[106] *See generally*, Frederick M. Abbott, *Regional Integration Mechanisms in the Law of the United States*; Starting Over, 1 IND.J. GLOBAL LEG. STUD. 155 (1993).

their success. The interest of the parties tends to manifest itself in cooperative behavior. Although it is important to pursue mechanisms intended to minimize destructive conflict, the historical record suggests that the NAFTA and WTO institutions should be able to cooperate and coexist, more or less peacefully.

Chapter Seven

THE NAFTA AND THE EUROPEAN UNION

There is no single dominant trading partner of the United States. In 1993 the European Union in the aggregate was the third leading merchandise exporter to the United States, behind Canada and Japan by a narrow margin, and was the second leading importer of merchandise from the United States, behind Canada.[1] The European Union is in the aggregate the leading services exporter to and importer from the United States, but the United States maintains a significantly higher services trade surplus with Japan than it does with the EU. Cross-investments between the European Union and the United States are very substantial, although Japan is the largest single country holder of foreign direct investment in the United States. Trends in trade and investment patterns may well suggest that both for the EU and the United States the principle focus of external economic relations for the next decade will be elsewhere than in their reciprocal sphere.[2] Nevertheless, it cannot be disputed that the U.S.- European Union economic relationship is of tremendous significance to both sides. The importance of the trans-Atlantic relationship is heightened by the intertwined political history of the United States and Europe, by cultural similarities, and by relatively similar approaches to social welfare issues.

The integration of the United States into the NAFTA was no doubt taken with an eye on developments involving the European Union. The pace of EU expansion is breathtaking and certainly was a cause for reasonable concern among U.S. trade policy planners.[3] The EU was moving to consolidate its relationship with the EFTA countries by completing the European Economic

---

[1] Supporting figures for these introductory observations are detailed *infra*.
[2] The U.S. shift of focus to the Asia-Pacific sphere is discussed in Chapters One and Eight. The shift in EU areas of opportunity is discussed in COMMISSION OF THE EUROPEAN COMMUNITIES, EUROPEAN ECONOMY, THE EUROPEAN COMMUNITY AS WORLD TRADE PARTNER, NO. 53 (1993) [hereinafter EUROPEAN ECONOMY].
[3] A thorough report on the progress of European Union integration is in EUROPEAN ECONOMY, *id*.

Area Agreement, was negotiating preferential arrangements with the former COMECON countries and continuing to extend its preferences to developing countries within the Lóme framework. As the NAFTA has entered into force, the EU has concluded formal accession agreements with Austria, Finland, Norway and Sweden. If and when the agreements are ratified, it will become the Union of the Sixteen.[4] Whether or not the EU had designs on a Fortress Europe, the market access bargaining power being assembled by the EU created a sufficient risk of imbalance in future trade negotiations with the United States that the latter perceived some urgency in creating a North American counterweight.

The North American integration process obviously will have some impact on the dynamic of commercial and political relations between the United States and the EU, and also between Canada, Mexico and the EU. Some of the ways in which this dynamic may be affected are discussed in official reports of the EU, discussed in sections II and III below. The absence of a mechanism for a coordinated NAFTA external commercial policy will be an important factor in shaping new relations. The EU will be able to negotiate separately with the governments of Canada, Mexico and the United States as a means of securing the most favorable terms of access to the NAFTA market.[5] In most cases regarding access to the EU market, on the other hand, the governments of Canada, Mexico and the United States must deal with the central authority of the European Commission.[6]

---

[4] See, e.g., Nevine Khalil & Debra Percival, *Europe: A Bigger and Better Union for Its New Members?*, INTER PRESS SERVICE, June 24, 1994 (LEXIS/NEXIS).

[5] For example, if in negotiations with the EU the United States were to threaten to restrict establishment rights within its territory and thereby limit the ability of EU-owned enterprises to supply services in the NAFTA market, the strength of the threat would be diminished because the EU could pursue alternative establishment arrangements with Canada and Mexico, thereby gaining comparable access to the NAFTA services market.

[6] There are of course grey areas where the division of competences between the Union and Member States may be contested and in which third countries may negotiate jointly or severally with the Commission and the Member States. See Frederick M. Abbott, *Crosscurrents in European Union External Commercial Relations: The Controversy Over the Germany-United States Treaty of Friendship*, 54 ZAöRV__ (1994) and Frederick M. Abbott, *NAFTA and the Future of United States-European Community Trade Relations: The Consequences of Asymmetry in an Emerging Era of Regionalism*, 16 HASTINGS INT'L & COMP. L. REV. 489 (1993). Although EU authority in the field of establishment rights may not be entirely clear, the Maastricht Treaty added provisions seeming to bolster the Union role in this area, and the Commission certainly acts as though it has the authority to control establishment access rights. See discussion *infra*.

I. THE TRANS-ATLANTIC RELATIONSHIP BY THE NUMBERS

In 1993, Canada, Japan and Mexico were, in that order, the leading single country merchandise export markets and the leading importers to the United States in dollar volume of trade.[7] In 1993 the European Union in the aggregate was the third leading merchandise exporter to the United States, behind Canada and Japan by a narrow margin, and was the second leading importer of merchandise from the United States, behind Canada.[8] For the European Union, while in 1990 the EFTA countries were in the aggregate its leading merchandise

---

[7] Exports by U.S. (in millions of dollars) to Canada (100,212.0), Japan (47,898.9) and Mexico (41,630.1). Imports by U.S. (in millions of dollars) from Canada (111,216.4), Japan (107,246.5) and Mexico (39,917.2). From U.S. Trade Data for 1993, furnished to the author on July 6, 1994 by the United States Department of Commerce, Bureau of Economic Analysis, Balance of Payments Division, Merchandise Trade Branch (Marc Bouchard).

[8] U.S. Dept. of Comm., *id*. Table below based on Department of Commerce data, *id.*, in millions of dollars. Left hand numeral indicates relative position among all U.S. trade markets (by country), up to 25th. Ranking from U.S. Dept. of Comm., Business America, Apr. 1994, at 39.

Exports from U.S. by Country			Imports to U.S. by Country		
4.	United Kingdom	26,381.3	5.	Germany	28,562.3
5.	Germany	18,946.4	7.	United Kingdom	21,730.0
8.	France	13,289.8	9.	France	15,295.4
9.	Netherlands	12,839.0	10.	Italy	13,216.8
12.	Belgium-Luxembourg	9,436.7	19.	Netherlands	5,443.3
17.	Italy	6,466.1	21.	Belgium-Luxembourg	5,402.0
22.	Spain	4,168.0		Spain	2,991.9
	Ireland	2,728.2		Ireland	2,519.4
	Denmark	1,092.2		Denmark	1,672.7
	Greece	879.4		Portugal	785.2
	Portugal	726.5		Greece	347.5
	Total of Twelve	96,953.6		Total of Twelve	97,966.5

In 1990, leading U.S. exports to the European Union included aircraft, computers and parts, and telecommunications equipment. *U.S. Foreign Trade Highlights 1990*, U.S. Dep't of Commerce, Int'l Trade Adm. (1991), at 80. Telecommunications equipment was ninth on the list at roughly $2 billion. This is of interest in light of existing discriminatory EU government procurement preferences with respect to telecommunications equipment. The leading EU export to the United States was automobiles, and parts thereof was sixth on the list, at $7.5 billion and $2.5 billion respectively. *Id*. at 81.

trading partners, the United States was by a substantial margin its leading single country trading partner.[9] In 1990, Canada was the European Union's eighth largest export market and tenth largest supplier of imports.[10] Mexico was the EU's 26th largest export market[11] and 31st largest supplier of imports.[12] It is of some interest to note that in 1993 the United States ran a slight merchandise trade deficit with the European Union, and that in the prior several years the United States had run a substantial merchandise trade surplus with the European Union.[13] This may perhaps be attributed to a U.S. economy which emerged from recession in 1992, prior to the recovery of the European Union economies.

In 1993 the United States exported services to the European Union valued at $56.7 billion.[14] The largest areas of gross receipts included travel, other private services and royalty payments. In 1993 the European Union exported services valued at $48.9 billion to the United States. The largest U.S. payment outflows involved travel, other private services and direct defense expenditures.[15] The United States thus had a substantial services trade surplus with the Union, even taking into account a substantial imbalance in defense expenditures in favor of the Union.[16] Viewing the Union services market from

---

[9] EUROPEAN ECONOMY, at 11. The EFTA countries accounted for 26.5% of Union exports and the United States 18.2%. Note that EFTA, less Switzerland, has been transformed into part of the European Economic Area so that these percentages are only a rough description of Union external trade. The EFTA countries accounted for 23.5% of Union imports, with the United States at 17-18%. *Id.* at 8. All in 1990 data.

[10] At 9,409 million ECU. *Id.* at 206.

[11] At 3,881 million ECU. *Id.* at 211.

[12] At 2,947 million ECU. *Id.* at 206.

[13] The overall merchandise trade balance between the United States and the European Union was a U.S. $.993 billion deficit in 1989, a $4.929 billion surplus in 1990, a $15.503 billion surplus in 1991, a $6.640 billion surplus in 1992 and $7.248 deficit in 1993. From U.S. Trade Data for 1993, furnished to the author on June 30, 1994 by the United States Department of Commerce, Bureau of Economic Analysis, Balance of Payments Division, Merchandise Trade Branch (Marc Bouchard). Note that these figures were calculated for 1991-1993 based on adjusted data which differs somewhat from that referred to in note 8, *supra*. Unadjusted final 1993 data as reported in note 8 shows only a $1.013 billion deficit for the United States.

[14] Christopher L. Bach, *U.S. International Transactions, Fourth Quarter and Year 1993*, 74 SURVEY OF CURRENT BUSINESS 44, 80 (TABLE 10) (U.S. DEPT. OF COMM.).

[15] *Id.* U.S. military-related services payments to the EU in 1993 were $7.9 billion. EU military-related services payments to the U.S. in 1993 were $ 2.3 billion.

[16] It is not clear, however, how meaningful the foregoing figures are for present purposes. Since these figures reflect payments flows, they do not necessarily reflect the dynamic of U.S. services investment in the Union (or EU services investment in the United States) which may not involve payments flows on a current basis, *e.g.*, an EU affiliate of a U.S. parent may, for a variety of reasons, not repatriate earnings on a current basis.

another useful perspective, aggregate internal gains from the integration of its financial services market are estimated at $26.4 billion.[17]

In the same 1993 period, the United States exported services valued at $16.7 billion to Canada and imported $9 billion in services trade from Canada.[18] The United States exported $27.1 billion in services to Japan and imported $15.1 billion in services trade from Japan.[19]

Although Japan is the leading single country holder of foreign direct investment (FDI) in the United States,[20] the European Union is in the aggregate the leading holder of FDI in the United States.[21] Canada maintains a very substantial FDI position in the United States, while Mexico's position is negligible.[22] The United Kingdom is the leading single country recipient of U.S. FDI, with Canada second. Mexico is a substantial recipient of U.S. FDI.[23] The European Union in the aggregate is the leading recipient of U.S. FDI.[24] The United States is by a large margin the leading recipient of foreign direct investment from the European Union, and the United States is second to the EFTA countries (in the aggregate) as holder of foreign direct investment in the EU.[25] Over 20 percent of FDI in Mexico originates from Western Europe.[26]

---

[17] See Bob Straetz, *European Community Liberalizes Financial Services Market to Become More Competitive*, BUSINESS AMERICA (U.S. Dep't of Comm.), Feb. 8, 1993, at 2, 3-5 *citing* the Cecchini Report on the "Costs of Non-Europe" prepared for the European Commission.

[18] *U.S. International Transactions, supra* note 14, at 82.

[19] *Id.* at 83.

[20] As of 1992, Japan held $96.743 billion in foreign direct investment (FDI) in the United States. *Foreign Direct Investment in the United States: Detail for Historical-Cost Position and Balance of Payments Flows, 1992*, U.S. DEPT. OF COMM., 73 SURVEY OF CURRENT BUSINESS 59, 67 (July 1993).

[21] As of 1992, the EU held in the aggregate $219.133 billion of FDI in the U.S., with the United Kingdom ($94.718 billion) and the Netherlands ($61.341 billion) dominating in this total. *Id.*

[22] As of 1992, Canadian FDI in the U.S. was valued at $38.997 billion, Mexican FDI at $.502 billion. *Id.*

[23] As of 1992, U.S. FDI in the U.K. was valued at $77.842 billion and in Canada at $66.432 billion. U.S. FDI in Mexico was valued at $13.330 billion. *U.S. Direct Investment Abroad: Detail for Historical-Cost Position and Balance of Payments Flows, 1992*, U.S. DEPT. OF COMM., 73 SURVEY OF CURRENT BUSINESS 88, 100 (July 1993).

[24] As of 1992, the United States held FDI valued at $200.535 billion in the EU. *Id.*

[25] See D. Greenaway, *Trade and foreign direct investment*, in EUROPEAN ECONOMY, at 103, 103-11.

[26] Commission of the European Communities, *Information Note on the North American Free Trade Agreement*, COM(93) 188 final, 12 May 1993 [hereinafter *Commission Note*], at 12.

II. THE EUROPEAN COMMISSION

As noted in Chapter One, the EU Commissioner for External Economic Relations, Sir Leon Brittan, reacted favorably to approval of the NAFTA by the U.S. Congress.[27] This favorable reaction is consistent with the analysis of the Commission as contained in its Information Note on the NAFTA of May 1993 [hereinafter Commission Note].[28]

The Commission Note observes that because Canada and the United States already entered into the CUSFTA, and because the NAFTA by and large preserves the structure of the CUSFTA, that the NAFTA's principal effects involve the integration of Mexico with two highly industrialized neighbors.[29] The Note suggests that the NAFTA will have the effect of gradually raising Mexican standards of living, and that "[b]y achieving duty free access to one of the largest and richest markets in the world, Mexico will become one of the most attractive investment destinations for third countries."[30] The Commission suggests that the trade diverting effects of the NAFTA will be offset by growth in the Mexican market should the objectives of its participants be met, and that success of the Uruguay Round negotiations will be a significant determinant of the trade creating-trade diverting effect of the NAFTA. A successful completion of the Uruguay Round will multilateralize many of the NAFTA preferences.[31]

The Commission says that: "The Community is in favour, as a matter of principle, of all free trade agreements *which respect the pertinent GATT rules.*"[32] It goes on to note that Article XXIV accepts that trade diversion will be a natural consequence of a free trade agreement, and that the GATT does not contemplate the payment of compensation as a consequence of trade diversion. It points to the requirements of Article XXIV:5 that duties and other restrictive regulations of commerce of constituent countries not be higher as a consequence of a free trade arrangement, and says that the NAFTA will be evaluated in the GATT under this rule.[33]

---

[27] *See* Chapter One, *supra*, text accompanying notes 14-15.

[28] *Commission Note.*

[29] The Commission Note also observes that because two-way Canada-Mexico trade is very small, and because this situation is not likely to change dramatically, the principal impact will be on U.S.-Mexico relations. This is quite consistent with the analysis of the U.S. International Trade Commission discussed in Chapters Four and Five, *supra*.

[30] *Commission Note*, at 4.

[31] *Id.* at 13.

[32] *Id.* at 14 (emphasis in original).

[33] *Id.* 14.

The specific concerns of the Commission with respect to the NAFTA are rather muted.[34] It notes that preferential tariff treatment of U.S. exports by Mexico, particularly in sectors in which Mexico maintains relatively high tariffs, will result in increased competition for Union exports, but does not suggest that this raises a legal issue. It says that problems will arise if the NAFTA restricts market access regarding financial services, insurance and investment to companies owned or controlled by NAFTA nationals, referring to the one Canadian restriction in this area.[35] It says that the Union places no discriminatory restrictions on foreign-owned firms, although the Commission fails to mention the several sectors as to which it has recently reserved the right to restrict third country market access.[36] As with respect to trade in goods, the Commission points out that successful conclusion of Uruguay Round GATS and TRIMS agreements will help by multilateralizing the preferences in the NAFTA services and investment sectors.[37]

The Commission observes that NAFTA rules of origin are more restrictive than those in the CUSFTA. Of some interest, it states: "Although not contrary to GATT, this is clearly against the interests of exporters of car parts to Canada and Mexico (whose car exports are almost entirely directed to the US)."[38] Some concern is expressed with respect to stricter textile rules of origin, but it is noted that there are some compensating developments with respect to textiles. It is suggested that EU access to the Mexican market in dairy products, sugar and meat could be restricted, but the Commission does not raise legal issues in this respect. The Commission seeks assurance that the NAFTA provisions which may be invoked to counter subsidized agricultural imports be operated in a GATT-consistent manner.

The Commission finally raises the potential for NAFTA and GATT dispute settlement conflict, concern that third country customs user fees not be raised to offset intra-NAFTA fee elimination, and says that the NAFTA patent pipeline rules create a "potentially serious discrimination against Community patent right holders." These issues have been addressed in Chapters Four through Six,

---

[34] *See id.* at 15-16.

[35] *See* discussion of Canadian restriction, *supra* Chapter Five.

[36] *See* Abbott, *NAFTA and the Future, supra* note 6, at 504-10 (1993) regarding, *e.g.*, the Second Banking Directive.

[37] The Commission expresses concern over whether Mexico's elimination of performance requirements is extended to non-NAFTA countries. The recent Mexican investment law, discussed *infra*, should ameliorate this concern.

[38] *Id.* at 15. Recall that in Chapter Four the question was considered whether more restrictive rules of origin are consistent with GATT Article XXIV:5.

supra.

The Commission sees the main effects of the NAFTA perhaps to be on the political side. It foresees that as Mexico's economic standing increases, it "will similarly achieve more equality in its relationship with the Community" and that as Mexico is drawn "more closely into the North American orbit, Mexico's relationship with the Community may gain importance as a counterweight."[39] In its summary conclusion, the Commission says:

> In summary, therefore, and notwithstanding some displacement of certain exports of the Community to the participants of the NAFTA, the impact of the NAFTA on the Community can be expected to be felt most strongly in terms of its political and economic relationship with Mexico; that impact is expected to be globally positive.[40]

III. THE REPORT OF THE EUROPEAN PARLIAMENT COMMITTEE ON EXTERNAL ECONOMIC RELATIONS AND RESOLUTION OF THE EUROPEAN PARLIAMENT

Another EU perspective on the NAFTA is reflected in the Report of the European Parliament Committee on External Economic Relations on the Free Trade Agreement between the United States of America, Canada and Mexico (NAFTA)[hereinafter European Parliament Report or Report].[41] The European Parliament Report notes first the likely positive economic and political consequences of the NAFTA for Mexico, and recognizes the interest of the United States in promoting these consequences.[42] After briefly summarizing the major substantive provisions of the NAFTA, the Report turns to the potential consequences for third countries, including the Union.[43] The Report suggests that the countries facing the most severe short term negative consequences of the NAFTA will be the countries of Latin America and the Caribbean which face diversion of their exports to the United States in favor of Mexico. The Report also suggests that Southeast Asian nations may be adversely affected as Asian investment capital is redirected toward Mexico. Specifically with respect to the Union, the Report identifies exports of yarn, principally to Canada, and exports

---

[39] *Id.* at 4.
[40] *Id.* at 5.
[41] A3-0378/92, 18 Nov. 1992, DOC_EN\RR\217\217513, PE 201.930/fin (Rapporteur: Mr. Gijs de Vries).
[42] *Id.* at 7.
[43] *Id.* at 13-14.

of automobile parts and components as likely to be adversely affected. Of some interest, however, is the strong perception of a silver lining in the grey clouds:

> It would appear that foreign investors in the NAFTA countries will receive no less favorable treatment than will American, Canadian or Mexican companies. Since 57% of foreign direct investments in the US are European, the presence of European affiliates may be an important factor in gaining competitive advantage against other third countries (notably Japan and Korea).[44]

Finally with respect to third countries, the Report asserts that the NAFTA dispute settlement mechanism may disadvantage third countries if the NAFTA develops a jurisprudence different from the GATT.[45] As with the Commission Note, the European Parliament Report fails to also note the comparable role of the European Court of Justice.

The Report considers the prospective GATT-legality of the NAFTA under GATT Article XXIV. The Report notes that deficiencies in Article XXIV preclude its meaningful application, as well as the unlikely prospect that the NAFTA will be disapproved in the GATT.

The Report finally considers the long term implications of the NAFTA for the global trading system and the Union in particular. The Report speculates that a two bloc American/Asian -- European trading system is more likely to emerge than a three bloc system including a separate Asian arrangement.[46] The Report is not inclined to exaggerate the dangers posed by such a development, but does note that "an expanded NAFTA would not necessarily be in the Community's best interest."[47] As a countermeasure, the Report strongly urges a successful completion of the GATT Uruguay Round and suggests that with adequate discipline free trade areas "can be useful building blocks of the world trade regime."[48]

---

[44] *Id.* at 14. The Report notes the possibility of discriminatory treatment of third-country-owned enterprises in the Canadian financial services market, but notes that the operative provision of the Canada-US Free Trade Agreement has not been invoked against a European-owned company. *Id.* at 13-14 & n. 9.

[45] *Id.* at 14.

[46] *Id.* at 16.

[47] *Id.* at 17.

[48] *Id.* at 17-18.

A. THE OPINION OF THE COMMITTEE ON FOREIGN AFFAIRS AND SECURITY FOR THE COMMITTEE ON EXTERNAL ECONOMIC RELATIONS

Appended to the European Parliament Report is an Opinion of the Committee on Foreign Affairs and Security for the Committee on External Economic Relations [Foreign Affairs Opinion].[49] The disparity between the views expressed in the European Parliament Report and the Foreign Affairs Opinion is striking. So striking, in fact, that a somewhat extended quotation is justified:

> The NAFTA agreement, for which US President George Bush campaigned vigorously, establishes a free trade area in which the United States will carry by far the greatest economic, trading, political, and strategic weight: Canada and Mexico cannot compete with the American giant on equal terms. No common institutions are to be set up under the agreement, nor will any steps be subsequently taken towards establishing more complex forms of cooperation. NAFTA, therefore, cannot be likened in any way to the process which has been continuing in Europe for over 40 years and is moving towards the ultimate goal of union.
>
> Outlining the philosophy behind the agreement when speaking to journalists, President Bush declared that the cold war was now over and the main challenge facing the United States was to compete on a rapidly changing and expanding global market.
>
> In fact, the other side of the coin is that the United States is having to contend with growing competition - not only in economic terms - from Japan and Europe. The downturn in the US economy (unemployment and balance of trade deficit) could ultimately place a question mark over the country's currently unchallenged world supremacy. To counter a Europe which is consolidating its strength and moving towards union, as well as an increasingly enterprising Japan which is continuing to extend its sphere of influence, the United States is thus expanding its hegemony over both halves of the American continent. The advent of NAFTA will bring a very severe predicament for the Central and South American countries, which may eventually be crushed under the weight of the new economic bloc.
>
> That being the case, the Community must ensure that the establishment of the North American Free Trade Area does not lead to greater protectionism, pose an obstacle to the development and expansion of transatlantic relations, or jeopardize the continuation of Community policy in relation to Latin America.
>
> In view of its close political, economic, and cultural ties with most Central and South American countries, for which it constitutes a vital reference point, the Community needs to consolidate its position in the region. The idea of a European plan for Latin America should be reactivated and explored further in order to save countries and markets from being swallowed up into the US sphere of influence and to avert the resulting heavy blow to Europe's political prestige as well as to its economy.[50]

---

[49] *Id.* at 19-22 (Draftsman: Mr. Titley).
[50] *Id.* at 21.

B. THE RESOLUTION OF THE EUROPEAN PARLIAMENT

On December 15, 1992 the European Parliament adopted a Resolution on the Free Trade Agreement between the United States of America, Canada and Mexico.[51] The resolution, *inter alia,* "welcom[es] the NAFTA agreement to the extent that it will prove trade-creating rather than trade-diverting"; and expresses concern with the impact of rules of origin on EU exporters of textiles and automobiles, with respect to possible Canadian restrictions in the financial services sector, and with the possible effect that NAFTA dispute settlement may have on the "effectiveness of the GATT dispute settlement mechanism."[52] The resolution, *inter alia,* calls on the Commission to prepare a report on the NAFTA's potential effects on the Union and Latin America for the Council and Parliament; requests the Commission and the Member States to make inquiry within the OECD concerning the compatibility of NAFTA financial services provisions with OECD rules concerning national treatment of foreign investment; calls for a rapid conclusion of the Uruguay Round (requesting the Commission to suggest ways to improve Article XXIV); and "[c]alls on the Commission and the Council to develop economic and political relations with Latin America and Asia as much as possible."[53]

IV. MARKET ACCESS BALANCE

Since the NAFTA in some measure reflects the intention of U.S. trade policy planners to maintain a balance of market power with the EU, it may be useful to briefly consider comparative market access elements of the two arrangements.

A. TRADE IN GOODS

The EU establishes a common outer tariff wall and free circulation for imported third-country goods which have paid the applicable tariff in the country of entry.[54] A NAFTA-origin good which enters the EU pays no additional tariffs

---

[51] Resolution A3-0378/92, PV 42 II, PE 163.452 (Official Minutes of the European Parliament, Dec. 15, 1992).
[52] *Id.*
[53] *Id.*
[54] *See* Chapter Three, *supra.*

upon movement between the Member States. However, while NAFTA-origin goods are not discriminated against on the basis of restrictive intra-EU rules of origin, the EU does maintain an extensive array of tariff preferences in favor of developing country parties to the Lóme agreements.[55] The EU therefor discriminates against NAFTA-origin goods, but principally in terms of favoring imports of primary products from developing countries, and EU exports do not in substantial measure appear to directly benefit from these measures.[56] In addition, the EU maintains substantial barriers to imports of agricultural products, such as variable levies, pursuant to its common agricultural policy.[57]

The NAFTA, on the other hand, maintains the separate tariff schedules of each Party, and provides free circulation within the NAFTA only to goods originating in its territory (including goods meeting its transformation requirements).[58] Although the tariff collection rules of the Parties may exempt third country goods from the double-payment of tariffs on intra-NAFTA transit, the NAFTA tariff system creates some substantial preferences (depending on sector) for goods of NAFTA origin, particularly in respect to exports to Mexico. Third country enterprises with factories in the United States, which supply those factories with parts from abroad, may find that the transformation requirements necessary to achieve free intra-NAFTA circulation create significant competitive impediments to penetrating the Mexican market.

In 1990, leading U.S. merchandise exports to the European Union included aircraft, computers and parts, and telecommunications equipment.[59] The leading EU export to the United States was automobiles, and parts thereof was sixth on the list, at $7.5 billion and $2.5 billion respectively.[60] The scale of EU exports of automobiles and parts to the United States suggests that the impact of NAFTA rules of origin on EU automotive exports directly and indirectly destined for Mexico may be significant.

From a legal standpoint, the EU's treatment of third country exports is more favorable than the NAFTA's. A more complete evaluation of the balance in

---

[55] *See* EUROPEAN ECONOMY, at 63-72.

[56] *Id.* at 68.

[57] For a description of the Common Agricultural Policy (CAP), *see* COMMISSION OF THE EUROPEAN COMMUNITIES, AGRICULTURE IN EUROPE, DEVELOPMENT, CONSTRAINTS AND PERSPECTIVES (1992). The dismantling of CAP barriers was a major objective of many participants in the GATT Uruguay Round. Though these efforts have initiated a process of tariffication and gradual elimination of agricultural market access barriers, it is too early to label these efforts a substantial success.

[58] *See* Chapter Four, *supra*.

[59] *See* note 8 *supra*.

[60] *Id.* at 81.

goods treatment between the EU and NAFTA must await a post-Uruguay Round evaluation of trade-weighted preferences in which EU agricultural barriers are considered against remaining NAFTA tariffs (and tariff preferences) across all sectors.

B. TRADE IN SERVICES AND INVESTMENT

The European Union generally treats third country service providers and investors in a non-discriminatory manner. Third country nationals who establish juridical entities in the Member States are assimilated to nationals of the Member States and thereby are subject to the same treatment as EU nationals.[61] The Treaty on European Union and secondary EU legislation do not grant to third country nationals a right of establishment in the EU territory. Establishment rights are for the most part within the competence of the individual Member States. There are, however, two important caveats. First, new provisions in the Maastricht Treaty give the Council the power to restrict the right of establishment.[62] Second, the Council and Commission have

---

[61] Article 52 of the establishment chapter of the EU Treaty provides for the gradual elimination of restrictions on the freedom of establishment of nationals of a Member State in the territory of another Member State. "Freedom of establishment" is defined to include the right to "set up and manage undertakings" on the condition of national treatment. Article 58 of the treaty provides that:

> Companies or firms formed in accordance with the law of a Member State and having their registered office, central administration or principle place of business within the Community shall, for purposes of this Chapter, be treated in the same way as natural persons who are nationals of the Member States.

The EU Treaty provides in Article 59 of the services chapter for the progressive elimination of barriers to the free provision of services within the Union "in respect of nationals of Member States who are established in a State of the Union other than that of the person for whom the services are intended." Article 66 provides that Article 58 of the establishment chapter, *inter alia*, shall apply to the matters covered by the services chapter. Thus, the rule that companies or firms formed in accordance with the laws of a Member State be treated as natural persons who are nationals of a Member State also applies to the services chapter. In order to benefit from treatment as nationals of a Member State, third country entities are subject to the requirement of maintaining a "continuous and effective link" in a Member State. *General Program for the Abolition of Restrictions on Freedom of Establishment* and *General Program for the Abolition of Restrictions on Freedom to Provide Services*, 1962 J.O. 32, reprinted in CCH *COMMON MKT. REP. (CCH)* ¶1335ff, ¶1545ff, (1962) [hereinafter General Program]. *See generally* Abbott, *NAFTA and the Future supra* note 6.

[62] The Maastricht Treaty on European Union would appear to clarify the position of the Union with respect to the power of Union organs to restrict third country access to the internal market. New article 73b to the Union Treaty would add that, within the framework of the Capital and Payments Chapter, all restrictions on the movement of capital and payments between Member States and between Member States and third countries would be prohibited. However, new article

132   *Chapter Seven*

adopted secondary legislation which necessarily infers that they have the authority, even prior to the Maastricht Treaty, to restrict establishment rights.[63]

Access of U.S. national enterprises to establishment in the EU is generally governed by bilateral Treaties of Friendship, Commerce and Navigation (FCN) between the United States and the individual Member States.[64] These treaties

---

73c(1) would preserve existing restrictions and new article 73(c)(2) would provide:

> Whilst endeavoring to achieve the objective of free movement of capital between Member States and third countries to the greatest extent possible and without prejudice to the other Chapters of this Treaty, the Council may, acting by qualified majority on a proposal from the Commission, adopt measures on the movement of capital to or from third countries involving direct investment - including investment in real estate -, establishment, the provision of financial services or the admission of securities to capital markets. Unanimity shall be required for measures under this paragraph which constitute a step back in Community law as regards the liberalization of the movement of capital to or from third countries.

[63] One clear manifestation of the Union's restricted view of the right of establishment and freedom to provide services appears in the Second Banking Directive. Second Council Directive of 15 December 1989 on the coordination of laws, regulations and administrative provisions relating to the taking up and pursuit of the business of credit institutions and amending Directive 77/780/EEC, 32 O.J. EUR. COMM. (no. L386) 1 (30 Dec. 1989)[hereinafter Second Banking Directive]. A report on the status of the Second Banking Directive and the actions of the Union in regard to it, as well as a report on the status of proposed directives in other Union services sectors, is in Bob Straetz, *European Community Liberalizes Financial Services Market to Become More Competitive*, BUSINESS AMERICA (U.S. DEPT. OF COMM.), Feb. 8, 1993, at 2. The Second Banking Directive is intended to establish uniform minimum standards for banking institutions in the Member States of the Union so that a single license issued by a Member State to a banking institution would permit that enterprise to function throughout the Union on the same conditions. *See generally*, Mark A. Goldstein, *1992 and the FCN and OECD Obligations of EEC Members States to the United States in the Financial Services Area*, 30 VIRG. J. INT'L L. 189, 221-30 (1990), and Michael Gruson & Werner Nikowitz, *The Second Banking Directive of the European Economic Community and Its Importance for Non-EEC Banks*, 12 FORDHAM INT'L L.J. 205 (1989) and *The Reciprocity Requirement of the Second Banking Directive of the European Economic Community Revisited*, 12 FORDHAM INT'L L. J. 452 (1989). The Second Banking Directive authorizes the Commission to direct Member States to limit or suspend decisions regarding authorizations to form new banking subsidiaries and decisions regarding the prospective acquisition of holdings by third-country-controlled enterprises when the Commission finds that: "Community credit institutions in a third country do not receive national treatment offering the same competitive opportunities as are available to domestic credit institutions and [that] the conditions of effective market access are not fulfilled." Second Banking Directive, art. 9(4). The Commission itself may only suspend or limit authorizations for a period of three months, but the Council may by qualified majority extend this period. *Id.*

[64] See Treaty of Friendship, Establishment and Navigation, Feb. 21, 1961, United States-Belgium, 14 U.S.T. 1284, T.I.A.S. No. 5432; Treaty of Friendship, Commerce and Navigation, Oct. 1, 1951, United States-Denmark, 12 U.S.T. 908, T.I.A.S. No. 4797; Convention of Establishment, Nov. 25, 1959, United States-France, 11 U.S.T. 2398, T.I.A.S. No. 4625; Treaty of Friendship, Commerce and Navigation, Oct. 29, 1954, United States-West Germany, 7 U.S.T. 1839, T.I.A.S. No. 3593; Treaty of Friendship, Commerce and Navigation, Feb. 2, 1948, United States-Italy, 63 Stat. 2255, T.I.A.S. No. 1965; Agreement Supplementing the Treaty of Friendship, Commerce and Navigation, Sept. 26, 1951; United States-Italy, 12 U.S.T. 131, T.I.A.S. No. 4685; Treaty of Friendship, Commerce and Navigation, Jan. 21, 1950, United States-Ireland, 1 U.S.T. 785,

contain some provisions for restricting non-discriminatory access in some sectors, but on the whole provide nationals from the United States with open access to establishment in the EU. The WTO GATS Agreement will alter the significance of the existing bilateral FCN treaties between EU Member States and third countries, including the United States.[65] The GATS includes among the commitments that Members may make with respect to liberalizing their services markets a commitment to permit the supply of a service within their territories "through commercial presence."[66] Such a commitment is not obligatory, however, even with respect to a sector which a Member has agreed to liberalize since each Member specifies its commitments and may choose to limit a particular mode of supply, *e.g.*, the establishment of a commercial presence, except in the case of the financial services sector in which a market access commitment must include the right to establish.[67] The author has been

---

T.I.A.S. No. 2155; Treaty of Friendship, Establishment and Navigation, Feb. 23, 1962, United States-Luxembourg, 14 U.S.T. 251, T.I.A.S. No. 5306; Treaty of Friendship, Commerce and Navigation, Mar. 27, 1956, United States-Netherlands, 8 U.S.T. 2043, T.I.A.S. No. 3942; Treaty of Friendship, Commerce and Navigation, Aug. 3, 1951, United States-Greece, 5 U.S.T. 1829, T.I.A.S. No. 3057; Treaty of Friendship and General Relations, July 3, 1902, United States-Spain, 33 Stat. 2105, T.S. No. 422; Convention of Commerce and Navigation, July 3, 1815, United States-United Kingdom, 8 Stat. 228, T.S. No. 110.

See UNITED STATES DEPARTMENT OF STATE, TREATIES IN FORCE ON JANUARY 1, 1992, at 17 (Belgium; at 59 (Denmark); at 79 (France); at 87 (Germany); at 94 (Greece); at 120 (Ireland); at 125 (Italy); at 151 (Luxembourg); at 172 (the Netherlands); at 223 (Spain); at 254 (United Kingdom).

See generally Abbott, NAFTA and the Future, *supra*, note 6; Abbott, *Crosscurrents*, *supra* note 6; Joseph J. Norton, *Status of U.S. Commercial Treaties with the E.E.C. Member States*, in EUROPEAN ECONOMIC COMMUNITY: TRADE AND INVESTMENT (J. NORTON ED., 1986), at 10-1, and Mark A. Goldstein, *1992 and the FCN and OECD Obligations of EEC Member States to the United States in the Financial Services Area*, id.

[65] In a number of areas the FCN treaties deal with subject matter not affected by the WTO Agreement and so will not be affected. Such subject matter areas include access to judicial proceedings generally, rights of freedom of expression and worship, treatment of estates and so forth.

[66] GATS, arts. I:2(c), XVI & XXVIII(d).

[67] Article XVI:1 of GATS provides:

With respect to market access through the modes of supply specified in Article I, each Member shall accord services and services suppliers of any Member treatment no less favourable than that provided for under the terms, limitations and conditions agreed and specified in its schedule.

A footnote to this paragraph states that if a Member has agreed to permit the supply of service through the establishment of a commercial presence, then it will allow related transfers of capital into its territory. This footnote by inference confirms that a member may choose *not* to permit the supply of a service through the granting of establishment rights.

Note, however, that with respect to the Financial Services sector, each Member making a market access commitment in that sector will generally be obligated to permit financial service suppliers of other Members to establish a commercial presence in their territory. *See* Understanding

advised by GATT Secretariat officials familiar with the GATS schedules that they for the most part reflect so-called "standstill" commitments, *i.e.*, GATS Members have generally not undertaken new liberalization commitments, but have agreed not to adopt new restrictions. In any event, it can be stated with some certainty that the schedules of the United States and the EU do not include all areas of commercial interest to enterprises of each side. The GATS negotiations simply were not so successful.[68] Moreover, in respect to the critical area of financial services it was agreed that changes could be made to the Members' market access commitments up to six months after entry into force of the WTO,[69] so that the effect of the GATS in this area will remain uncertain until perhaps late 1995.[70] Thus the effect which the GATS will have on establishment provisions in the bilateral EU Member State - U.S. context cannot be evaluated at this point. In some sectors, market access and the right of establishment are likely to be governed by GATS. In other sectors, the FCN treaties will continue to govern. It may be some years before this situation sorts itself out.

The NAFTA treatment of third country national investors and service providers is similar to that of the EU. Third country nationals who establish a juridical entity in the NAFTA territory are assimilated to NAFTA nationals, and are subject to the same treatment as those nationals.[71] With respect to the United States, investors of the European Union are granted access to establishment in the U.S. territory by the same FCN Treaties which govern access of U.S. nationals to the Member States of the EU. Unlike the provisions of the Maastricht Treaty which give the Council the right to restrict establishment rights, and unlike the secondary EU legislation which permits the Council and Commission to restrict market access rights, the NAFTA does not contemplate the centralized restriction of the right of establishment.

One of the more interesting developments accompanying the formation of the NAFTA is the adoption by Mexico of the Foreign Investment Act of 1993.[72] By this legislation the government of Mexico multilateralizes substantial

---

on Commitments in Financial Services, 33 I.L.M. 145, at para. 5 (1994).

[68] As only one well-known example, EU/US market access in the field of audio-visual services was taken off the table. *See France, U.S. Held Secret Talks*, REUTER EUR. COMM. REP., Dec. 24, 1993 (LEXIS/NEXIS).

[69] GATS, Second Annex on Financial Services.

[70] This assumes a January 1, 1995 coming into force of the WTO Agreement plus six months. *See* Chapter Three, *supra*, regarding target date for WTO entry into force.

[71] *See* Chapter Five, *supra*, and requirement of "substantial business activities".

[72] Mexico: Foreign Investment Act of 1993, Dec. 27, 1993, 33 I.L.M. 207 (1994).

elements of the investment-related benefits of the NAFTA for U.S. and Canadian nationals. The Investment Act permits 100 percent foreign ownership of Mexican enterprises, except in a fairly large number of reserved sectors.[73] Reserved sectors are in some cases closed to foreign investment (*e.g.*, the petroleum sector),[74] or varying percentages of foreign participation are permitted (*e.g.* 30 percent for stockmarket offices and 49 percent for insurance institutions and basic telephone services).[75] In some cases approval of a Commission on Foreign Investments is required for investments in excess of 49 percent (*e.g.* legal services), and in some other cases such approval is required only when this will exceed aggregate foreign capital limitations as annually established by the Commission.[76] Transitional provisions in the automotive, videotext and switchboards, and construction sectors limit participation to 49 percent until December 31, 1999, July 1, 1995, and January 1, 1999, respectively, at which time 100 percent ownership is permitted.[77] The Investment Act is understood to eliminate performance requirements applicable to foreign investments,[78] although this is not expressly provided for in the Act.

While the Mexican Foreign Investment Act imposes considerably more restrictions on third country investors than EU, U.S. or Canadian legislation, it is nevertheless a strong signal of Mexican determination to liberalize its investment market on a multilateral basis. The European Commission Information Note adopts this view when it says:

> one of the reasons that Mexico engaged in the NAFTA negotiations, and that Canada also participated fully, was to increase their attractiveness as investment destinations. It is therefore fully in the interests of Mexico and Canada, as well as the United States, not to make investment by non-members such as the Community more difficult.[79]

It adds: "it is considered unlikely that Mexico or indeed its two NAFTA partners will seek to raise obstacles against foreign investment (except perhaps in specific, sensitive sectors)."[80]

---

[73] *Id.* art. 4.
[74] *Id.* art. 5.
[75] *Id.* art. 7.
[76] *Id.* arts. 8-9. The legislation does not indicate which sectors may be covered by the latter procedure.
[77] *Id.* Transitory Articles.
[78] Jorge A. Vargas, *Introductory Note. Id.* at 209.
[79] *Commission Note, supra* note 28, at 13.
[80] *Id.* at 15.

V. THE ENTENTE

The architects of the NAFTA have achieved the purpose of a relative parity in aggregate market size with the European Union. Although there are dissimilarities with respect to NAFTA and EU approaches to commercial market integration, on the whole both arrangements remain open to traders and investors of third countries. Neither the NAFTA nor the EU has to date demonstrated discriminatory tendencies which might be cause for serious concern among third countries which are not parties to these arrangements. This is not to discount the difficulties and controversies. The EU, for example, maintains discriminatory legislation in its audio-visual sector which is of legitimate concern to the United States and other third countries.[81] Discrimination is the exception to the rule for the NAFTA and EU and is in sharp contrast to the ideas of a Fortress North America and a Fortress Europe.

The formation of the NAFTA creates a shared interest between its Parties and the Member States of the European Union. This is an extremely important development from the standpoint of the development of the WTO. WTO rules are made and interpreted by its Members. The greater the interest of its Members in providing flexibility for regional arrangements, the more likely it is that flexible rules will be adopted. It is a difficult question whether Members of the WTO will be able to maintain the discipline of broad multilateral rules in the face of two competing regional rule systems backed by enormous market power. In this regard, the formation of the NAFTA represents an important juncture for the WTO/GATT system.

It is also important to note that the NAFTA and EU countries share social welfare perspectives which are substantially similar. The social welfare programs of the more highly developed EU Member States, the United States and Canada are very expensive to maintain. Maintaining expensive social welfare programs -- paid for by taxes on workers wages -- is difficult if enterprises based outside the regions do not maintain similar programs. The same point can be made with respect to expensive programs designed to protect the environment. The WTO will have to deal with the problem of disparities in social welfare systems. If it does not, these disparities may push the EU and NAFTA toward regional protectionism.

It would be possible for the EU and NAFTA regions to move toward a

---

[81] Council Directive of 3 Oct. 1989 on the coordination of certain provisions laid down by law, regulation or administrative action in the Member States concerning the pursuit of television broadcasting activities, O.J.E.C. L 298/23, 17 Oct. 1989.

reciprocal system of granting or denying market access in which at least part of the basis upon which the "openness" of a market would be evaluated is its maintenance of minimum labor, environmental and competition standards. At present, such a reciprocity test is not WTO consistent. Two points, however, deserve to be made in this respect. First, there may be subtle ways by which such a reciprocity system could be pursued by the EU and NAFTA so as not to create the too direct appearance of WTO inconsistency. For example, in GATS market access negotiations social welfare programs could be taken into account by EU and NAFTA negotiators as part of their internal evaluation criteria with respect to other GATS Members. The GATS market access negotiation process will not be entirely transparent, and such a process might disguise the consideration of non-GATS-specific factors.

Second, an inability of the WTO to deal adequately with social welfare program disparities may be a factor which will encourage an emphasis on the regional development and implementation of trade rules, as opposed to an emphasis on the broad multilateral approach. If a strong tendency develops among the major economic powers to deal with trade-related issues on a regional basis, the vitality of the WTO system may be significantly diminished through inattention. There are limits within all national governments on the attention which can be paid to any set of issues and to international organizations. This was demonstrated quite clearly with respect to the U.S. government as negotiation and conclusion of the NAFTA brought the GATT Uruguay Round negotiations to a virtual halt for an extended period. The degree of attention which governments and others interested in trade and social welfare policy pay to particular institutions, of course, is a relative matter.

There is no doubt that EU trade and social welfare policy officials presently are more concerned with EU-specific matters than with WTO matters, and this is not an unreasonable attitude. Recognizing therefore that this question is one of balance, it nevertheless seems apparent that if the WTO proves unresponsive to social welfare issues, there is a danger that it will simply be ignored. This is not to suggest that there is an immediate threat to the WTO system resulting from social welfare concerns. It is necessary, however, that trade policy-makers continue to consider options for ameliorating the likelihood that social welfare disparities will lead to a breakdown of the multilateral system which the WTO embodies. It is perhaps ironic that the relative compatibility of the NAFTA and EU social welfare systems may provide an impetus more for a bi-regional Fortress Atlantic than for either a Fortress North America or a Fortress Europe.

Chapter Eight

THE NAFTA AND JAPAN

Japan in 1993 was second to Canada as the leading merchandise exporter to and importer from the United States.[1] Japan is the leading single country market for U.S. services exports, as well a leading exporter of services to the United States.[2] Japan is the leading single country holder of foreign direct investment (FDI) in the United States, while the United States maintains substantial FDI in Japan.[3] Japan's persistently large merchandise trade surplus with the United States is a seemingly perpetual source of political friction between the two countries. It has been suggested that Japan's strength in high-technology industries and its market access barriers with respect to imports in this sector presents a particular problem for the United States.[4] Since 1990, Japan and the United States have pursued on a bilateral basis the Structural Impediments Initiative (SII), directed, *inter alia*, at reducing the adverse trade effects of Japan's restrictive distribution system, exclusive dealing practices and inter-locked corporate relationships.[5]

The NAFTA can be viewed in part as a response by the United States to economic competition from Japan. The United States sought in the NAFTA to

---

[1] In 1993, Japanese merchandise exports to and imports from the United States were $107,246.5 and $47,898.9 million respectively. Chapter Seven *supra* note 7.

[2] In 1993 Japanese services exports to and imports from the United States were $15.1 and $27.1 billion respectively. Chapter Seven *supra* note 7. Only $1.1 billion of the $15.1 billion in 1993 payments from the United States to Japan were military-related. *Id.*

[3] As of 1992, Japanese FDI in the United States was valued at $96,743 million. *Foreign Direct Investment in the United States: Detail for Historical-Cost Position and Balance of Payments Flows, 1992*, U.S. DEPT. OF COMM., 73 SURVEY OF CURRENT BUSINESS 59, 67 (July 1993). At the same time, U.S. FDI in Japan was valued at $26,213 million. *U.S. Direct Investment Abroad: Detail for Historical-Cost Position and Balance of Payments Flows, 1992*, U.S. DEPT. OF COMM., 73 SURVEY OF CURRENT BUSINESS 88,100 (July 1993).

[4] *See* TYSON and THUROW, *supra* Chapter One, note 21.

[5] *See generally*, MITSUO MATSUSHITA, INTERNATIONAL TRADE AND COMPETITION LAW IN JAPAN (1993), at 200-07; TYSON, *id., e.g.*, at 83-84.

expand its export opportunities in an environment protected on a relative basis from Japanese competition. Japan has not pursued a strategy comparable to that of the European Union in creating a formally structured regional market and so the NAFTA cannot be said to be a response to Japanese regionalization efforts in the same sense that it is a response to EU activities. On the other hand, as Japan's MITI White Paper makes very clear, Japan has emerged as a major market force throughout the Asian region by means of extensive direct investment holdings.[6] It may well be argued that Japan's direct investment strategy will be as successful as the European and North American strategies in creating a relatively protected environment in which to conduct trade. The Japanese strategy of investing in overseas manufacturing facilities to supply domestic factories, as well as to supply third markets directly, may well do as much or more to control the destination and pricing of products as does the formation of a formal preferential regional arrangement.[7]

This Chapter first sets out the results of my various meetings in Japan with government officials, scholars and business executives to discuss the implications of the NAFTA. The NAFTA analysis contained in the 1994 report of the Industrial Structure Council of Japan, an official advisory body to MITI, is then reviewed. The rules governing investment access between Japan and the NAFTA countries are described, and finally some general observations are made concerning the implications of the NAFTA for Japan.

I. CONVERSATIONS IN JAPAN

In 1992 and 1993 I visited Japan three times to discuss the NAFTA and its implications, making several presentations and participating in informal discussions at the Fair Trade Center and the University of Tokyo. In June 1993 I interviewed officials at the Ministry of Foreign Affairs and the Ministry of International Trade and Industry (MITI), and met with representatives of

---

[6] MINISTRY OF INTERNATIONAL TRADE AND INDUSTRY, WHITE PAPER ON INTERNATIONAL TRADE, JAPAN 1992 (1992) [hereinafter MITI WHITE PAPER].

[7] One might see the outline of historical-cultural factors at work in the various approaches to economic ordering undertaken by the Europeans, the Japanese and the North Americans. The Europeans, with a principally positivistic civil law approach to the ordering of society, have created an intensely rule-based system in the EU. The Japanese, whose social order is defined largely by custom and the appreciation of complex but subtle social relationships, have approached relative market protection by an informal system (which may nevertheless yield a very firm result). The North Americans, with a relative lack of social history and custom, and a generally hostile attitude toward authority, have created a rule framework with considerable operational flexibility.

industry groups and business executives. I have had the opportunity to discuss the implications of the NAFTA on a number of occasions with Professor Mitsuo Matsushita, Japan's leading trade scholar and Chair of the Unfair Trade Policies and Measures Subcommittee of the Industrial Structure Council (ISC), as well as with Mr. Ken Matsumoto, Director of the Fair Trade Center and Member of the ISC Subcommittee.

My conversations in Japan uncovered varying levels of concern with respect to the NAFTA, but not a uniformity in opinion, even between government agencies. The concerns expressed by the business community tended to be quite pragmatic and to reflect a well informed approach to a new reality. While acknowledging the grey clouds, Professor Matsushita sees the silver lining of the NAFTA in its potential for creating an expanded North American economy and enhanced export opportunities for Japan. Following is a summary of my conversations, divided among the political, public economic and private economic perspectives.

A. THE POLITICAL PERSPECTIVE

An official at the Ministry of Foreign Affairs expressed disappointment that the U.S. government had not consulted with Japan to a greater extent regarding either the initiation of the NAFTA negotiations or their progress because, in his view, the NAFTA raises important political concerns for Japan. The Japanese have watched the European Union pursue increasingly close economic and political cooperation, and recently begin to incorporate Eastern Europe into its sphere of influence. If the United States were to assume a dominant role with respect to North and Latin American economic and political affairs, Japan could be left in a relatively isolated position.[8] This official suggested that concern over U.S. political insensitivity to the ramifications of its strategy of forming more cohesive regional blocs was not limited to the Japanese, but was shared by other nations. He also expressed a general sense of uneasiness about the tendency of the United States and the European Union to focus on their mutual interests and not to include Japan in consultations. This tendency is evidenced not only by U.S. and EU officials, but by the international media, and this creates a sense of isolation in Japan.

---

[8] As an example of U.S. insensitivity to the political ramifications of the NAFTA, he cited a Commerce Department official's public suggestion that Australia/New Zealand and the ASEAN nations might be incorporated into the NAFTA, without having mentioned this in advance to Japanese officials.

At the Ministry of International Trade and Industry there was not the same level of concern over the lack of U.S. consultation regarding the initiation or conduct of the NAFTA negotiations. MITI believes that the United States did not meaningfully consult with any third country regarding the NAFTA and so, in any event, it does not feel that Japan was discriminated against.

I asked at the Foreign Affairs Ministry whether Japan would find it necessary to pursue its own regional arrangement in response to the NAFTA. The view expressed was that Japan could pursue its strategy *vis-à-vis* Asia without a formal arrangement. A formal arrangement might threaten the U.S. and Europe and escalate inter-regional tensions. Japan would prefer to pursue an informal cooperative arrangement.[9]

At the Ministry of Foreign Affairs it was suggested that many Asian countries would be comfortable with a reduced U.S. military-strategic presence in Asia. In response to my question, I was told that Japan is not particularly worried about a Chinese military threat.[10]

B. THE PUBLIC ECONOMIC PERSPECTIVE

An important observation which can be made on the basis of a number of conversations, as well as from the MITI White Paper, is that from an economic perspective, Japan should not be thought of as a group of islands in the North Pacific. Japanese economic interests are spread throughout the world and to a growing extent constitute a major portion of Southeast Asian economies, so that Japan and its interests should be considered from a multinational perspective. This observation applies from the perspective of industries as diverse as the textile, automobile and computer manufacturing industries, and was made either directly or indirectly by members of government, industry and the academy.

A second observation made by a number of those with whom I spoke was that Japan perceives itself as overly dependent on the United States market for exports.[11] As a numerical value, Professor Matsushita suggested that Japan would try to reduce its export dependence on the United States from 40 percent of its external market share down to 20-25 percent of its external market share.

---

[9] This view -- that Japan prefers to maintain informal arrangements in Asia -- was subsequently reiterated by Japan's representative, Foreign Minister Tsutomo Hata, at the Nov. 18-19 APEC meeting. Paul F. Horwitz, *A Non-Starter*, INT'L HER. TRIB., *supra* Chapter One, note 17.

[10] The North Korean nuclear threat was not discussed.

[11] This view was not shared at the Ministry of Foreign Affairs.

It was also apparent throughout the my discussions that the Japanese perceive the People's Republic of China as their major growth opportunity. This is in addition to the already large inroads Japan has made into Southeast Asian markets. Professor Matsushita added a practical observation with respect to Japan's preference for maintaining informal trade relations with other Asian countries. Japan maintains substantial trade surpluses with most of these countries, which protect their markets with relatively high tariff and non-tariff barriers. It is not so clear that many of them would find it desirable to structurally enhance Japanese market access, particularly since Japan presents relatively few formal barriers to imports and therefore may not be offering substantial reciprocal concessions.

The official at the Foreign Ministry with whom I spoke offered an interesting perspective on the U.S.-Japan merchandise trade imbalance. He suggested that Japanese trade advantages with the United States were largely in so-called "mid-tech" products such as stereos and VCRs, and not in high-tech goods. The U.S., it was posited, could reenter the mid-tech market without great difficulty and thereby significantly reduce its trade imbalance if its industries so chose. He noted that the U.S. has a substantial agricultural surplus with Japan. Also, he intimated that one reason the Japanese market is perceived as closed is that U.S. companies which successfully penetrate the market do not publicize this success.

As a general policy matter the Japanese were not overly concerned about the formation of the NAFTA. This assumed, however, that the NAFTA was not a substitute for completion of the GATT Uruguay Round. It was indicated on several occasions that success of the NAFTA and failure of the GATT Uruguay Round would be perceived as a very serious threat to Japanese economic interests.

A repeated theme of my meetings in Japan was that Japan is increasingly interested in strengthening the role of the WTO/GATT in international trade law-making and dispute settlement. At MITI, for example, I was asked whether I believed the United States would be disturbed by increased use of the GATT dispute settlement forum with respect to trade disputes with the United States. It might be suggested that the Japanese have a strong interest in WTO/GATT dispute resolution since it tends to favor their approach of maintaining modest formal external trade barriers while continuing to maintain relatively invisible internal trade barriers that are largely outside the WTO/GATT's purview.

Professor Matsushita took a fairly optimistic view of the NAFTA from the Japanese perspective. He suggested that the NAFTA will accelerate North American economic growth and thereby create an expanded market for Japanese exports. Even if the NAFTA favors American exports to a certain extent, since

Japan will be playing by a set of rules in which it is competitive with third countries, Japan should still be able to expand its export market.

Both the Ministry of Foreign Affairs and the consensus view of business executives was that the NAFTA would not generate a flood of Japanese foreign direct investment into Mexico. In the first place, Mexico must be evaluated in comparison to other capital-export markets, especially those of Southeast Asia and the PRC. The Japanese are not terribly impressed by the state of the Mexican infrastructure. The business community is concerned to a certain extent with political instability.[12] Concern was also expressed with respect to investment restrictions which would remain applicable to Japanese companies after the NAFTA comes into effect.[13] Moreover, in discussions with business executives, a view emerged that Japanese companies -- and particularly automobile companies -- may for a variety of reasons be more inclined to accelerate or enhance their investments in the United States as a consequence of the NAFTA, rather than pursuing investments in Mexico. Among concerns expressed about Mexico were those involving the lack of infrastructure development, a less highly trained labor force and political instability. It was also pointed out that the United States -- and particularly some southern States such as South Carolina -- offer very attractive investment climates and wage rates which are not unattractive. Therefore, all other things being equal, Japanese companies may well chose to take advantage of the NAFTA by expanding direct investments in the United States.

I asked each of the constituencies I spoke with whether rapidly increasing Japanese investments in Chile represented a Japanese strategy to enter the NAFTA through the back door. While this seemed to me an intuitively apparent Japanese strategy, none of those with whom I spoke was in any way inclined to acknowledge this as a possibility. Other motives were suggested. In particular, it was suggested that Chile has the cleanest balance sheet in Latin America, a stable government, and laws favorable to foreign investment. Therefore, when Japanese companies consider the possible locations for Latin American facilities, Chile is a natural choice. These points were specifically made at MITI.

At MITI I discussed with officials the GATT Article XXIV implications of the NAFTA. The MITI officials raised the following concerns:

1. New automobile rules of origin are the *de facto* raising of a tariff on

---

[12] The Ministry of Foreign Affairs did not discuss the issue of political stability.

[13] Note that these discussions took place prior to Mexico's adoption of a new foreign investment law. *See* discussion Chapter Seven, text accompanying notes 72-80.

Japanese-produced goods shipped from Canada to the United States, since fewer such goods will qualify for tariff-free entry into the United States.[14]
2. The removal of Maquiladora benefits also constitutes a *de facto* increase in tariff barriers because companies which previously enjoyed effective duty-free importation into Mexico will lose their tariff-exempt status with respect to components coming from outside the NAFTA.
3. The "yarn forward" rule in the textile sector constitutes the *de facto* raising of a tariff barrier or the application of a more restrictive regulation of commerce (since the CUSFTA principally employed a "fabric forward" rule).
4. There was some concern with whether there were preferences accorded to NAFTA Party banks under the financial services and investment provisions, but as of June 1993 the government had not completed its evaluation in these sectors.
5. Quota discrimination was, as with the CUSFTA, raised as a general problem.
6. Agricultural snap-backs were considered an abstract issue as under the CUSFTA, but it was made clear that this was only a theoretical problem for Japan since it had little interest in the agricultural export sector.
7. Concern was expressed over Mexico's auto parts sourcing rules which favor established enterprises, and that these rules may discriminate against new third country inward investment.

A hope was expressed at MITI that a GATT working party would begin to examine the NAFTA as soon as possible.

C. The Private Economic View of the NAFTA

Business executives expressed concern with various provisions of the NAFTA. The subject of greatest interest by far was the new rules of origin. There was a general apprehension that the rules were not sufficiently clear and that this would expose Japanese companies to the risk of unwarranted interpretations by administrative authorities. The question was raised several times why the NAFTA negotiators could not have made the rules more clear. I suggested that

---

[14] This observation might be reformulated to refer to the imposition of more restrictive regulations of commerce, but the text employs the terminology used by MITI officials in mid-1993. *See* discussion of the ISC Report, *infra*, for a reformulation.

it is a customary facet of international negotiations that agreements are reached with some "play in the joints." This permits each party to lend its own self-interested interpretation to the agreement and avoids forcing the negotiators to battle to a firm conclusion on each issue. Some uncertainty will always be present, even though this may create an uncomfortable situation for business enterprises. This being said, it may be worth noting that as of June 1994 the implementation of NAFTA rules of origin at the U.S.-Mexico border had posed great difficulties for customs officials and U.S. business enterprises.[15]

A representative of a major Japanese automobile manufacturer suggested that the NAFTA presented his company with some very difficult choices. Its current manufacturing facility in Canada would not be able to meet local content requirements unless it significantly expanded its local production or acquisition of parts. However, in order for it to economically produce parts locally, it would have to increase considerably vehicle production at its plant. It was not clear that such a ramp-up would be justifiable; and, in any event, if the company were going to dramatically increase the scale of its investment, it may well choose to do so within U.S. territory where it would have improved access to U.S. components, *e.g.*, auto engines. The company might elect to increase its U.S. production of parts and sell surplus production to American producers. This business executive indicated that his company planned to make its decision regarding expansion of North American production by 1998 in order to be able to meet the 2002 phase-in of the NAFTA automobile content rules.

A representative from a large Japanese automobile parts industry group also raised concern over parts origin rules which he suggested may result in a *de facto* 80 percent local content requirement.[16]

One industry representative indicated that Japan would take a much more cautious and analytical approach with respect to the NAFTA than it had with respect to other recent ventures in the United States, *e.g.* investment in the real estate market. A strong impression was generally conveyed that Japanese companies view Southeast Asia and the PRC as much more dynamic market opportunities than North America. There was little expectation of a flood of Japanese investment into Mexico. The U.S. market was characterized as a *relatively* low risk but also a low reward market. No business executive was willing to suggest that Japan was pursuing a Chilean "back door" investment

---

[15] Allen R. Myerson, *Under the Free Trade Pact, Snarls on the Mexican Border*, N.Y. TIMES, June 21, 1994, at A1.

[16] A representative from the steel industry expressed concern over USTR Kantor's suggestion that U.S. companies buy locally produced parts (outside the specific NAFTA context), as well as with new U.S. transfer pricing rules.

strategy with respect to the NAFTA.

I found a general lack of information about the present status of Japan-Mexico treaty relations (or other formal Japan-Mexico investment-related relations), and I found no indication that there was any immediate intent or urgency connected to clarifying this area. Both the Ministry of Foreign Affairs and MITI disclaimed familiarity with the state of formal Japanese-Mexican commercial relations.

II. THE REPORT OF THE INDUSTRIAL STRUCTURE COUNCIL

Japan prepares a report comparable to the National Trade Barriers Estimate Report of the United States Trade Representative and the Annual Report on United States Trade and Investment Barriers of the European Commission. The 1994 Japan report [hereinafter "ISC Report"] was drafted and issued by a subcommittee of the Industrial Structure Council (ISC), an official advisory body to MITI.[17] The ISC Report raises a number of concerns with respect to the NAFTA.[18]

The ISC Report first suggests that NAFTA rules of origin may be inconsistent with the Article XXIV requirement that regulations of commerce not be made more restrictive. The Report specifically refers to textile, color television and automotive rules of origin.[19] It discusses changes to the "roll up" rules which are used to trace automobile parts, suggesting that the NAFTA rules (which do not blend foreign and domestic subparts) certainly are more restrictive than the CUSFTA rules.

The ISC Report notes that the NAFTA does not provide for the complete elimination of quantitative restrictions on agricultural trade between the United States and Canada, and between Canada and Mexico. It suggests therefore that the NAFTA may not eliminate regulations on substantially all trade between the constituent territories of the FTA.

The ISC Report observes that the NAFTA provides that its Parties will

---

[17] INDUSTRIAL STRUCTURE COUNCIL, 1994 REPORT ON UNFAIR TRADE POLICIES BY MAJOR TRADING PARTNERS (1994) [hereinafter ISC REPORT]. This is the third annual report drafted by the Subcommittee on Unfair Trade Policies and Measures of the WTO Committee of the ISC. The Subcommittee is chaired by Professor Mitsuo Matsushita.

[18] *Id.* at 315-21.

[19] The ISC Report notes that the CUSFTA and NAFTA automotive rules are not directly comparable, although suggesting that NAFTA parts "roll up" rules are certainly more restrictive. *Id.*

exempt each other from global safeguards actions under GATT Article XIX in certain circumstances, and it questions the GATT-consistency of this provision. However, the Report acknowledges that there is not a consensus in the GATT as to whether RIAs are entitled to global safeguards exemptions.

The ISC Report takes note of the fact that the NAFTA intellectual property provisions provide in some cases for more favorable treatment among Parties than comparable WTO TRIPS provisions. It says that the TRIPS MFN principle will require that the NAFTA standards be extended to third countries.

The ISC Report finally refers to the use of 15 year transition periods for elimination of tariff and non-tariff measures with respect to certain products. It suggests that this may be inconsistent with the requirement that measures be eliminated within a reasonable length of time, and says that "[a]ccording to the Final Act, this 'reasonable length of time' is interpreted to be ten years."[20]

The ISC Report raises concerns which have been discussed in Chapters Four and Five, *supra*. The concerns with respect to whether the NAFTA eliminates barriers on substantially all trade within a reasonable time must be evaluated in the context of the extensive product coverage and generally short transition periods of the NAFTA. It is most unlikely that the NAFTA will be considered not to meet Article XXIV standards in this context. The WTO/GATT NAFTA Working Party will certainly give serious attention to the changes in rules of origin between the United States and Canada. It must again be noted, however, that there is no consensus in the GATT on the Article XXIV implications of changes in RIA rules of origin.

III. RECIPROCAL ACCESS RIGHTS

The access of Japanese nationals to establishment in the United States is governed by an FCN treaty.[21] This treaty is comparable to those in force between the United States and the Member States of the EU discussed in Chapter Seven. Article VII of the Japan - U.S. FCN Treaty generally accords the right of establishment on a national treatment basis to the enterprises of each party.[22] It also accords MFN treatment to such enterprises with respect to the

---

[20] *Id.* at 321.

[21] Japan - United States Treaty of Friendship, Commerce and Navigation of 1953. Signed in Tokyo on April 2, 1953, entered into force on Oct. 3, 1953, 4 U.S.T. 2063, T.I.A.S. No. 2863 [hereinafter Japan - U.S. FCN Treaty].

[22] Japan - U.S. FCN Treaty, art. VII(1).

conduct of business activities.[23] Each party, however, reserves the right to limit investment in public utilities, shipbuilding, air or water transport, banking involving depository or fiduciary functions, and the exploitation of land or other natural resources.[24] As noted also in Chapter Seven with respect to the Member States of the EU, the provisions of the Japan-United States FCN Treaty with respect to the right of establishment may be superseded in some sectors by GATS market access commitments. The United States, of course, maintains potential restrictions on Japanese and other third country investment for national security purposes on the basis of the Exon-Florio statute.[25]

U.S. access to establishment in Japan is likewise governed by the Japan-United States FCN Treaty and applicable GATS market access commitments. Japan maintains legislation which generally requires the filing of reports on direct investment with the Ministry of Finance, and permits the imposition of emergency controls for national security purposes.[26]

Japan, just as the EU, will benefit from the Mexican Law on Foreign Investment which may substantially level its investment playing field with the United States.[27]

IV. THE IMPLICATIONS OF THE NAFTA FOR JAPAN

Japan is the single leading exporter to the United States which is not a party to the NAFTA.[28] Japan's indirect automobile exports to the United States through Canada will be affected by changes to rules of origin which will probably add to the tariffs borne by such indirect exports. Nevertheless, U.S. tariffs on automobiles and parts are generally low,[29] and the impact of the rules of origin

---

[23] *Id.*, art. VII(4). It is not clear the extent to which this MFN obligation would permit Japan to piggyback on FCN treaties which do not expressly contain limits equivalent to those in the Japan - U.S. FCN Treaty, but it can be argued that it should.

[24] *Id.* art. VII(2). The FCN Treaty has been relied upon by Japan in a number of cases in which it has challenged the application of U.S. anti-discrimination law to Japanese-owned companies in the United States. *See* Frederick M. Abbott, *Regional Integration Mechanisms in the Law of the United States: Starting Over*, 1 INDIANA J. GLOBAL L. STUD. 155, 160-61 (1993).

[25] *See, e.g.*, Patrick L. Schmidt, *The Exon-Florio Statute: How it Affects Foreign Investors and Lenders in the United States*, 27 INT'L LAWYER 795 (1993).

[26] *See* MITSUO MATSUSHITA, INTERNATIONAL TRADE AND COMPETITION LAW, *supra* note 5, at 242-47.

[27] *See, supra* Chapter Seven, text accompanying notes 72-78.

[28] Canada is the leading single exporter to the United States and, of course, a party to NAFTA. *See* Chapter Seven, *supra*.

[29] The U.S. duty on passenger cars is 2.5% ad valorem. USITC, The Likely Impact on the United

changes should not significantly effect Japanese-controlled trade between Canada and the United States. For Japan, the major issue with respect to automobiles concerns access to Mexico which maintains tariffs (prior to any Uruguay Round-related adjustments) of 15 percent ad valorem on automobiles and 13.2 percent on automobile parts.[30] The 1980s strategy of the Japanese automobile industry to locate production facilities in the United States should ameliorate much of the adverse effect which the NAFTA might otherwise have had on Japanese exports to Mexico. No doubt U.S. facilities of Japanese-owned automobile companies may be required to source more parts purchases in the United States, but savings in transportation costs from Japan should to some extent offset any higher costs associated with these sourcing changes. Perhaps it will be Japanese parts manufacturers that are most affected by the NAFTA. They, like the integrated manufacturers in the 1980s, will need to consider establishing additional North American facilities. In the short to intermediate term, Japanese automotive investment plans seem likely to focus on the United States as opposed to Mexico or Canada. It seems reasonable to expect that over the longer term, as Mexico's industrial infrastructure improves, Japanese attention increasingly will be directed to the Mexican territory.

The other areas in which Japanese exports are most likely to be affected by the NAFTA are in those sectors in which Mexico will continue to maintain relatively high external tariffs. The Japanese electronic products (including computer and telephone equipment)[31] and machinery and equipment (including machine tools)[32] export industries would appear likely to suffer from NAFTA tariff preferences in favor of U.S.-based manufacturers.

Japan's services export strengths are in the capital intensive sectors such as banking. As pointed out in the European Commission Information Note on the NAFTA,[33] if Mexico intends to substantially increase its rate of economic growth, it will have very little incentive to restrict the importation of capital through foreign owned banks. It therefore seems rather unlikely that the Japanese financial services sector will find itself at any significant competitive disadvantage as respects U.S. and Canadian service providers in Mexico. In the short to intermediate term, Japanese providers of transportation, construction and professional services are for a variety of reasons unlikely to have a

---

States of a Free Trade Agreement with Mexico, Feb. 1991, at 4-18 to 4-19 (USITC Pub. 2353).
[30] *Id.* at 4-19.
[31] 1991 ad valorem Mexican tariffs of 16% average. *Id.* at 4-26.
[32] 1991 Mexican ad valorem 10-20% tariffs. *Id.* at 4-32.
[33] *Commission Note*, Chapter Seven *supra*, note 28, at 15.

significant interest in the Mexican market.[34] In any event, favorable NAFTA rules applicable to established services providers and the favorable attitude toward foreign direct investment evidenced by Mexico's new Foreign Investment Law present little reason for Japanese service providers to be concerned about services access discrimination.

Japan's principal concern with the NAFTA is not with the immediate effect of its present structure. It is a concern with the future of the global trading system and whether the formation of large and powerful regional organizations will undermine the multilateral framework embodied in the WTO/GATT. The 1994 ISC Report voices this concern, saying:

> regional integration, even when it charts a course to a more open market, can be the starting point for economic blocs that could destroy the free-trade system.
> It will therefore be necessary to monitor regional integration on a continuing basis to ensure that it is in compliance with WTO rules and open to the outside world.[35]

In conversations with Japanese trade policy experts in mid-1994, I detected a somewhat greater willingness to consider the possibilities for enhanced formal commercial arrangements with other Asian countries, particularly in respect to investment access and protection agreements. Although some confidence is expressed that APEC will provide an appropriate forum for pursuing some agreements of limited scope, there remains considerable skepticism as to whether a formal RIA in the Asia-Pacific region comparable to either the NAFTA or EU would be a pragmatic way to address regional interests.

Japan faces perhaps the gravest danger among industrialized countries from a breakdown of the WTO system and emergence of a tightly regionalized world. This results from a combination of factors, not the least of which is that historical political animosity between Japan, South Korea and the PRC does not readily lend itself to close Asian regional cooperation. Economic necessity may make strange bedfellows, but it perhaps should not be surprising if Japanese trade policy-makers, working on behalf of a highly export-oriented domestic economy, seek to emphasize the importance of containing regional protectionism. Nor should it be surprising if Japanese interest in Latin American as a whole proves to be greater than that previously expressed, as a vital counterweight to U.S. influence in the region.

---

[34] The Mexican market for many of these services is presently small on a relative scale, and Japan is not a significant exporter of professional services. Japan faces obvious disadvantages *vis-à-vis* U.S. land transport companies in providing services in the Mexican territory.

[35] ISC Report, at 314.

Chapter Nine

THE NAFTA AND THE REST OF THE WORLD

The potential impact of the NAFTA on third countries played a very small role in the debate preceding its approval.[1] This might be explained by a variety of factors. Perhaps the most important is that the United States House of Representatives was the central actor in the approval drama. There are 435 members of the House of Representatives, they represent relatively small voting districts and are subject to election every two years.[2] Members of the House tend to focus on narrow domestic concerns, and they paid most of their attention to the impact the NAFTA would have on the U.S. economy and subsectors relevant to their districts. The Bush and Clinton Administrations had little choice but to deal with members of the House of Representatives on their own terms, and so had little reason based in the domestic approval process to address the NAFTA's potential impact on third countries. The task of the Executive Branch in the NAFTA approval process was one of moderating parochial demands by House members for extensive protective measures.

As is widely acknowledged, the European Union was not in a position to challenge the NAFTA because of its own extensive scheme of preferences.[3] The Japanese were concerned about the potential impact of the NAFTA, but seemed to recognize that approval was very much a matter of local American politics and that the NAFTA would rise or fall on local concerns.[4]

---

[1] This observation is made in Carlos Alberto Primo Braga, *NAFTA and the Rest of the World*, in NORTH AMERICAN FREE TRADE: ASSESSING THE IMPACT 210, 211 (Donna Lustig et. al. eds., 1992). Primo Braga also speculates as to the reasons for this lack of attention, suggesting both that it may have been understood to have minor economic consequences, and that third countries chose not to address the issues for a variety of political reasons. *Id.* at 211-13.

[2] The U.S. Senate by way of contrast is composed of 100 members, two representing each of the 50 States, and are subject to election every 6 years on a staggered basis.

[3] Presaged by Thomas Cottier, *Die Bedeutung des GATT im Process der europäischen Integration*, in EG-RECHT UND SCHWEIZERISCHE RECHTSORDNUNG (O. Jacot-Guillarmod et al. eds., 1990). *See* Comment by Jeffrey Schott regarding paper by Primo Braga, *supra* note 1, at 238.

[4] The Japanese chose to focus their attention and lobbying on amelioration of excessive rule of

Potential criticism by the Latin American countries may have been muted for a number of reasons. First, Mexico is one of their own and so such criticism might have been perceived as fratricidal. Second, when President Bush announced his intention to negotiate a free trade agreement with Mexico, he presented this plan as the first step toward a hemisphere-wide free trade zone, stretching from Anchorage to Tierra del Fuego.[5] Because of the implicit promise of subsequent incorporation into a broader Western Hemispheric plan, the Latin American countries may reasonably have concluded that there was no reason to raise objection to initiation of the process with the NAFTA, even if this might have short term negative consequences for them.[6] The principal expressions of anxiety from the Western Hemisphere came from the Caribbean countries.[7] These countries would be affected by NAFTA preferences in favor of Mexico both in sectors in which they presently enjoy preferential treatment by the U.S. and in sectors not enjoying such preferential treatment.[8] In response to Caribbean concerns, a legislative proposal was introduced (but not approved) during the NAFTA approval process in 1993, and a similar proposal was scheduled to be introduced with the support of the Clinton Administration in 1994, to provide the Caribbean countries with relief from potential NAFTA-induced trade diversion in the textiles sector.[9]

---

origin-related demands by U.S. industry.

[5] In 1990 President Bush announced the Enterprise for the Americas Initiative (EAI), intended to lead to a Western Hemispheric FTA. *See* Richard Bernal, *Regional Trade Arrangements in the Western Hemisphere*, 8 AM. U.J. INT'L L.& POL'Y 683, 708-09 (1993), for description of the EAI. The announcement by Presidents Bush and Salinas of U.S.-Mexico negotiations was made on June 11, 1990. President Bush announced the EAI initiative on June 27, 1990, and the announcement of the trilateral NAFTA negotiations was made by President Bush on February 24, 1991. *See* GARY CLYDE HUFBAUER & JEFFREY J. SCHOTT, NORTH AMERICAN FREE TRADE, ISSUES AND RECOMMENDATIONS (1992) [hereinafter ISSUES AND RECOMMENDATIONS], at 24 and *Bush Transmits Legislative Proposal to Implement Latin American Reform Package*, 8 BNA INT'L TR. REPTR. 349, Mar. 6, 1991.

[6] *See* Primo Braga, *NAFTA and the Rest of the World*, *supra* note 1, at 211-12, referring to "strategic behavior of the potential 'victims'."

[7] *See, e.g., Small Nations Fear Bush Enterprise Initiative, Mexico FTA May Dim Their Economic Prospects*, 7 BNA INT'L TR. REPTR. 1892, Dec. 12, 1990.

[8] *See, e.g.*, HUFBAUER AND SCHOTT, ISSUES AND RECOMMENDATIONS, at 275. The relationship of the various Latin American integration programs and the NAFTA is considered in Chapter Ten, *infra*.

[9] *See* Caribbean Basin Free Trade Agreements Act, H.R. 1403, 103rd Cong., 1st sess., March 18 1993 and S1155, 103rd Cong., 1st sess., June 24, 1993; and Canute James, *New hope for clothes makers - A look at the Caribbean welcome for US tariff plans*, FIN. TIMES, June 14, 1994, World Trade News, at 4. The Clinton Administration intended to request that all tariffs and quotas on textile and apparel imports be removed for the 24 countries which are beneficiaries of the Caribbean Basin Initiative (CBI). The CBI program provides GSP duty free trade for 90% of Central American and Caribbean products entering the U.S., but has excluded apparel, textiles and

South Korea and Taiwan, among other Asian countries, voiced concern over the potential trade diverting impact of the NAFTA.[10] Australia and New Zealand also raised concerns, but their voices may too have been muted by identification as candidates for NAFTA accession or free trade agreements with the United States and Canada.[11] On the whole, the expressions of concern by third countries with respect to the NAFTA's potential trade diverting effect were voiced in a measured business-like manner. The NAFTA was not characterized by third country governments as a grave threat to their national economic security.

As Primo Braga has suggested, third countries may have stayed in the background in the NAFTA debate because they perceived that the NAFTA would not have significant negative economic consequences for them.[12] First, the NAFTA may have been viewed as a relatively open regional arrangement unlikely to have significant trade diverting effects. Second, the NAFTA might have been seen to include a prospective "growth dividend" which would outweigh any potential discriminatory characteristics.

I. THE ECONOMICS OF THE NAFTA

A. THE STATE OF THE ART IN RIA ECONOMICS

Economists have found it difficult to provide a definitive perspective on the welfare benefits and costs of RIAs because of their enormous complexity and dynamism. In 1950 economist Jacob Viner described the basic economic impact

---

leather goods. *See New hope for clothes makers, id.,* and Richard Bernal, *Regional Trade Arrangements in the Western Hemisphere, supra* note 1, at 705. The legislation introduced in 1993 called for monitoring of the situation with respect to sugar.

[10] *See* regarding Taiwan, *e.g.,* Paul F. Horwitz, *Looking to Asia for Growth, Clinton Vows to Open Markets,* INT'L HER. TRIB., Nov. 20-21, 1993, at 1; Paul F. Horwitz, *A Non-Starter in Seattle: Asian-Pacific Community, id.* at 1. Comments from South Korea are cited in Jisu Kim, *Impact of the North American Free Trade Agreement on East Asia: A Korean Perspective,* 8 AM. U.J. INT'L L.& POL'Y 881, 891. Concerns of Southeast Asian nations are reported in K.T. Arasa, *NAFTA Seen Cutting ASEAN Exports by $2 Billion,* REUTERS BUS. REP., Nov. 23, 1992 (LEXIS/NEXIS); regarding the PRC, *see, e.g., China Concerned About NAFTA,* SOURCEMEX, Feb. 17, 1993 (LEXIS/NEXIS).

[11] *See, e.g., NAFTA Could Hit Asian Exports; Australian Govt Report,* AFX NEWS, May 5, 1994 (LEXIS/NEXIS); *Effect of Pact on Australia Will Be Mixed, Report Says,* 11 BNA INT'L TR. REPTR. 750, May 11, 1994; *Canada Prefers NAFTA Accession Over Bilateral Pacts, Maclaren Says,* 11 BNA INT'L TR. REPTR. 862, June 1, 1994.

[12] Primo Braga, *NAFTA and the Rest of the World, supra* note 1, at 211.

of the RIA,[13] and his observations remain at the core of RIA economic analysis. Viner observed that RIAs may both create trade among RIA members by shifting production and imports from higher-cost RIA members to lower-cost RIA members, and divert trade by shifting production and imports from non-RIA member country exporters (with former cost advantages) to member country producers/exporters awarded cost advantages by new preferences. According to Viner, whether an RIA would produce a global economic welfare benefit would depend upon whether its trade creating (*i.e.*, new trade between the member countries) or trade diverting (*i.e.*, member country trade which is substituted for third-country trade) forces were predominant. Though not so assumed by Viner,[14] Dam (among others) subsequently concluded that it would be possible to predict whether a particular RIA would, as a whole, be trade creating or trade diverting and therefor beneficial or detrimental to global economic welfare.[15]

Forty years following Viner's pathfinding work, predicting or even determining after the fact the trade creating/trade diverting impact of an RIA remains an elusive goal of the economist. Moreover, a substantial consensus has developed that a meaningful evaluation of the effects of an RIA must involve more than a determination of its effects on trade.

A 1989 Note prepared by the GATT Secretariat which reviewed the literature on the trade creation and trade diversion effects of RIAs suggested that as economic analysis had become increasingly sophisticated and the dynamic effects of market manipulating mechanisms became better understood, the complex effects of trade barrier adjustment on local production and consumption, external production and consumption, employment, social welfare, monetary policy (including balance of payments effects), etc., challenged the

---

[13] JACOB VINER, THE CUSTOMS UNION ISSUE 41-81 (1950).

[14] Viner wrote with respect to trade creating ("TC") and trade diverting ("TD") effects:

> None of these questions [of effect] can be answered *a priori*, and the correct answers will depend on just how the customs union operates in practice. All that *a priori* analysis can do, is to demonstrate, within limits, how the customs union must operate, if it is to have specific types of consequences.

Id. at 42-43.

[15] *See* Kenneth W. Dam, *Regional Economic Arrangements and the GATT: The Legacy of a Misconception,* 30 U.CHI.L. REV. 615 (1963). For Dam it followed from this conclusion that the best legal formula for evaluating a prospective RIA would employ at its core a determination whether the RIA was likely to generate a preponderance of trade creating or trade diverting effects. Certain economists have suggested trade creation/trade diversion-based rules as the appropriate RIA evaluation criteria. *See, e.g.,* Wonnacott & Lutz, *Is There a Case for Free Trade Areas?, in* FREE TRADE AREAS AND U.S. TRADE POLICY 59 (Jeffrey Schott ed., 1989).

most sophisticated empirical and modeling capacities of the economist. Beyond that, the 1989 Note suggested that an evaluation of RIAs involves "public choice" issues which are not answerable by economic modeling alone.[16]

Following a thorough review of economic studies with respect to the economic impact of RIAs (including the EU) and an identification of the more prudent and realistic of these studies, the 1989 Note observed, *inter alia*, a "considerable variation" in the estimated trade creation and trade diversion effects of the EU.[17] The Note added that "with few often striking exceptions . . . most studies [of customs unions] have produced estimates of substantial absolute values for TC, net TC and/or welfare gains, which nevertheless are extremely small as percentages of national income or GNP,"[18] and that the difficulties encountered by leading economists in estimating after the fact the impact of the creation of an RIA "underlines the limits in the logic and practice of *ex ante* prediction of TC-TD [trade creation-trade diversion]."[19]

A collection of economic papers concerning RIAs prepared under the auspices of the GATT Secretariat was published in 1993.[20] The contributors to this study point out that modern era preferential trading arrangements, for example in the form of British Imperial preferences, date back to the early 1800s.[21] Srinivasam, Whalley and Wooten canvassed *ex ante* and *ex post*

---

[16] *A Brief Review of the Literature on Trade Creation and Trade Diversion Effects of Regional Arrangements,* Group of Negotiations on Goods (GATT), Negotiating Group on GATT Articles (June 6, 1989) [hereinafter Note of GATT Secretariat]. An extensive bibliography is appended to the Note. The Note states that the major extensions in customs union theory have "sought to broaden the focus of Viner's analysis" by including assessment of the additional effects referred to in the text. *Id*. at 6, para. 11. However, the Note adds that studies of the trade effects of tariff changes involving trade creation and trade diversion "reaffirm the feasibility of the underlying calculus that a [Customs Union] will increase overall world welfare if it created more trade than it diverted." *Id*. at 11, para. 20.

[17] *Id*. at 13, para. 24.

[18] *Id*. The Note refers to one economist's conclusion that because of certain studies which exceptionally suggested a large trade creation effect for the EC/EFTA (European Free Trade Association), "a persistent bias has emerged which underestimated TD [trade diversion]." *Id*. at 12-13, para. 23.

[19] *Id*. at 12, para. 23. *See also* Balassa, *Trade Creation and Trade Diversion in the European Common Market,* 77 ECON. J. 1 (1967), in which the conclusion about predicting the impact of RIAs is reinforced: "[W]hile a number of criteria have been put forward for appraising the chances of trade creation and trade diversion in a union, it seems to be generally agreed that an *a priori* judgment regarding the *net* effect of a customs union on trade flows cannot be made." *Id*.

[20] REGIONAL INTEGRATION AND THE GLOBAL TRADING SYSTEM (Kym Anderson and Richard Blackhurst eds., 1993).

[21] Kym Anderson & Hege Norheim, *History, Geography and Regional Economic Integration, in* REGIONAL INTEGRATION AND THE GLOBAL TRADING SYSTEM *id*. at 19, 39. T.N. Srinivasam et al., *Measuring the Effects of Regionalism on Trade and Welfare, in* REGIONAL INTEGRATION AND THE GLOBAL TRADING SYSTEM *id*. at 52, 57.

studies of the trade and welfare effects of RIAs.[22] Their general conclusions include the following:

> It is difficult to generalize over the results of all these ... groups of studies because their individual characteristics are so varied, as are the results. While some studies provide detailed analysis of the trade impacts, their analysis of welfare impacts may be more limited. Also, some of the model-based studies, while providing analysis of trade and welfare impacts, do not provide results in a form which makes it easy to disentangle the various influences on trade and welfare.
>
> We, therefore, see these studies as shedding somewhat incomplete and at times conflicting light on the effects of post-War RIAs on trade and welfare, to say nothing of what may be the likely effects of prospective RIAS.[23]

The debate preceding approval of the NAFTA seemed to confirm the indeterminacy of economic analysis as interest groups assembled or affiliated themselves with economic studies yielding highly divergent results concerning the potential impact of the arrangement.[24] The use by propagandists for and against the NAFTA of conflicting economic studies created confusion and perhaps ultimately became counterproductive. It was not uncommon for politicians and bureaucrats to discount the generally inconclusive economic studies of the NAFTA.

Even as the indeterminacy of *ex ante* and *ex post* economic analysis of RIAs made its way into conventional wisdom during the NAFTA debate, it is also apparent that the state of the art in the economic analysis of RIAs is improving. A noteworthy example of a new generation of economic studies with respect to RIAs is "Implications of NAFTA for East Asian Exports" by Primo Braga, Safadi and Yeats.[25] In this study the authors both review the serious economic studies of the potential trade diverting impact of the NAFTA and present their own analysis of the potential effects of the NAFTA on East Asian exports. In their own study, the authors employ both a partial equilibrium model and a gravity flow model. The gravity flow model permits the incorporation of a significant number of variables.[26] Though even this model remains incomplete

---

[22] When economists use the term "welfare effects" they are generally referring to effects on gross national (or domestic) product (GNP or GDP) as an aggregate economic measure of national well-being. The term "welfare effects" is not generally used in reference to effects on social welfare in a broad sense.

[23] Srinivasam et al., *supra* note 21, at 72.

[24] *See* Thomas J. Schoenbaum, *The North American Free Trade Agreement (NAFTA): Good for Jobs, for the Environment, and for America*, 23 GA. J. INT'L & COMP. L. 161, 149-80 (1993) for references to various studies.

[25] C.A. Primo Braga, Raed Safadi & Alexander Yeats, *Implications of NAFTA for East Asian Exports* (1994) [hereinafter Primo Braga et al., *Implications of NAFTA*], draft paper furnished to author.

[26] *See* Appendix II to Primo Braga et al., *Implications of NAFTA*.

-- for example, it does not appear to incorporate potential changes in investment flows -- the sophisticated nature of the model nevertheless demonstrates that economists are working diligently to remedy deficiencies in their existing tools, in particular by seeking to incorporate in their models a more complete set of the variables which may determine the economic impact of the RIA.

The distinction between a customs union along the European Union model, and a free trade area along the NAFTA model, from the standpoint of economic analysis of their potential impact on third country trade and investment, is discussed in Appendix I to this chapter.

B. NAFTA Trade and Welfare Effects

Bearing in mind the present limitations of economic analysis, serious studies of the NAFTA's effects with respect to third countries suggest that it may have a modest trade diverting impact. Primo Braga, Safadi and Yeats estimate that the NAFTA will reduce East Asian exports to the United States by less than one percent.[27] They analyzed the East Asian region specifically because of its heavy reliance on the North American market and the fact that it produces a relatively high level of labor-intensive products "that often face North American trade barriers."[28] In other words, they chose to analyze the potential impact of the NAFTA on a group of countries which might have been expected to bear its brunt. A portion of their summary and conclusion may be useful to quote because of the perspective it suggests:

> While there has been considerable apprehension among many non-member countries about NAFTA's trade diverting effects, the evidence reported in this study suggests that the impact on East Asian exporters might be small. Under current (pre-Uruguay Round) trade restrictions, East Asia's trade diversion is projected to be between $384 and $680 million annually with the latter figure representing approximately four-fifths of one percent of the region's total exports to the United States. These loss projections are probably upward biased since they do not incorporate any supply constraints on the capacity of Mexico or Canada to expand exports, nor do they reflect the influence of NAFTA's rules of origin that could limit members' ability to fully capitalize on the agreement's trade preferences.
>
> One way of placing the importance of the NAFTA in perspective is to compare the projected East Asian NAFTA-induced losses with estimates of the export gains this region

---

[27] Primo Braga et al., *Implications of NAFTA*, *id.* at 35. The authors note that the United States is used as the import market because East Asian exports to Canada and Mexico are very small by comparison. *Id.* at 21. The discussion in this section relies heavily on this paper by Primo Braga, et al. which itself refers to a substantial number of "working papers" of economists.

[28] *Id.* at 3. They note that "[h]igh trade barriers are one pre-condition for NAFTA to divert third countries' exports." *Id.*

should achieve as a result of a successful completion of the Uruguay Round. The World Bank ... estimates that exports from East Asian low-and middle-income economies (i.e., all East Asia less Hong Kong, Singapore, Taiwan (China) and OECD Asia) would increase by $16.2 billion annually under a 30 percent Uruguay Round reduction in trade barriers; an increase of $27.1 billion is forecast for a 50 percent liberalization. For these East Asian economies, the gains from these kinds of Uruguay Round result are 60 to 100 times the upper range of NAFTA-induced losses estimated in this study. [citations omitted][29]

With respect to the trade diverting effects of the NAFTA on regions other than East Asia, even in those sectors in which it is almost certain that the NAFTA will have trade diverting consequences, those consequences are not projected to be catastrophic. In perhaps the most dramatic case, if it is assumed that the NAFTA results in a doubling of Mexican citrus output, then by the year 2000 Brazilian citrus production may decline by 4.5 percent.[30] Under certain assumptions, Caribbean countries might experience a welfare loss (*i.e.* GDP reduction) of $128 million from reductions in their sugar exports.[31] In the textile and steel sectors, the NAFTA is expected to reduce quota rents for third countries. In the textile sector this might produce a 0.03 percent reduction in third country GDP.[32] The principal impact of the NAFTA in the automotive sector may be to dramatically increase automobile exports from Mexico, but this is predicted to result in only modest reductions in third country exports.[33]

In the aggregate, NAFTA's trade diverting effects are estimated to be very modest, generally at less than one percent of third country exports.[34] The overall consistency of serious studies tends to reinforce the general conclusion that the NAFTA should not have dramatic trade diverting consequences for third countries.

The potential effects of the NAFTA with respect to investment flows have not been subject to the same level of analysis as its potential effects on trade flows, yet economists acknowledge that investment flows will be an important

---

[29] *Id.* at 35-36.

[30] *Id.* at 12, *citing* Spreen, Thomas et al. (1992) *NAFTA Effects on Agriculture* (Park Ridge: Illinois, American Farm Bureau Federation).

[31] *Id.* at 13, citing Borrell, Brent and Coleman, Jonathan R. (1991), *Gains from Trade in Sugar and the U.S.-Mexico Free Trade Agreement,* Working Paper of the Center for International Economics, Canberra.

[32] *Id.* at 14-16, *citing* Trela, Irma and Whalley, John (1992), *Trade Liberalization in Quota Restricted items; US and Mexico in Textiles and Steel,* WORLD ECONOMY, Jan. 15, 1992.

[33] *Id.* at 16-19, *citing* Hunter, Linda, et al.(1992), *US-Mexico Free Trade and the North American Auto Industry; Effects on the Spatial Organization of Finished Autos,* WORLD ECONOMY, Jan. 15, 1992.

[34] *Id.* at 3-11, citing various studies, and summary chart on page 8.

determinant of the effect of the NAFTA on third countries.[35] Analysis of the NAFTA's potential impact on investment flows is complicated by the fact that increases of foreign investment into Mexico may be based as much on the change in its general attitude towards foreign investment (and its commitment to stable macroeconomic policies) as it is attributable to the NAFTA.[36] The increased attractiveness of Mexico to foreign investors will increase inward investment and, since investment capital is a limited resource, to some extent reduce the level of foreign investment directed to third countries. A reduction in inward investment into third countries will reduce their economic growth rate (*i.e.* welfare). Potential investment diversion must be considered along with potential trade diversion in the panoply of NAFTA effects on third countries. The extent of NAFTA-induced investment diversion is an open question.[37]

C. A FINAL OBSERVATION ON RIA ECONOMICS

Andre Sapir, in an article written prior to conclusion of the GATT Uruguay Round, pointed to the economic dangers of regional protectionism in an environment of imperfect competition.[38] New economic theory, he said, suggests that trade protectionism exacerbates the tendency of firms to engage in anti-competitive behaviors, in addition to interfering with the operation of comparative advantage. Sapir concluded that regional integration coupled with managed trade/protectionism may present a more serious economic threat than prior studies of the RIA phenomenon have suggested.

Sapir also observed that regional integration undertaken in an open cooperative manner may be a productive complement to a liberal multilateral trading system.[39] This sentiment is echoed by other leading economists. The two major RIAs in operation today, the EU and NAFTA, are both by and large open to third country trade and investment. The facts at present therefor suggest that regional integration will not have a significantly adverse effect on world

---

[35] *See* conclusion of Primo Braga et al. on this point, *id.* at 9-10.

[36] *See* Jeffrey Schott, Comments on Primo Braga, *supra* note 3, at 240.

[37] *See* Appendix I *infra*, regarding this author's suggestion that the NAFTA may result in investment diversion, first made in Frederick M. Abbott, *Integration Without Institutions: The NAFTA Mutation of the EC Model and the Future of the GATT Regime*, 40 AM.J.COMP.L. 919, 922 (1992).

[38] Andre Sapir, *Regionalism and the New Theory of International Trade: Do the Bells Toll for the GATT? A European Outlook*, 16 WORLD ECONOMY 423 (1993).

[39] *Id.* at 432.

trade and investment flows.

II. MARKET ACCESS

The United States maintains an array of FCN treaties and Bilateral Investment Treaties (BITs) with other countries.[40] In recent years the United States has entered into a number of bilateral agreements and understandings directed at investment and intellectual property rights protection with countries formerly in the Soviet orbit, as well as with the PRC.[41] The United States is also party to the OECD Code on Capital Movement which provides rules governing the movement of investment capital among OECD countries.[42] As discussed in Chapters Seven and Eight, *supra*, the WTO GATS Agreement will govern establishment rights in sectors in which Members have made market access commitments which include establishment rights.

United States laws with respect to inward foreign direct investment generally do not discriminate on the basis of the country of origin of the investment.[43] There is legislation which permits the blocking of acquisitions based on national

---

[40] *See* Chapters Seven and Eight for discussion of FCN treaties with Europe and Japan. Regarding BITs, *see most recently*, Kenneth J. Vandevelde, *U.S. Bilateral Investment Treaties: The Second Wave*, 14 MICH. J. INT'L L. 621 (1993).

[41] Regarding former Soviet orbit, *see, e.g., United States, Azerbaijan Sign Bilateral Trade Accord*, 10 BNA INT'L TR. REPTR. 638, Apr. 14, 1993; *United States, Bulgaria Sign Trade Agreement with MFN, Intellectual Property Protection*, 8 BNA INT'L TR. REPTR. 627, Apr. 24, 1993; and references in Vandevelde, *id*. Regarding the PRC, *see U.S. China Agree to Negotiate Memorandum on High-Tech Exports*, 9 BNA INT'L TR. REPTR. 2163, Dec. 23, 1992; *U.S.-China Intellectual Property Accord Ends Threat of U.S. Retaliatory Duties*, 9 BNA INT'L TR. REPTR. 139, Jan. 22, 1992.

[42] OECD, Code of Liberalisation of Capital Movements (1990 ed.). Like the FCN Treaties, the OECD Code establishes binding obligations with respect to OECD members. The OECD Code provides, subject to various reservations, that the country parties will permit establishment of foreign-owned enterprises within their territory. Extension of the right of establishment does not strictly involve the grant of national treatment. *See id*. arts. 1-2, Annex A, list A, pt. 1. A "Remark" following the provision relating to the right of establishment prohibits "measures that raise special barriers or limitations with respect to non-resident (as compared to resident) investors, and that have the intent or effect of preventing or significantly impeding direct investment by non-residents." The condition that to be prohibited differential measures must prevent or "significantly impede" inward investment would seem to offer less protection to third country investors than a genuine national treatment requirement. There is an obligation not to discriminate with respect to parties to the Code, *id*. art. 9, but this is subject to an exception for customs unions, *id*. art. 10. Article 10 provides: "Members forming part of a special customs or monetary system may apply to one another, in addition to measures of liberalisation taken in accordance with the provisions of article 2(a), other measures of liberalization without extending them to other members." *Id*. art. 10.

[43] *See United States: President's Statement Announcing United States Foreign Direct Investment Policy*, 31 I.L.M. 488 (1992), para. 1.

security grounds, but this legislation does not identify particular foreign countries of concern.[44] U.S. treaty commitments with respect to FDI might be considered largely superfluous to the non-discriminatory treatment enjoyed by inward foreign investors. However, foreign national investors who are parties to FCN treaties have invoked those treaties to seek more favorable than national treatment in U.S. courts.[45] Also, the United States has on a number of occasions acted under national security-related legislation to seize and/or freeze assets of foreign nationals in the United States.[46] Finally, U.S. Section 301 legislation appears broad enough to permit the USTR to impose investment-related restrictions on foreign nationals doing business in the United States,[47] and the United States has invoked Section 301 to challenge investment-related restrictions in foreign countries.[48] While this is not to suggest that a bilateral investment treaty with the United States would provide a third country investor with protection in all situations, it cannot be excluded that foreign investors in the United States who are the beneficiaries of rights under treaties with the United States may be at least somewhat better off from the standpoint of security of investment and non-discriminatory treatment than are foreign nationals who are not beneficiaries under such treaties.

As discussed in Chapter Five, the establishment of an enterprise anywhere in the NAFTA entitles a third country investor to the treatment enjoyed by NAFTA Party nationals with respect to the provision of services and, with an exception regarding access to the Canadian banking sector, investment

---

[44] *See* Schmidt, *The Exon-Florio Statute*, Chapter Eight, *supra* note 25.

[45] *See, e.g.*, the *Sumitomo* line of cases in which Japanese-owned U.S. subsidiaries have claimed exemption from U.S. laws prohibiting discrimination on the basis of an FCN treaty provision entitling these companies to employ managers of their choice. This is not intended to suggest that the courts have found the FCN treaties to in fact constitute a bar to application of anti-discrimination laws. The circuits have divided on this question with various middle ground results. Avigliano v. Sumitomo Shoji America, 638 F.2d 552 (2d Cir. 1981), *rev'd*, 457 U.S. 176 (1982); MacNamara v. Korean Airlines, 863 F.2d 1135 (3rd Cir. 1988); Wickes v. Olympic Airways, 745 F.2d 363 (6th Cir. 1984); Spiess v. C. Itoh, 643 F.2d 353 (5th Cir. 1981).

[46] Referring to actions under the Trading with the Enemy Act and International Emergency Economic Powers Act, and their predecessors, pursuant to which at various times the U.S. has acted against German, Cuban, Iranian, Nicaraguan and Iraqi assets. *See, e.g.*, Switzerland v. United States *(The Interhandel Case)*, 1959 I.C.J. Rep. 6, and Dames & Moore v. Regan, 453 U.S. 654 (1981).

[47] *See, e.g.*, Section 301(c)(1), Pub. L. No. 93-618, 19 U.S.C. § 2411 (as amended) authorizing USTR to suspend or withdraw application of trade agreement concessions, and Section 301(c)(2)(A) authorizing services sector access restriction. *See also Press Conference with U.S. Trade Representative Mickey Kantor regarding Executive Order Reinstating Super 301*, FED. NEWS SERV., Mar. 3, 1994 (LEXIS/NEXIS).

[48] *See, e.g.*, Korean Insurance case discussed in Judith H. Bello and Alan F. Holmer, *Significant Recent Developments in Section 301 Unfair Trade Cases*, 21 INT'L LAW. 211 (1987).

opportunity. In Mexico, the new Foreign Investment Law generally governs establishment rights.[49] According to the USITC 1993 Report on the NAFTA, Canada's foreign investment laws are generally favorable to inward investment.[50] Both Mexican and Canadian investment legislation may of course be supplemented by bilateral treaty obligations.

III. THE BALANCE OF POWER

A major NAFTA-related question facing third countries is how the combination of the Canadian, Mexican and U.S. markets will affect their future trade negotiations with these countries. As discussed in Chapter Two, the NAFTA does not establish a coordinated external policy or negotiating arm and so, at least in the near term, market access negotiations will continue to be conducted on a bilateral basis. The European Commission observed in its NAFTA Information Note that as Mexican economic development increased, and in light of Mexico's access to the U.S. market, it expected the political dynamic of EU-Mexico relations to change to one more characterized by equality. The countries of Latin America also should have begun to alter their perspectives on economic and political negotiations with Mexico. If the NAFTA in fact produces accelerated economic growth for Mexico, that country should prove to be a major market for Latin American exports. Furthermore, as will be discussed in the next Chapter, the accession clause in the NAFTA gives Mexico joint control over the entry of new members. Even though alternatives to direct NAFTA accession exist with respect to future Western Hemispheric arrangements, Mexico will certainly play a major role in determining further steps in integration and therefore must be considered a key international actor by its fellow Latin American states.

The United States has enhanced its international bargaining position as a consequence of the NAFTA. This flows largely from the inherent power which it and the other NAFTA Parties maintain to shift course from open- to managed-trade regionalism. At present, U.S. leverage is particularly strong in relation to the automotive sector where restrictive rules of origin, along with its attractive infrastructure and geographic proximity, make it the primary duty-free gateway to the Mexican market. If and when Mexico begins to lower its tariff and non-tariff barriers to third countries (*i.e.* providing parity with Canada and the

---

[49] *See* discussion of new Mexican Foreign Investment Law, *supra* Chapter Seven.
[50] *See* ITC 1993 Report, *supra* Chapter Four, note 1, at 42-2 to 43-3.

United States), U.S. bargaining power *vis-à-vis* third countries will of course erode.

Canada perhaps does not gain as much bargaining power from the NAFTA arrangement as either Mexico or the United States. First, Canada, unlike Mexico, is not expected to undergo a dramatic increase in its economic growth rate as a consequence of the NAFTA. Second, Canada has a significantly smaller domestic market than the United States and is highly dependent on the United States as an export market. It has minimal leverage with the United States should their interests diverge. Canada's position on the world stage will to a certain extent be enhanced by providing an alternative to the United States for NAFTA market access, but its smaller domestic market and higher transportation costs to Mexico are limiting factors.

IV. THE TREND IMPLICATIONS OF THE NAFTA FOR THE REST OF THE WORLD

The NAFTA is a relatively open arrangement which is unlikely to have a significant impact on third country trade. A principal risk inherent in the NAFTA is that, perhaps as a consequence of a future U.S. balance of payments crisis, it will become a tool of managed trade. Such a development would have adverse consequences for the global community. NAFTA market access restrictions would contract worldwide demand and reduce world economic welfare. The risk that the NAFTA and other RIAs will move toward protective trade management is a serious one, and one that has attracted the attention of those concerned with preserving an open multilateral trading system.[51]

The NAFTA represents part of a trend toward the structural regionalization of the world economy. As noted in Chapter One, the Clinton Administration has promoted further structural regionalization of the Asia-Pacific region, though yet without great success. In the next chapter the trend toward regionalization in the Western Hemisphere will be examined. European integration proceeds at a rapid pace.

---

[51] *See, e.g.,* Sapir, *Regionalism and the New Theory, supra* note 38, and JAGDISH BHAGWATI, THE WORLD TRADING SYSTEM AT RISK 58-79 (1991). It should be mentioned that in light of the importance of the U.S. economy within the global framework, a move toward protective managed trade in the United States alone would have an effect quite similar to such a move in the NAFTA.

A. A Threat to Multilateralism?

The regional integration process raises concern for the future of the multilateral trading system as embodied in the World Trade Organization. These general concerns have been well-articulated by Stefan Riesenfeld:

> Let me remind you that the basic blueprint of a new world order designed at Bretton Woods was that of a peaceful, nondiscriminating, and open system of economic and trade relations of global dimensions and that both bilateralism and regionalism were viewed, at best, as an exception and transitional phase in the realization of the ultimate goal. Thus the General Agreement on Tariffs and Trade (GATT), which survived as the remnant of the idea of the International Trade Organization planned in Havana, was instituted as the instrument governing worldwide liberalized, if not free, trade.
>
> It was clear from the beginning of that system that the building of a free global trade system would not be easy and would take a sequence of negotiating rounds. For that reason and to accommodate perceived benefits of customs unions and free trade areas, Article XXIV of GATT excepted arrangements of that type from the sweep of the most favored nation treatment requirement which is the central provision of the system. . . .
>
> Regional cooperation in trade and resource conservation and sharing is both necessary and desirable. Nevertheless, regionalism should not be at the expense of a global perspective of the ultimate needs of mankind.[52]

The foundation of the post-war GATT system was the idea of most favored nation treatment (MFN). MFN is not an economic end in itself. It might well be that a greater overall level of global trade liberalization could be achieved by conditioning access to favorable trade treatment on case-by-case reciprocal concessions. MFN is a political expedient. It attempts to divorce trade from the political arena by prohibiting countries from favoring certain trading partners over others. RIAs exempt themselves from providing generalized MFN treatment; establishing two-tier MFN networks. The countries of the customs union or free trade area grant to each other a special form of treatment, and then within the WTO/GATT framework grant to outsiders a separate level of MFN treatment. The RIA thus chips away at the MFN principle by creating special and more favored entities within the global trading framework. Whether the RIA exemption from MFN treatment will gradually swallow the multilateral MFN principle cannot be predicted. It is, however, well to be aware of what the RIA in principle stands for.

RIAs represent a potential threat to the WTO/GATT system not only because they may undermine the MFN principle and because they threaten the operation of global comparative advantage. RIAs constitute separate international rule systems, and the rules of the RIA and those of the WTO/GATT may diverge.

---

[52] Stefan Riesenfeld, *Pacific Ocean Resources: The New Regionalism and the Global System*, 16 ECOLOGY L. Q. 355-56, 359 (1989).

The potential for conflict between NAFTA rules and dispute settlement, and WTO rules and dispute settlement, was discussed in Chapter Six. A fundamental question now facing the WTO system is whether RIAs such as the NAFTA and EU are growing so powerful and are so sufficiently self-contained that they will chose to ignore WTO rules and rulings in favor of their own rules and rulings in the event of conflict. If these RIAs opt in favor of their own rule systems, then it may be difficult for the WTO to retain an authoritative character strong enough to protect those countries outside the RIA systems.

It is sometimes suggested that the global trading system will break into two or three major regional systems which will engage in fierce economic competition.[53] The likely consequences of such a development are exceedingly difficult to predict.[54] The operation of comparative advantage could be severely restricted if these RIAs acted to close themselves off from each other. Global productivity might increase if they engaged in active inter-regional trade. A scenario is certainly foreseeable in which the trend toward regionalization continues unabated, and in which the WTO plays the role of inter-regional mediator. This scenario may on the whole be one to encourage if the RIAs can be persuaded to maintain an open character.[55]

B. DEVELOPMENTAL EFFECTS

Concern with the potentially closed nature of a global trading system composed of several powerful RIAs is also a developmental concern. If regional preferences are granted among groups of countries at an advanced stage of economic development, this may widen the schism between more and less developed countries by permitting those with existing advantages to enhance their level of economic development. If the benefits of expanded trade opportunities are not extended to the less developed countries, an RIA-based system may function to widen the gap between rich and poor.[56] The addition

---

[53] *See* LESTER THUROW, HEAD TO HEAD, Chapter One *supra*, note 21, at, *e.g.*, 75-85.

[54] On the difficulties of predicting the future course of regionalization and its impact on the multilateral trading system, *see* John H. Jackson, *Reflections on the Implications of the NAFTA for the World Trading System*, 30 COLUM.J.TRANAT'L L. 501, 510-11 (1992).

[55] The potential advantages and disadvantages of open versus closed regionalism have been widely noted. *See, e.g.*, Sapir, *Regionalism and the New Theory*, *supra* note 38; C.A. Primo Braga, Raed Safadi and Alexander Yeats, *Regional Integration in the Americas: "Deja Vu All Over Again?"*, draft of February 1994 furnished to author, at 3-4; BHAGWATI, THE WORLD TRADING SYSTEM, *supra* note 51.

[56] The concerns of developing countries with respect both to the schism which may be exacerbated

of Spain, Portugal and Greece to the European Union may have ameliorated some of the basis for concern regarding the creation of a developmental schism in Europe. The close association with the EU of former COMECON countries perhaps will demonstrate the capacity of RIAs to accelerate growth in less developed regions.

The NAFTA breaks new ground by the attempted integration of economies at radically different levels of development. The southward extension of the NAFTA would alleviate concern over the potential for creation or maintenance of an isolated region of wealth in North America.

C. THE SOCIAL WELFARE EFFECTS OF RIAS

The potential effects of the NAFTA on working conditions and the environment were central to the NAFTA approval debate. Labor unions in the United States expressed concern that the lower wages and benefits of Mexican workers would lead to a rapid migration of U.S. jobs to Mexico. Environmental interest groups suggested that U.S. firms would move to Mexico in order to escape from regulatory restrictions. They also suggested that U.S. health and safety standards would be lowered as U.S. businesses lobbied for a level (and lower) playing field on which to compete. Ultimately the political process was obliged to consider and begin to address these social welfare issues in respect to the NAFTA.

The NAFTA and other RIAs must be evaluated for their potential impact on labor, the environment and other areas of social welfare concern. The European Union has demonstrated that an RIA can take a highly sophisticated approach to social issues; one that accounts for differences in national levels of economic development and disparate national philosophies on issues of social concern. A critique of the NAFTA's approach to environmental and labor concerns should not be understood *per se* as a critique of the RIA process. RIAs can be adapted to meet the governance goals of their constituent countries.

---

between rich and poor, and to the potential for isolation from RIAs were articulated on Mar. 27, 1990 by the Hon. Ambassador Tommy T.B. Koh of Singapore at the "Around the Uruguay Round Conference" sponsored by the American Society of International Law, in cooperation with the Oceana Group (Washington, D.C., Mar. 27-28, 1990).

D. THE RIA AS LABORATORY

The WTO system will soon comprise most of the countries of the world. These countries are at very different stages of economic development, they have different political systems and political philosophies, they have different approaches to domestic economic management and to trade. It is exceedingly difficult to produce a consensus in such an organization on any issue which is controversial. As a consequence, the WTO will move very slowly into new areas and its approach to new issues will often be of the least common denominator variety.

RIAs have a considerable advantage over the WTO in their capacity to generate agreement on new issues. RIAs will develop new policies and implement them while the WTO remains locked in debate over whether to place issues on its agenda. This is not a criticism of the WTO. It is simply a fact.

As the RIAs develop and implement new policies, the practical consequences of these policies can be observed and analyzed. Positive results can be extracted and applied in the broader multilateral forum. The RIAs will thus act as laboratories for the global integration process. The fact that the NAFTA and European Union take very different approaches to the integration process may prove to be a valuable asset in this regard.

RIAs are complex phenomenon that affect the broad spectrum of human interests. The RIA phenomenon cannot be adequately evaluated in terms of trade creation/trade diversion or GDP gains and losses. RIA affects must be evaluated from the political, economic, social and legal perspectives. The World Trade Organization rules governing RIAs are principally directed toward regulating their potential economic impact. This focus is understandable and may represent the practical limitations of a single international organization. Nevertheless, policy-makers and scholars concerned with RIAs cannot afford to ignore the other dimensions of the phenomenon.

V. CONCLUDING OBSERVATIONS

The critical question raised by the regionalization movement is whether the WTO can hold together at the center, providing a forum for maintaining global liberal trade. Alternatively, the centrifugal force of expanding regionalization may pull the WTO apart (or marginalize it). As the power of the RIAs expands -- as is clearly happening -- the incentive of the regional actors to abide by WTO rules may diminish. Look at the conduct of the European Union in the

Uruguay Round negotiations and consider whether any individual European country could have withstood U.S. pressure on any number of important issues (take audio-visual market access, for example) on its own. One might also consider that European Union negotiating positions were not infrequently market restrictive as opposed to market opening (take the agricultural negotiations, for example).

What will be the consequence when several large and powerful multistate actors begin to displace individual states in WTO negotiations? On the one hand, there is the potential for more rapid progress in trade liberalization through simplified bargaining by fewer actors. On the other hand, the risks of catastrophic failure would appear to increase as each major player is more confident in "going it alone" if the system breaks down. And what will be the effect of this new order on the marginalized actors, those states without regional alliances? How will their interests be adequately represented?

These questions have moved out of the realm of mere abstraction and may, in the not too distant future, reach center stage. There is no practical way to establish the probability that the international trading system will pursue one path or another, or to project with any degree of certainty how the various components of the system will react to future developments. There is without doubt a consensus view among serious students of the international economic system that, all other things being equal, open markets are preferable to closed markets. Open markets are a prerequisite to economic efficiency, and efficiently operating economies are the key to enhanced global wealth creation. In a perfect economic world, specialization would be undertaken without regard to national or regional boundaries, and wealth creation would be maximized.

From Adam Smith onward, however, economists have recognized that the world economy is subject to many kinds of efficiency constraints, based upon considerations ranging from important social welfare concerns, such as the need to protect the environment and to provide adequate working conditions for labor, down to the corruption of bureaucrats.[57] The trend toward regionalization of the global economy is, from the standpoint of the perfect economic world, an efficiency constraint. We do not live in a perfect economic world, and the implications of the RIA-constraint phenomenon involve questions of degree and considerable uncertainty. It may be suggested with respect to future developments in the NAFTA and other RIAs that, from the perspective of global economic welfare, developments which favor market opening will be preferable to developments which favor market closing, provided that the social

---

[57] See Frederick M. Abbott, *Trade and Democratic Values*, 1 MINN.J.GLOBAL TR. 9 (1992).

welfare implications of market opening measures have been adequately considered and that legitimate social welfare concerns have been addressed. A principal question facing the WTO and the states that are protected by it is whether they are sufficiently willing to deal with social welfare issues, in addition to purely economic issues. If they are not, they may accelerate the trend toward structural regionalization of the world economy, to their own detriment.

Chapter Nine

APPENDIX I -- THE ECONOMICS OF CUSTOMS UNIONS AND FREE TRADE AREAS DISTINGUISHED

In Chapter Three the technical distinction between the "customs union" and "free trade area" is discussed from a legal perspective. In brief, the customs union (such as the European Union) eliminates tariffs between its constituent countries and establishes a common outer tariff wall, while the free trade area (such as the NAFTA) eliminates tariffs between its constituents as each maintains its own external tariff. Although a free trade area may seem to have a more limited purpose than a customs union,[58] and while this might imply that it is less likely to impose an economic burden on third countries, this appearance may be deceiving.[59]

In the European Union model of a customs union (CU), a common tariff wall is established, inter-member barriers are dismantled, and goods which enter the CU from outside have the benefit of free circulation within the common wall.[60] This gives rise to an economic advantage for certain external exporters; namely, a single tariff is paid in return for access to a more substantial intra-CU market. Of course, this does not benefit all exporters to the CU; rather, only those whose goods may be distributed to more than one CU country from a single point of entry (and whose goods would not otherwise qualify for intra-CU tariff free transit, *e.g.*, because of distribution in bond).

Whatever economic benefit this intra-CU free circulation may provide to external traders, it is not provided to them by an FTA along the lines of the NAFTA which expressly (a) maintains its members' border tariff measures as applicable to goods originating outside the regional territory, and (b) rules of origin which restrict goods which enter one country in the FTA from obtaining

---

[58] On the economic impact of FTAs, see Jeffrey Schott, *More Free Trade Areas?* and Wonnacott & Lutz, *Is There a Case for Free Trade Areas?*, *supra* note 15, at 1 & 59; ITC 1993 REPORT, Chapter Two. These references do not suggest, as this author does, that FTAs following the NAFTA model are inherently more trade diverting than CUs following the EU model.

[59] It may therefore perhaps be misguided to suggest that an FTA's institutions are necessarily more limited than a CU's because it is a less economically important phenomenon than a CU. The author first developed this theme in Frederick M. Abbott, *Integration without Institutions: The NAFTA Mutation of the EC Model and the Future of the GATT Regime*, 40 AM.J.COMP.L. 917, 920-22 (1992).

[60] As noted in Chapter Three, GATT Article XXIV does not require a CU to grant free circulation to goods from third countries on which tariffs have been paid on initial entry into the CU (nor does Article XXIV impose such a requirement on FTAs). However, such free circulation is expressly provided for by Article 10 of the EU Treaty. *See* Chapter Three, *supra*, text accompanying note 20.

a local character after having cleared the first tariff hurdle.[61] In essence, an external exporter to an FTA does not generally enjoy the privilege of free circulation and the corresponding economic advantage. It logically follows that an FTA will be somewhat less successful in attracting imports than a CU because it offers fewer advantages, and that, all other things being equal, it will divert more trade than the CU. This same argument can be made in the terms that the CU will create comparatively more trade by presenting a more open and complete single market.

An FTA will offer an offsetting benefit if its members elect to reduce their third country tariff barriers though under no trade law obligation to do so, and will approximate a CU if it does not preclude foreign goods from obtaining a local character through the establishment of restrictive rules of origin. The NAFTA, as detailed in Chapter Four, establishes complex and restrictive rules of origin. Nevertheless, the NAFTA attempts to ameliorate the adverse impact of its rules of origin on third country exporters by rules which generally provide that imported goods will be subject to a maximum total of the single highest tariff of any Party into which they are shipped.[62] That is, imported goods will not be subject to "double duties". Goods may also be shipped in bond or unprocessed through a Party without payment of duties.[63]

A NAFTA-model FTA should have one significant capital-related effect, and in this sense a long-term trade creation effect. Namely, foreign direct investors should be encouraged to establish manufacturing facilities within the FTA in order to produce goods of "local" origin which will thereby enjoy "acquired free circulation." A CU will create somewhat less incentive for capital movement, and thereby for trade creation, because it eliminates its inter-member tariff barriers. The decision by an external party to export production capital into the FTA probably means an export-directed plant foregone in a non-FTA country, so there is also a corresponding long-term trade diversion effect because of the FTA's propensity to attract capital away from alternative non-FTA sites. The capital attracting/capital diverting features of the FTA may well offset each other from the perspective of potential trade creation/trade diversion.

From an economic perspective there is little reason to believe that a free trade area such as the NAFTA is less likely to cause trade diversion than a customs union such as the European Union.

---

[61] *See* Chapter Four, *supra*.
[62] *See* discussion of rules on duty drawback and remission in Chapter Four.
[63] *See* Chapter Four, *supra*.

Chapter Ten

THE FUTURE OF WESTERN HEMISPHERIC INTEGRATION

The Latin American region is in the midst of a dynamic transformation. This transformation spans the political, economic and social spheres. The extent and pace of this transformation are in many respects as startling as those which have overtaken Eastern Europe following the collapse of Soviet hegemony, with the principal difference being that the Latin American transformation has resulted principally from the push of internal forces rather than from the evaporation of an external force. This transformation is evident in Argentina, for example, where in the space of only a few years the economy has been largely transformed from statist to *laissez-faire*, privatization has been accomplished to a significant extent, the size and influence of the military establishment have been substantially reduced, trade barriers have been cut dramatically, and inflation has been brought almost completely under control.[1]

The process of transformation in Latin America has just begun and the benefits of that transformation may not accrue to the average Latin American individual for a number of years. There is therefore a strong likelihood that political and social disruption will affect the economic development process in Latin America for quite some time.[2] For those who have followed this process

---

[1] The author visited Argentina in August 1994 and attended presentations by the President, the Economics Minister, the Environmental Minister, and a number of other Argentinean government officials. He spoke with several Argentinean government officials and attended a briefing on the situation in Argentina by the U.S. Ambassador to Argentina, James Cheek, a career diplomat with many years of service in Latin America. Political and economic developments in Argentina are well documented. *See, e.g.*, Nathaniel C. Nash, *Argentina Is Booming But There Is No Rest for Its Tortured Soul*, N.Y.TIMES, July 17, 1994, sec. 4., at 6 and *Testimony July 20, 1994 Bernard Aronson, Former Asst. Sec'y State Inter-Amer. Aff., House Comm. For. Aff./Econ. Pol'y, Trade and the Environment in the Americas*, FED.DOC.CLEARING HOUSE CONG. TEST., July 20, 1994 (LEXIS/NEXIS).

[2] To take Argentina again as an example, the impact of transformation from a statist to free market economy has had the consequence of increasing unemployment and reducing the power of organized labor, creating internal political difficulties. *See, e.g., Commentary Views Political Events*, LAT. AM. INTELLIGENCE REPTS, July 10, 1994 (LEXIS/NEXIS). Moreover, a history of political corruption and human rights abuse apparently is not easily overcome. *See* Nash, *Argentina*

over the past few decades, the general change in atmosphere and approach is sufficiently startling that there is a natural temptation to question whether the present situation is entrenched or transitory.

The general transformation of Latin American perspective with respect to economic development evidences itself very clearly in the regional integration process. The MERCOSUR arrangement that presently includes Argentina, Brazil, Paraguay and Uruguay is striking in this regard.[3] Prior Latin American integration arrangements have tended to focus on the creation of rather elaborate institutional structures.[4] The text of the MERCOSUR agreement, by contrast, contains only the most limited institutional provisions.[5] Senior government officials of the MERCOSUR countries have explained that the decision to minimize the MERCOSUR institutional structure was taken with deliberation, and followed an analysis of the reasons prior Latin American integration efforts had produced notably little success.[6] The conclusion was reached that the establishment of regional bureaucracies had interfered with the practical task of negotiating reductions in trade barriers. It was determined that the process of eliminating barriers would be accomplished only by direct inter-governmental negotiations, which preferably would avoid an item-by-item approach in favor

---

is Booming, supra note 1 and Martin Andersen, *The Dark Side of Carlos Menem's Argentina,* WASH. TIMES, June 24, 1994, at A23 (Op-Ed).

[3] Treaty of Asuncion Establishing a Common Market Among Argentina, Brazil, Paraguay and Uruguay (MERCOSUR) [done at Asuncion, Mar. 26, 1991], 30 I.L.M. 1041 (1991).

[4] For a legal description and analysis of Latin American regional integration mechanisms in the 1960s and early 1970s, including the Latin American Free Trade Association (LAFTA) established by the Treaty of Montevideo (signed in 1960), *see* Stefan A. Riesenfeld, *Legal Systems of Regional Economic Integration,* 22 AM.J.COMP.L. 415, 431-43 (1974). For a description and analysis of the Andean Pact and its novel provisions with respect to foreign direct investment and technology transfer, *see* Frederick M. Abbott, *Bargaining Power and Strategy in the Foreign Investment Process: A Current Andean Code Analysis,* 3 SYR.J.INT'L L.& COMM. 319 (1975).

[5] *See* Treaty of Asuncion, *supra* note 3, arts. 9-18. For example, the Common Market Group is the executive organ of the MERCOSUR, and consists of members of the Foreign Affairs and Economics Ministries, and the Central Bank of each member. Its functions are stated in four sentences, including "to propose specific measures for applying the trade liberalization programme, coordinating macroeconomic policies and negotiating agreements with third parties" (*id.* art. 13). Article 18 provides that:

> Prior to the establishment of the common market on 31 December 1994, the States Parties shall convene a special meeting to determine the final institutional structure of the administrative organs of the common market, as well as the specific powers of each organ and its decision-making procedures.

[6] Presentations by Marcos Castrioto de Azambuja (Ambassador of Brazil to Argentina), Carlos Ceballos (Charge d'Affaires of Uruguay to Argentina), and Jorge Hugo Herrera Vegas (Subsecretary for MERCOSUR of Argentina), at Workshop on Regional Integration, International Law Association, 66th Conf., Buenos Aires, Aug. 15, 1994 (author's notes).

of across-the-board staged barrier reductions. Thus, the executive branches of the MERCOSUR governments, in consultation with their parliaments, industry and labor groups, have directly undertaken negotiation and implementation of the economic integration process.[7] Intra-MERCOSUR tariff reductions and the establishment of a common external tariff have been agreed upon in a remarkably short time.[8]

I. WESTERN HEMISPHERIC INTEGRATION PROGRAMS

The Western Hemisphere is replete with integration arrangements. These include bilateral and multilateral (or minilateral) arrangements. The multilateral arrangements include the Andean Pact,[9] the Central American Common Market (CACM),[10] the Caribbean Community (CARICOM),[11] the Latin American Integration Association (LAIA or ALADI),[12] the MERCOSUR,[13] the NAFTA (and CUSFTA), and the Rio Group.[14] In July 1994 thirty-seven Caribbean states and territories signed a regional cooperation agreement establishing the

---

[7] It is of interest to note that, according to government officials, in each of the MERCOSUR countries the constitution allocates the power over foreign commerce to the executive. Parliamentary approval of trade barrier elimination is not required. Responses of Brazilian and Uruguayan officials, *id.*, to author's question regarding manner in which MERCOSUR negotiations are conducted.

[8] *See Presidents of MERCOSUR Nations Ratify Common External Tariffs*, 11 BNA INT'L TR. REPTR. 1268, Aug. 17, 1994 and *MERCOSUR Lowers Internal Import Duties; Brazil, Argentina Trade Charges, Bans*, 11 BNA INT'L TR. REPTR. 58, Jan. 12, 1994.

[9] Bolivia, Colombia, Ecuador, Peru and Venezuela. Chile withdrew in 1976 and Peru's membership is under review. *See* Abbott, *Bargaining Power and Strategy in the Foreign Investment Process*, *supra* note 4, regarding the Andean Pact. *See generally,* Augusto de la Torre and Margaret R. Kelly, *Regional Trade Arrangements*, IMF Occasional Paper 93 (1992); C.A. Primo Braga, Raed Safadi and Alexander Yeats, *Regional Integration in the Americas*, "Deja Vu All Over Again?", draft paper furnished to author (February 1994), and; Richard Bernal, *Regional Trade Arrangements in the Western Hemisphere*, *supra* Chapter Nine, note 5.

[10] Costa Rica, El Salvador, Guatemala, Honduras and Nicaragua.

[11] Antigua and Barbuda, Dominica, Grenada, Montserrat, St. Kitts and Nevis, St. Lucia, and St. Vincent. There is also a subgroup, the seven member Organization of East Caribbean States.

[12] Argentina, Bolivia, Brazil, Chile, Colombia, Ecuador, Mexico, Paraguay, Uruguay and Venezuela.

[13] Argentina, Brazil, Paraguay and Uruguay.

[14] Eleven members of the LAIA (including Mexico, excluding Guyana), with a representative of each Central America and the Caribbean sitting as observers. *See, e.g.,* de la Torre and Kelly, *Regional Trade Arrangements*, *supra* note [], and *Debate Over Hemispheric Free Trade Zone Gains Force*, CHRON. LAT. AM. ECON. AFF., Mar. 3, 1993 (LEXIS/NEXIS).

Association of Caribbean States (ACS).[15] The ACS is intended to promote economic integration in the Caribbean region.[16] There is a trilateral agreement between Colombia, Mexico, and Venezuela (the Group of 3), an FTA agreement between Chile and Mexico, an agreement between the Group of 3 and CACM, an FTA between El Salvador and Guatemala, and an FTA between Argentina and Brazil.[17] There is an FTA agreement between Colombia and CARICOM.[18] There is the Enterprise of the Americas Initiative (EAI) announced by President Bush in June 1990 to address trade, investment and debt reduction.[19] The EAI envisaged the establishment of special funds within the Inter-American Development Bank to focus on investment reform and privatization,[20] with the long-term goal of establishing a hemisphere-wide FTA.[21] The EAI also contemplated the creation of councils and a consultative process to discuss trade and investment issues. By the end of 1993, all of the nations of the Western Hemisphere except Cuba had signed framework agreements with the United States to establish the consultative arrangements envisaged by the EAI.[22] The MERCOSUR countries and the United States have signed a joint framework agreement to monitor and consult on trade and investment matters.[23] The Organization of American States (OAS) envisages a major role for itself in the Western Hemispheric integration process.[24]

---

[15] *See Caribbean States Sign Regional Cooperation Pact*, 11 BNA INT'L TR. REPTR. 1179, July 27, 1994. There are twenty-five signatories with full member status, including Colombia, Cuba, Mexico and Panama, and twelve signatories with observer status, mostly overseas territories (*e.g.*, the U.S. Virgin Islands).

[16] *Id.*

[17] *See* de la Torre and Kelly, *Regional Trade Arrangements, supra* note 9, at 7-10; Primo Braga et al., *Regional Integration, supra* note 9, at Table 2.

[18] *See Caribbean States Sign Regional Cooperation Pact*, 11 BNA INT'L TR. REPTR. 1179, July 27, 1994.

[19] *See Bush Announces New Initiatives on Trade, Aid and Debt Reduction for Latin America*, 7 BNA INT'L TR. REPTR. 983, July 4, 1990; Walt Schaffer, *Enterprise for the Americas Initiative offers new trade, investment opportunities*, BUS. AM., March 23, 1992, at 2.

[20] The Multilateral Investment Fund has a planned capitalization of $1.5 billion, including a $500 million commitment from the United States. *Id.* Schaffer.

[21] *Id.*

[22] *See* Juanita Darling, *Spotlight on Trade; Latin American Countries Are Lining Up to Be Part of NAFTA*, L.A. TIMES, Nov. 20, 1993, pt. D, at 1.

[23] *U.S. Signs Framework Agreement with Four Latin American Countries*, 8 BNA INT'L TR. REPTR. 963, June 26, 1991.

[24] *See O.A.S. & Other Regional Organizations to Promote Hemispheric Integration Initiative*, CHRON. LAT. AM. ECON. AFFAIRS, Apr. 7, 1994 (LEXIS/NEXIS) and *OAS Special Trade Representative to Hold May Meeting; Agenda Includes NAFTA*, 11 BNA INT'L TR. REPTR. 704, May 4, 1994.

As noted above, Latin American integration efforts from the 1960s through the 1980s proved largely unsuccessful in terms of eliminating intra-regional trade barriers, stimulating trade and accelerating economic growth. Institutional failures, as the MERCOSUR countries determined, were certainly a major cause of this lack of success. Policies of import substitution and hostility toward foreign investment prevalent throughout Latin America certainly were major causes as well.[25] Primo Braga, et al. suggest that new Latin American attitudes toward trade and investment provide a much improved basis for current integration efforts and plans.[26]

The extensive array of integration programs being pursued in Latin America is positive from the standpoint of accelerating regional economic growth. These programs focus attention on the removal of unjustifiable trade barriers and will force regional industries to become competitive on a world scale. However, it is plain that coordination and simplification of the various programs is needed. Integration programs improve economic efficiency by permitting business enterprises to take advantage of larger markets in the absence of tariffs and other trade barriers that increase costs. Overly complex regulatory frameworks are in themselves a significant trade barrier. Customs officials are required to apply multiple, and perhaps inconsistent, sets of rules. Administrative agencies and courts become involved in sorting out the attendant difficulties. Business enterprises spend time and labor studying and complying with regulations from multiple sources. The lack of coordination among Latin American integration programs is recognized by the governments involved, and is the subject of study.[27] Nevertheless, the proliferation of Latin American integration mechanisms does not appear to be slowing.

II. WESTERN HEMISPHERIC INTEGRATION, THE UNITED STATES AND THE NAFTA

Plans for the future economic integration of the Western Hemisphere have been

---

[25] *See* Primo Braga et al., *Regional Integration, supra* note 9, at 1-4.
[26] *Id.*
[27] *See, e.g., Chaotic Pattern of FTAs Makes Future of Free Trade in Latin America Unpredictable,* 9 BNA INT'L TR. REPTR. 940, May 27, 1992; *Americas: RIO Group Leaders Decide to Harmonize Integration Pacts,* INTER PRESS SERV., Dec. 2, 1992 (LEXIS/NEXIS); *OAS Special Trade Representative to Hold May Meeting; Agenda Includes NAFTA,* 11 BNA INT'L TR. REPTR. 704, May 4, 1994; *Latins Envision a Single Trade Zone,* N.Y. TIMES, June 17, 1994, sec. D, at 2.

the subject of extensive discussion and reporting. The politics and economics of such prospective arrangements are extremely complex and in continuous flux. To begin with, the domestic political situation in the United States must be considered. NAFTA approval, as discussed in Chapter One, involved a coalition of conservative Republican and moderate Democratic members of the Congress brought together by the particular circumstance of outgoing Republican and incoming Democrat Presidents. The Republicans, having furnished President Clinton with an important legislative victory in approval of the NAFTA, have already signalled their opposition to future Western Hemispheric plans that might include social welfare components such as the NAFTA Supplemental Agreements on the Environment and Labor.[28] There is no reason to expect that U.S. labor unions will change the hostile position they took in the NAFTA approval debate in respect to future integration efforts. If Democratic congressional representatives backed by labor unions join Republicans in opposing future integration proposals, or in making demands on U.S. and Latin American negotiators that are untenable, the prospects of future integration proposals will be dimmed.

As respects the Latin American countries, it should not be assumed that they are all anxious to join in the NAFTA or a comparable FTA in the near term. Most of these countries have introduced economic liberalization programs quite recently. Liberalization followed many years of pursuing import substitution policies that resulted in industrial infrastructures that are non-competitive on a world scale. Joining the NAFTA might require them to eliminate tariff and other import barriers more rapidly than they would prefer.[29] A somewhat slower program of external barrier liberalization would give domestic industries a better chance to upgrade their operations before being subject to direct exposure to more efficient U.S. producers. Since the U.S. maintains generally low tariffs on merchandise imports, Latin American manufacturers would not gain significantly from a reduction in U.S. tariffs. Latin American agricultural producers might gain substantially from U.S. reductions in agricultural tariffs and quotas, but at least some Latin American trade negotiators question whether the United States is prepared to significantly enhance market access in the field

---

[28] *All 44 Republican Senators Oppose Administration's Fast Track Proposal*, 11 BNA Int'l Tr. Reptr. 1026, June 26, 1994 and *Finance Panel Passes Proposal Implementing Uruguay Round*, 11 BNA INT'L TR. REPTR. 1196, Aug. 3, 1994 (noting exclusion of fast track authority as a consequence of Republican objections).

[29] *See, e.g., Argentine Business Not Anxious for Immediate NAFTA Membership*, 11 BNA INT'L TR. REPTR. 655, Apr. 27, 1994 and *Brazil Views NAFTA with Caution; Some Exporters Fear Losses in U.S. Market,* 10 BNA INT'L TR. REPTR. 2013, Dec. 1, 1993.

of agriculture.[30]

Latin American trade policy planners appear to be focusing on integration in their immediate region, where they directly control the process.[31] Chile is in the process of negotiating either accession to the MERCOSUR or an FTA with the MERCOSUR countries.[32] This would create a large and dynamic Southern Cone bloc. The MERCOSUR countries have indicated their intention to pursue close ties with the European Union.[33] If a formal integration arrangement is concluded between the MERCOSUR and EU, this will complicate MERCOSUR negotiations with the United States regarding the NAFTA.

In March 1994, a U.S. inter-governmental working group was reported to have under consideration three alternative proposals for carrying out the EAI agenda of an eventual Western Hemispheric Free Trade Area (WHFTA).[34] These alternatives were: (1) to conduct country-by-country negotiations for accession to the NAFTA; (2) to conduct negotiations between the NAFTA and existing Latin American integration groups such as MERCOSUR and the Andean Pact (a "cluster by cluster" approach), and (3) a "building block" approach in which all of the Western Hemispheric integration arrangements would jointly act to coordinate their trade, macro-economic and regulatory structures with the goal of eventual hemispheric integration. A fourth possibility which has been widely discussed, but which was not reported as under consideration, is the so-called "hub and spoke" arrangement in which the United States (or Mexico) would negotiate separate free trade agreements with other Western Hemispheric countries, forming an arrangement involving bilateral free trade with the United States (or Mexico), but not multilateral free trade among all constituents.[35]

The U.S. government has indicated that the next step in its program for

---

[30] This was a particular concern of Argentine officials with whom the author met. *See supra* note 1. Argentina is, of course, a major exporter of agricultural products such as wheat which directly compete with U.S. agricultural products. Brazilian citrus exporters might well recall that U.S. citrus producers were among the principal opposition to the NAFTA.

[31] *See, e.g., Latins Envision a Single Trade Zone*, N.Y. TIMES, June 17, 1994, sec. D, at 2.

[32] *MERCOSUR to Start Negotiations with Chile on a Free Trade Area*, 11 BNA INT'L TR. REPTR. 1268, Aug. 17, 1994.

[33] *MERCOSUR Presidents Issue Declaration Urging Closer Ties with European Union*, 11 BNA INT'L TR. REPTR. 1268, Aug. 17, 1994.

[34] *Debate Over Hemispheric Free Trade Zone Gains Force*, CHRON. LAT. AM. ECON. AFF., Mar. 3, 1993 (LEXIS/NEXIS).

[35] *See, e.g.,* Richard Bernal, *Regional Trade Arrangements in the Western Hemisphere, supra* note 9, at 714.

hemispheric integration will be Chile's accession to the NAFTA (or conclusion of a bilateral FTA with the United States).[36] As of mid-1994, these negotiations continued to be hampered by the unwillingness of the U.S. Congress to extend fast-track negotiating authority to the President.[37]

The selection of Chile as first candidate for post-NAFTA negotiations is very sensible. As Japanese investors have already discerned, Chile's economy is stable, its external debt is low, its investment laws are favorable to FDI, and its tariffs are lower than those of its neighbors.[38] Chile also appears to have made a relatively smooth transition to democracy following a period of rule by the military. It is not so easy, however, to identify another Latin American country that at present approximates Chile as a candidate for NAFTA accession. Argentina presents a number of attractive features. However, its long history of repressive government and economic instability may dictate a rather cautious approach by U.S. trade policy planners. Venezuela has been mentioned, but in 1994 its economy and government are in shambles. Brazil presents a very complicated picture of economic and political transition, with unhealthy internal social conditions and a history of environment-related conflicts with U.S. interest groups. Colombia remains mired in internal political upheaval and violence, though the situation there appears to be improving.

Domestic political factors in the United States and the situation among Latin American countries suggest that the future of Western Hemispheric integration may first involve a fairly rapid accession by Chile to the NAFTA (or negotiation of an FTA with the United States). The United States is then likely to wait for the MERCOSUR to complete additional steps in its integration process, reducing its members' external tariffs. In the meantime, it should become more clear whether the political and economic situation in Argentina is sufficiently stable for the United States to enter into close political and economic cooperation with that country. Argentina may be determined to be the next candidate for accession.[39] Brazil, Colombia and Venezuela are all reasonable prospects in a more or less comparable time frame, as is the MERCOSUR as a whole, but the

---

[36] *See, e.g., Clinton Reaffirms Commitment to Chile During Talks with Frei*, 11 BNA INT'L TR. REPTR. 1073, July 6, 1994; *U.S. Hails Latin "Jaguars" But No Quick Trade Ties Seen*, REUTER EUR. BUS. REP., July 20, 1993 (LEXIS/NEXIS).

[37] *See supra* note 28, regarding fast-track objections. *See* Chapter one, Annex, regarding details of fast-track procedure.

[38] *See* Chapter Eight, *supra*, regarding Japanese basis for preferring Chile as Latin American investment recipient. *See also Chile Weighs MERCOSUR Link While Exploring NAFTA Ties*, 11 BNA INT'L TR. REPTR. 824, May 25, 1994.

[39] Uruguay may also be included in such a determination.

attractiveness of these countries as accession candidates will depend on highly indeterminate political and economic developments. The Andean Pact countries other than Colombia and Venezuela, and the CACM and CARICOM countries, are at sufficiently disparate levels of economic development as compared with the United States that their incorporation in a hemispheric free trade arrangement will most likely follow that of the countries previously mentioned.[40]

The present political and economic situation in the Western Hemisphere suggests that a unified hemispheric integration arrangement is at least a decade in the future. The integration process is likely to be a gradual one, incorporating within the NAFTA framework in fairly short order, and on a country-by-country basis, the most stable and successful national economies in the region. This may be followed over the longer term by bloc accessions to the NAFTA, or by more complex mergers among Western Hemispheric RIAs.

III. STRUCTURAL ISSUES

A. ACCESSION

The NAFTA contains an accession clause with four principle features.[41] First, the Free Trade Commission is authorized to negotiate the terms of accession of new members. This is the only express recognition in the NAFTA of an external relations competence for the Commission. Second, because the Commission acts by consensus, each NAFTA Party holds a veto over third country accessions. Third, accession can be agreed to on the condition that the NAFTA will not be applied between the acceding country[ies] and an existing Party[ies]. Fourth, accession must be approved according to applicable procedures in each Party. For the United States, the addition of a new member to the NAFTA would be

---

[40] There may, of course, be exceptional cases such as that of Costa Rica.
[41] NAFTA, Article 2204: Accession

1. Any country or group of countries may accede to this Agreement subject to such terms and conditions as may be agreed between such country or group of countries and the Commission and following approval in accordance with the applicable legal procedures of each country.

2. This Agreement shall not apply as between any Party and any acceding country or group of countries if, at the time of accession, either does not consent to such application.

considered a major amendment to the treaty and would be subject to congressional approval.[42] The NAFTA accession procedure is comparable to the European Union procedure.[43]

If bilateral free trade agreements are used by the United States to extend hemispheric integration, the customary treaty negotiation and approval procedures will be followed.[44] In the United States there are a number of constitutionally permissible mechanisms for the approval of trade agreements. In recent years the "fast-track" procedure has been used in order to facilitate the conclusion of such agreements. It is reasonable to expect that the fast-track procedure would be used for the negotiation and approval of bilateral WHFTA agreements.[45]

B. INSTITUTIONS

The United States body politic is averse to supra-national authority.[46] Additional WHFTA treaty commitments will restrict U.S. options in the conduct of its trading relations. If these treaty commitments are proposed to include institutional structures that will further limit U.S. freedom of trade policy action, they will meet with stiff congressional resistance. Although properly designed regional institutions may be the most efficient mechanisms for regional

---

[42] See Stefan A. Riesenfeld and Frederick M. Abbott, *The Scope of U.S. Senate Control Over the Conclusion and Operation of Treaties*, supra Chapter Two, note 35, for applicable principles and processes. The power of the Congress to regulate foreign commerce essentially excludes the possibility that the President could extend the NAFTA on his or her own authority. The fast track authorization by which the NAFTA was proposed and subsequently approved did not encompass parties other than Canada and Mexico. It cannot reasonably be argued that the NAFTA accession clause approves the accession of additional parties under U.S. law.

[43] Accession to the European Union requires, pursuant to Article 237 of the Treaty on European Union, unanimous assent by the Council, majority vote approval by the European Parliament, an agreement between the Member States and the applicant state and "ratification by all the Contracting States in accordance with their respective constitutional requirements."

[44] See Riesenfeld and Abbott, supra note 42, at 637-38, regarding the Congress and trade agreements.

[45] Although a regional arrangement with more extensive institutions than the NAFTA is not presently under consideration, the possibility cannot be precluded that such an arrangement might be the object of constitutional debate. See generally Frederick M. Abbott, *The Maastricht Judgment, the Democracy Principle, and U.S. Participation in Western Hemispheric Integration*, 37 [1994] GERM Y. B. INT'L L. __ (1995 forthcoming).

[46] This fact is well chronicled. See Frederick M. Abbott, *Integration Without Institutions: The NAFTA Mutation of the EC Model and the Future of the GATT Regime*, 40 AM.J.COMP.L. 917, 931-32 (1992).

integration,[47] it is most likely that the NAFTA orientation of leaving principal decision-making authority in the hands of national decision-makers within a consensual framework will be employed in the Western Hemispheric integration process for the foreseeable future.

The NAFTA Free Trade Commission/Secretariat structure can be used in arrangements involving accession to the NAFTA. The basic structure is entirely consensual and should not require adaptation. If a "cluster by cluster" or "building block" approach is followed, and the NAFTA is integrated with other RIAs, a new regional institutional structure may be required. A study of Latin American integration mechanisms prior to the MERCOSUR would have suggested difficulties in attempting to synthesize the U.S./NAFTA approach of consultative/consensual decision-making and the Latin American regional bureaucracy approach. However, MERCOSUR "integration-realism" implies that in the 1990s there is no insurmountable barrier between Northern and Southern institutional approaches to integration.

For the foreseeable future, it seems doubtful that the approach to dispute settlement taken by U.S./Western Hemispheric integration arrangements will stray significantly from that taken by the NAFTA. The European Union system, which involves a permanent judicial organ, the European Court of Justice, with the authority by majority vote to require Member States to disapply their own law in favor of Union primary and secondary law, is inconsistent with the general U.S. perspective on international organizational competence. The NAFTA approach, which permits a majority of non-U.S. arbitrators to render a decision against the United States, but does not require the United States to implement the decision, more closely reflects the present U.S. orientation. Even if the U.S. were in general more sympathetic to the EU approach, a Western Hemispheric arrangement in which a U.S. judicial representative had only a single vote among a substantial group of judicial representatives from developing Latin American countries, might not be appropriately balanced from a U.S. perspective. It appears most probable that any U.S./Western Hemispheric integration arrangement of the foreseeable future will include a dispute settlement arrangement in which the country parties can elect to suffer the withdrawal of trade concessions in lieu of complying with arbitral decisions.

---

[47] *See* Abbott, *Integration Without Institutions, id.* at 544-45 and *The North American Free Trade Agreement and Its Implications for the European Union*, 4 TRANSNAT'L L. & CONTEMP. PROBS. 119, 122 (1994). The determination by MERCOSUR member country officials that Latin American regional institutions have impeded the integration process does not preclude the possibility that the subject institutions and RIAs were not well designed.

IV. PRELIMINARY ECONOMIC ESTIMATES

Primo Braga, et al., have already attempted to predict the trade effects of a "Western Hemisphere Free Trade Area (WHFTA)", both for inter-member trade and for third countries. They suggest that a WHFTA may substantially increase intra-hemispheric trade and may have a significant trade diverting effect with respect to imports from the EU and Japan.[48] The extent to which such an arrangement would divert trade is dependent on the extent to which it is open or closed to third country imports. Primo Braga, et al., conclude:

> ... regionalism in the Americas may have non-trivial effects if the "deepening" of economic relations in the region parallels the experience of the EC. These results, however, do not say much about the welfare implications of the new regionalism in the Americas. Previous attempts of regional integration in the continent were instruments for trade diversion favoring special interests at the expense of society at large. The rhetoric of the new regionalism presents these initiatives as "open" trading blocs, which will foster intra-regional trade without promoting significant trade diversion.
>
> .....
>
> To the extent that these agreements are kept as "open" trading blocs they will not necessarily detract from unilateral and multilateral liberalization efforts and they can be welfare enhancing. If, however, they become mechanisms for export protection through non-transparent trade practices (e.g. restrictive rules of origin) or to roll-back unilateral liberalization efforts they may end up having more in common with their forerunners than our study suggested.[49]

V. WESTERN HEMISPHERIC INTEGRATION AND THE WTO

An RIA encompassing the Western Hemisphere would have great bargaining power *vis-à-vis* other states and regions. Its power to impose its own regulatory rules and decisions would be substantial. The role of the WTO in the governance of global trade could easily diminish in consequence of such a development. If a Western Hemispheric economic power were mirrored by similar economic power in the European Union, the role of the WTO might be reduced to arbitrating between the two great RIA powers. It is exceedingly

---

[48] Intra-Americas trade is predicted to increase to 1.5 times its current share. Imports from the EU may decline by as much as 13.2 percent, and from Japan by as much as 4.0 percent. Exports from the Americas to the EU may decline by as much as 7.2 percent, and exports to Japan may decline by as much as 2.8 percent. Primo Braga et al., *Regional Integration, supra* note 9, at 10-11. The authors note that the trade-diversion figures are overestimated because their model assumes WHFTA integration at the depth of EU integration.

[49] *Id.* at 11.

difficult to predict the consequences of such a development. Two open and democratic regional powers might well provide the foundation for a smoothly functioning global economy attendant to social welfare interests. Two closed regional powers might regress to hostile competition for scarce resources.

The beauty of the future is its indeterminacy. In the case of Western Hemispheric integration, little is clear. The historic resistance of the U.S. Congress to participation in multilateral endeavors suggests a real prospect that U.S. domestic considerations will stall movement toward hemispheric integration or limit the scope of its ambition. The political and economic situation in many Latin American countries makes it difficult to predict the extent of their participation in market-opening exercises. Nonetheless, the prospects for Western Hemispheric integration in the mid-1990s are better than at any other time in modern history. Democracy has become the norm in the Western Hemisphere. Market economics is succeeding state planning. Freedom of expression is gaining acceptance. Even if the integration process does not advance as rapidly as it might in a more perfect world, there is good reason to have hope for the future.

APPENDIX

GENERAL AGREEMENT ON TARIFFS AND TRADE

Article XXIV

Territorial Application - Frontier Traffic - Customs Unions and Free-trade Areas

1. The provisions of this Agreement shall apply to the metropolitan customs territories of the contracting parties and to any other customs territories in respect of which this Agreement has been accepted under Article XXVI or is being applied under Article XXXIII or pursuant to the Protocol of Provisional Application. Each such customs territory shall, exclusively for the purposes of the territorial application of this Agreement, be treated as though it were a contracting party; *Provided* that the provisions of this paragraph shall not be construed to create any rights or obligations as between two or more customs territories in respect of which this Agreement has been accepted under Article XXVI or is being applied under Article XXXIII or pursuant to the Protocol of Provisional Application by a single contracting party.

2. For the purposes of this Agreement a customs territory shall be understood to mean any territory with respect to which separate tariffs or other regulations of commerce are maintained for a substantial part of the trade of such territory with other territories.

3. The provisions of this Agreement shall not be construed to prevent:

(a) Advantages accorded by any contracting party to adjacent countries in order to facilitate frontier traffic;

(b) Advantages accorded to the trade with the Free Territory of Trieste by countries continuous to that territory, provided that such advantages are not in conflict with the Treaties of Peace arising out of the Second World War.

4. The contracting parties recognize the desirability of increasing freedom of trade by the development, through voluntary agreements, of closer integration between the economies of the countries parties to such agreements. They also recognize that the purpose of a customs union or of a free-trade area should be to facilitate trade between the constituent territories and not to raise barriers to the trade of other contracting parties with such territories.

5. Accordingly, the provisions of the Agreement shall not prevent, as between the territories of contracting parties, the formation of a customs union or of a free-trade area or the adoption of an interim agreement necessary for the formation of a customs union or of a free-trade area; *Provided* that:

- (a) with respect to a customs union, or an interim agreement leading to the formation of a customs union, the duties and other regulations of commerce imposed at the institution of any such union or interim agreement in respect of trade with contracting parties not parties to such union or agreement shall not on the whole be higher or more restrictive than the general incidence of the duties and regulations of commerce applicable in the constituent territories prior to the formation of such union or the adoption of such interim agreement, as the case may be;

- (b) with respect to a free-trade area, or an interim agreement leading to the formation of a free-trade area, the duties and other regulations of commerce maintained in each of the constituent territories and applicable at the formation of such free-trade area or the adoption of such interim agreement to the trade of contracting parties not included in such area or not parties to such agreement shall not be higher or more restrictive than the corresponding duties and other regulations of commerce existing in the same constituent territories prior to the formation of the free-trade area, or interim agreement, as the case may be; and

- (c) any interim agreement referred to in sub-paragraphs (a) and (b) shall include a plan and schedule for the formation of such a customs union or of such a free-trade area within a reasonable length of time.

6. If, in fulfilling the requirements of sub-paragraph 5(a), a contracting party proposes to increase any rate of duty inconsistently with the provisions of Article II, the procedure set forth in Article XXVIII shall apply. In providing for compensatory adjustment, due account shall be taken of the compensation already afforded by the reductions brought about in the corresponding duty of the other constituents of the union.

7. (a) Any contracting party deciding to enter into a customs union or free-trade area, or an interim agreement leading to the formation of such a union or area, shall promptly notify the CONTRACTING PARTIES and shall make available to them such information regarding the proposed union or area as will enable them to make such reports and recommendations to contracting parties as they may deem appropriate.

(b) If, after having studied the plan and schedule included in an interim agreement referred to in paragraph 5 in consultation with the parties to that agreement and taking due account of the information made available in accordance with the provisions of sub-paragraph (a), the CONTRACTING PARTIES find that such agreement is not likely to result in the formation of a customs union or of a free-trade area within the period contemplated by the parties to the agreement or that such period is not a reasonable one, the CONTRACTING PARTIES shall make recommendations to the parties to the agreement. The parties shall not maintain or put into force, as the case may be, such agreement if they are not prepared to modify it in accordance with these recommendations.

(c) Any substantial change in the plan or schedule referred to in paragraph 5(c) shall be communicated to the CONTRACTING PARTIES, which may request the contracting parties concerned to consult with them if the change seems likely to jeopardize or delay unduly the formation of the customs union or of the free-trade area.

8. For the purposes of this Agreement:

(a) A customs union shall be understood to mean the substitution of a single customs territory for two or more customs territories, so that

(i) duties and other restrictive regulations of commerce (except, where necessary, those permitted under Articles XI, XII, XIII, XIV, XV and XX) are eliminated with respect to substantially all the trade between the constituent territories of the union or at least with respect to substantially all the trade in products originating in such territories, and,

(ii) subject to the provisions of paragraph 9, substantially the same duties and other regulations of commerce are applied by each of the members of the union to the trade of territories not included in the union;

(b) A free-trade area shall be understood to mean a group of two or more customs territories in which the duties and other restrictive regulations of commerce (except, where necessary, those permitted under Articles XI, XII, XIII, XIV, XV and XX) are eliminated on substantially all the trade between the constituent territories in products originating in such territories.

9. The preferences referred to in paragraph 2 of Article I shall not be affected by the formation of a customs union or of a free-trade area but may be eliminated or adjusted by means of negotiations with contracting parties affected. This procedure of negotiations with affected contracting parties shall, in particular, apply to the elimination of preferences required to conform with the provisions of paragraph 8(a) (i) and paragraph 8(b).

10. The CONTRACTING PARTIES may by a two thirds majority approve proposals which do not fully comply with the requirements of paragraphs 5 to 9 inclusive, provided that such proposals lead to the formation of a customs union or a free-trade area in the sense of this Article.

11. Taking into account the exceptional circumstances arising out of the establishment of India and Pakistan as independent States and recognizing the fact that they have long constituted an economic unit, the contracting parties agree that the provisions of this Agreement shall not prevent the two countries from entering into special arrangements with respect to the trade between them, pending the establishment of their mutual trade relations on a definitive basis.

12. Each contracting party shall take such reasonable measures as may be available to it to ensure observance of the provisions of this Agreement by the

regional and local governments and authorities within its territory.

Ad Article XXIV

Paragraph 9

It is understood that the provisions of Article I would require that, when a product which has been imported into the territory of a member of a customs union or free-trade area at a preferential rate of duty if re-exported to the territory of another member of such union or area, the latter member should collect a duty equal to the difference between the duty already paid and any higher duty that would be payable if the product were being imported directly into its territory.

Paragraph 11

Measures adopted by India and Pakistan in order to carry out definitive trade arrangements between them once they have been agreed upon, might depart from particular provisions of this Agreement, but these measures would in general be consistent with the objectives of the Agreement.

UNDERSTANDING ON THE INTERPRETATION OF ARTICLE XXIV OF THE GENERAL AGREEMENT ON TARIFFS AND TRADE 1994

Members,

Having regard to the provisions of Article XXIV of the GATT 1994;

Recognizing that customs unions and free trade areas have greatly increased in number and importance since the establishment of the GATT 1947 and today cover a significant proportion of world trade:

Recognizing the contribution to the expansion of world trade that may be made by closer integration between the economies of the parties to such agreements;

Recognizing also that such contribution is increased if the elimination between the constituent territories of duties and other restrictive regulations of commerce extends to all trade, and diminished if any major sector of trade is excluded;

Reaffirming that the purpose of such agreements should be to facilitate trade between the constituent territories and not to raise barriers to the trade of other Members with such territories; and that in their formation or enlargement the parties to them should to the greatest possible extent avoid creating adverse effects on the trade of other Members;

Convinced also of the need to reinforce the effectiveness of the role of the Council for Trade in Goods in reviewing agreements notified under Article XXIV, by clarifying the criteria and procedures for the assessment of new or enlarged agreements, and improving the transparency of all Article XXIV agreements;

Recognizing the need for a common understanding of the obligations of Members under Article XXIV:12;

Hereby agree as follows:

1. Customs unions, free trade areas, and interim agreements leading to the formation of a customs union or free trade area, to be consistent with Article

XXIV, must satisfy the provisions of its paragraphs 5, 6, 7 and 8 *inter alia*.

Article XXIV:5

2. The evaluation under Article XXIV:5(a) of the general incidence of the duties and other regulations of commerce applicable before and after the formation of a customs union shall in respect of duties and charges be based upon an overall assessment of weighted average tariff rates and of customs duties collected. This assessment shall be based on import statistics for a previous representative period to be supplied by the customs union, on a tariff line basis and in values and quantities, broken down by MTO country of origin. The MTO Secretariat shall compute the weighted average tariff rates and customs duties collected in accordance with the methodology used in the assessment of tariff offers in the Uruguay Round. For this purpose, the duties and charges to be taken into consideration shall be the applied rates of duty. It is recognized that for the purpose of the overall assessment of the incidence of other regulations of commerce for which quantification and aggregation are difficult, the examination of individual measures, regulations, products covered and trade flows affected may be required.

3. The "reasonable length of time" referred to in Article XXIV:5(c) should exceed ten years only in exceptional cases. In cases where Members believe that ten years would be insufficient they shall provide a full explanation to the Council for Trade in Goods of the need for a longer period.

Article XXIV:6

4. Paragraph 6 of Article XXIV establishes the procedure to be followed when a Member forming a customs union proposes to increase a bound rate of duty. In this regard it is reaffirmed that the procedure set forth in Article XXVIII, as elaborated in the guidelines adopted by the GATT 1947 CONTRACTING PARTIES on 10 November 1980 (27S/26) and in the Understanding on the Interpretation of Article XXVIII of the General Agreement on Tariffs and Trade 1994, must be commenced before tariff concessions are modified or withdrawn upon the formation of a customs union or an interim agreement leading to the formation of a customs union.

5. It is agreed that these negotiations will be entered into in good faith with a view to achieving mutually satisfactory compensatory adjustment. In such negotiations, as required by Article XXIV:6, due account shall be taken of reductions of duties on the same tariff line made by other constituents of the customs union upon its formation. Should such reductions not be sufficient to provide the necessary compensatory adjustment, the customs union would offer compensation, which may take the form of reductions of duties on other tariff lines. Such an offer shall be taken into consideration by the Members having negotiating rights in the binding being modified or withdrawn. Should the compensatory adjustment remain unacceptable, negotiations should be continued. Where, despite such efforts, agreement in negotiations on compensatory adjustment under Article XXVIII as elaborated by the Understanding on the Interpretation of Article XXVIII of the General Agreement on Tariffs and Trade 1994 cannot be reached within a reasonable period from the initiation of negotiations, the customs union shall, nevertheless, be free to modify or withdraw the concessions; affected Members shall then be free to withdraw substantially equivalent concessions in accordance with Article XXVIII.

6. The GATT 1994 imposes no obligation on Members benefiting from a reduction of duties consequent upon the formation of a customs union, or an interim agreement leading to the formation of a customs union, to provide compensatory adjustment to its constituents.

Review of Customs Unions and Free Trade Areas

7. All notifications made Under Article XXIV:7(a) shall be examined by a working party in the light of the relevant provisions of the GATT 1994 and of paragraph 1 of this Understanding. The working party shall submit a report to the Council for Trade in Goods on its findings in this regard. The Council for Trade in Goods may make such recommendations to Members as it deems appropriate.

8. In regard to interim agreements, the working party may in its report make appropriate recommendations on the proposed timeframe and on measures required to complete the formation of the customs union or free trade area. It may if necessary provide for further review of the agreement.

9. Substantial changes in the plan and schedule included in an interim

agreement shall be notified, and shall be examined by the Council for Trade in Goods if so requested.

10. Should an interim agreement notified under Article XXIV:7(a) not include a plan and schedule, contrary to Article XXIV:5(c), the working party shall in its report recommend such a plan and schedule. The parties shall not maintain or put into force, as the case may be, such agreement if they are not prepared to modify it in accordance with these recommendations. Provision shall be made for subsequent review of the implementation of the recommendations.

11. Customs unions and constituents of free trade areas shall report periodically to the Council for Trade in Goods, as envisaged by the GATT 1947 CONTRACTING PARTIES in their instruction to the GATT 1947 Council concerning reports on regional agreements (BISD 18S/38), on the operation of the relevant agreement. Any significant changes and/or developments in the agreements should be reported as they occur.

Dispute Settlement

12. The provisions of Articles XXII and XXIII of the GATT 1994 as elaborated and applied by the Understanding on Rules and Procedures Governing the Settlement of Disputes may be invoked with respect to any matters arising from the application of those provisions of Article XXIV relating to customs unions, free trade areas or interim agreements leading to the formation of a customs union or free trade area.

Article XXIV:12

13. Each Member is fully responsible under the GATT 1994 for the observance of all provisions of the GATT 1994, and shall take such reasonable measures as may be available to it to ensure such observance by regional and local governments and authorities within its territory.

14. The provisions of Article XXII and XXIII of the GATT 1994 as elaborated and applied by the Understanding on Rules and Procedures Governing the Settlement of Disputes may be invoked in respect of measures affecting its observance taken by regional or local governments or authorities within the

territory of a Member. When the Dispute Settlement Body has ruled that a provision of the GATT 1994 has not been observed, the responsible Member shall take such reasonable measures as may be available to it to ensure its observance. The provisions relating to compensation and suspension of concessions or other obligations apply in cases where it has not been possible to secure such observance.

15. Each Member undertakes to accord sympathetic consideration to and afford adequate opportunity for consultation regarding any representations made by another Member concerning measures affecting the operation of the GATT 1994 taken within the territory of the former.

GENERAL AGREEMENT ON TRADE IN SERVICES

Article V

Economic Integration

1. This Agreement shall not prevent any of its Members from being a party to or entering into an agreement liberalizing trade in services between or among the parties to such an agreement, provided that such an agreement:

   (a) has substantial sectoral coverage, and

   (b) provides for the absence or elimination of substantially all discrimination, in the sense of Article XVII, between or among the parties, in the sectors covered under sub-paragraph (a), through:

   (i) elimination of existing discriminatory measures, and/or

   (ii) prohibition of new or more discriminatory measures,

   either at the entry into force of that agreement or on the basis of a reasonable time-frame, except for measures permitted under Articles X, XII, XIV and XIV bis.

2. In evaluating whether the conditions under paragraph 1(b) are met, consideration may be given to the relationship of the agreement to a wider process of economic integration or trade liberalization among the countries concerned.

3. (a) Where developing countries are parties to an agreement of the type referred to in paragraph 1, flexibility shall be provided for regarding the conditions set out in paragraph 1, in particular sub-paragraph (b), in accordance with the level of development of the countries concerned, both overall and in individual sectors and sub-sectors.

   (b) Notwithstanding paragraph 6 below, in the case of an agreement of the type referred to in paragraph 1 involving only developing countries, more favorable treatment may be granted to juridical persons owned or controlled by natural persons of the parties to such an agreement.

4. Any agreement referred to in paragraph 1 shall be designed to facilitate trade between the parties to the agreement and shall not in respect of any Member outside the agreement raise the overall level of barriers to trade in services within the respective sectors or sub-sectors compared to the level applicable prior to such an agreement.

5. If, in the conclusion, enlargement or any significant modification of any agreement under paragraph 1, a Member intends to withdraw or modify a specific commitment inconsistently with the terms and conditions set out in its schedule, it shall provide at least 90 days advance notice of such modification or withdrawal and the procedure set forth in paragraphs 2-4 of Article XXI shall apply.

6. A service supplier of any other Member that is a juridical person constituted under the laws of a party to an agreement referred to in paragraph 1 shall be entitled to treatment granted under such agreement, provided that it engages in substantive business operations in the territory of the parties to such agreement.

7. (a) Members which are parties to any agreement referred to in paragraph 1 shall promptly notify any such agreement and any enlargement or any significant modification thereto the Council for Trade in Services. They shall also make available to the Council such relevant information as may be requested by it. The Council may establish a working party to examine such an agreement or enlargement or modification thereto and to report to the Council on its consistency with this Article.

   (b) Members which are parties to any agreement referred to in paragraph 1 which is implemented on the basis of a time-frame shall report periodically to the Council for Trade in Services on its implementation. The Council may establish a working party to examine such reports if it deems it necessary.

   (c) Based on the reports of the working parties referred to in paragraphs (a) and (b), the Council may make recommendations to the parties as it deems appropriate.

8. A Member which is a party to any agreement referred to in paragraph 1 may not seek compensation for trade benefits that may accrue to any other

Member from such agreement.

Article V bis
Labour Markets Integration Agreements

This Agreement shall not prevent any of its Members from being a party to an agreement establishing full integration of the labour markets between or among the parties to such an agreement, provided that such an agreement;

(a) exempts citizens of parties to the agreement from requirements concerning residency and work permits;

(b) is notified to the Council for Trade in Services.

INDEX

Accession, 28, 60, 155, 164, 181-85
Advanced Skills Through Education and Training (ASETS), 22
Agreement Concerning the Establishment of a Border Environment Commission, 30
Agreement on Sanitary and Phytosanitary Measures, *see Sanitary and phytosanitary measures*
Agreement on Technical Barriers to Trade, *see Technical barriers to trade rules*
Agricultural Grading Working Group, 98
Agriculture, 62-64, 125, 180-81
    apples, 63
    barriers, 130-31
    coffee, 63
    Common agricultural policy (CAP), 130
    dairy, 125
    exports, 145
    fruit, 11, 63, 160, 181
    imports, 45, 125
    livestock, 63
    market access, 130, 180-81
    meat, 63, 125
    Mexican competition, 11
    Mexican tariffs, 63
    non-tariff barriers, 63
    pork, 63
    potatoes, 63
    -related measures, 98
    sanitary and phytosanitary measures, 73-77, 98, 100, 103
    snapback, 41-42, 63-64, 145
    subsidies/subsidization, 11, 125
    sugar, 11, 70, 125, 155
    surplus, 143
    tariff, 62-63, 180
    trade, 147
    U.S.-Mexico bilateral agreements, 62
    vegetables, 11, 63
    wheat, 11
Air transportation/aviation services, 80, 87-88, 149
    aircraft, 121, 130
American/Asian-European trading system, 127
Andean Pact, 177, 183
Antidumping and countervailing duty (AD/CVD), 24, 101-04
Antigua and Barbuda, 177
Applied rates of duty, 40
Approval process (NAFTA), 4, 5, 7-22
Arbitration, *see also Dispute*
    binding international, 102
    ICSID, 102
    recognition, 102
    UNCITRAL, 102
Arbitrators
    excess of power, 102
    misconduct, 102
Argentina, 175-78, 182-83
ASEAN, 10, 13, 141

Asia, 13, 126, 140, 142-44, 146, 151, 155, 158-60
Asia–Pacific Economic Cooperation group (APEC), 10, 11, 12, 13, 151
Asia–Pacific free trade arrangement, 10
Asia–Pacific region, 10, 13, 119, 151, 165
Association of Caribbean States, 178
Asunción, Treaty of, 176
Australia, 10, 141, 155
Austria, 120
Automobiles/industry, 7, 65-68, 121, 125, 129-30, 135, 142, 144, 146, 149, 150, 160
    Honda, 68
    rules of origin, 65-68, 125, 130, 144, 147, 155
Automotive Standards Council, 98-99
Automotive Standards Subcommittee, 98
Auto Pact, 66
Auto parts, 66, 127, 130, 145-47, 149-50
Aviation, *see Air transportation*

Balance of Payment(s), 44, 156
    restrictions, 45
    U.S., 161
Banking, 46, 85-87, 92, 145, 150, 163
    liberalization, 86-87
    minimum standards, 132
    Second Banking Directive (EU), 132
Banks
    subsidiaries/branches, 85-88, 132
Barriers
    agricultural, 130-31
    disguised trade, 113
    elimination of, 36, 53, 130-31, 176, 180
    market access, 139
    non-tariff, 1, 44, 63
    removal of, 1, 16, 19
    services, 1, 16, 36, 51, 53
    tariff, 1, 44, 143, 145, 165, 173, 180
    to trade rules, technical, 74, 99, 100, 113
    trade, 19, 36, 44, 54, 67, 143, 148, 156, 159, 175-76, 179
Basel Convention on the Transboundary Movement of Hazardous Waste, 23-24, 112
Belgium, 121, 132-33
Bilateral agreements, 58, 162, 184
Bilateral Investment Treaties (BITs), 162
Bilateralism, 166
Blair House Accord, 10
Bolivia, 177
Border environment projects, 30
Border measures, 45
Brazil, 160, 176-78, 181-82
Bretton Woods, 166
British Imperial preferences, 157
Brittan, L., 11, 124
Brunei, 10
Building block approach, 181, 185
Bus companies/operators, 88-89
Bush, President, 8, 9, 18, 21, 22, 128, 153-54, 178

Cabotage, 88
California, 17
Canada
    agricultural subsidies, 11
    cultural industries, 94-95
    economic growth, 23
    economic interests, 20
    economy, 19
    financial services, 127, 129
    hemispheric isolation, 19
    investment in Mexico, 19
    trade with Mexico, 19
Canada-United States Free Trade Agreement (CUSFTA) (1988), 5, 19, 23-25, 41-42, 62-72, 76, 93, 103-04, 124-25, 145, 147, 180
    and NAFTA, 23-25, 65-66
Capital, transfers/movement of, 52, 132-34, 150, 173

Caribbean Basin Free Trade Agreements Act, 154
Caribbean Community (CARICOM), 177-78, 183
Caribbean countries, 9, 126, 154, 160, 177-78
Caribbean States, Association of, 176
Cartels, 44
Carter, President, 8
Central American Common Market (CACM), 177, 184
Chile, 9, 10, 13, 144, 146, 177-78, 181-82
China (PRC), 4, 10, 12, 19, 142-144, 151, 162
Clinton, President, 8, 9, 10, 11, 12, 21, 22, 153-54, 165, 180
"Cluster by cluster" approach, 181, 185
Code of Liberalisation of Capital Movement (OECD), 162
Colombia, 177-78 182-183
COMECON, 120, 168
Commercial presence, 52, 80, 82, 133
Commission for Environmental Cooperation, 27, 29, 110
Commission for Labor Cooperation, 29, 113
Committee on Sanitary and Phytosanitary Measures, 98
Committee on Small Business, 98
Committee on Standards-Related Matters, 98-99
Committee on Trade in Goods, 98
Committee on Trade in Worn Clothing, 98
Common outer tariff, 129, 172, 177
Comparative advantage, 161, 166-67
Competition
    imperfect, 161
    Japanese, 139-40
    laws, 98
Competitive disadvantage, 99, 150
Computer products, 66, 121, 130, 142, 150
    rules of origin, 66

Concessions, withdrawal of, 40, 59
Congress (U.S.), 2, 7, 8, 9, 10, 11, 21, 22, 31-32, 73, 116, 124, 180, 182, 187
Congressional approval, 9, 21
Consensus, 28, 41, 64, 69, 101, 113, 148, 184
Conservation measures, 100
Construction and engineering, 89–90, 135, 150
Consumer(s), 15, 16, 44, 99
Costa Rica, 177, 183
Council for Trade in Goods, 39, 41, 57
Council for Trade in Services, 53-54
Countervailing duty, 101-02
Court of International Trade, 115
Cuba, 178
Cultural industries, 94
Customs union(s), 14, 37-41, 45, 54, 156-57, 159, 162, 166, 172-73
    economics of, 172-73
Customs user fees, 71-72
Customs valuation, 55

Dam, K., 156
Debt reduction, 178
Democratic party (U.S.), 8, 9, 11, 180
Denmark, 121, 132-33
Developing countries, 32, 54, 120, 130, 185
Direct investment(s), *see Foreign direct investment*
Discrimination against third countries, 12, 36, 50-51
Discrimination, protection against, 10, 36, 51
Discriminatory preferences, 43
Discriminatory treatment, 36, 43-54, 64, 66, 76, 79-80, 87, 90, 95, 125, 130-31, 136, 155, 157
Dispute(s)
    environmental, 3, 29, 76, 103, and *see North American Agreement on Environmental Cooperation*
    labor, 22, and *see North American Agreement on Labor Cooperation*

settlement, 3, 4, 5, 24-30, 33, 36, 43, 54, 57-59, 75, 97, 100-15, 129, 143, 185
settlement panels, 28-30, 58, 76, 101-02, 111, 114
Understanding on, 36, 102-04
Diversion, trade, 6, 9, 126, 129, 154-61, 169, 173, 186
Domestic regulation procedures, 48
Domestic trade law, 58
Dominica, 177
Double duties, 70, 130, 173
Dumping, 55
Dunkel Draft, 51-52, 73, 75, 93
Duties, *see Tariff(s)*
Duty, drawback and remission of, 39, 69-71, 173

Economic
 blocs, 151
 competition, 139-40, 167
 development, 15, 18, 109, 164, 168-69, 175, 183
 growth, 18, 23, 143, 150, 161, 164-65, 179
 instability, 182
 integration, 2, 14, 49-54, 173
 liberalization, 1, 180
 planning, 15
 security, 155
 trends, 5
Economy
 Canadian, 19
 Japanese, 16, 143, 151
 Mexican, 18
 structural evolution of, 1
 U.S., 15, 16, 61, 122, 128, 153, 165
Ecuador, 177
EFTA, 119, 121-23, 157
Electric power, 13
Elimination of tariffs, 12, 24, 37, 39, 44-45, 61-64, 91-92, 148, 172, 180
El Salvador, 177-78

Emergency action(s) (safeguards), 22, 48, 54, 63-64, 147
Employment/opportunities, 15
Engineering, 89-90
Enterprise for the Americas Initiative (EAI), 9, 154, 178, 181
Environment
 Border Commission, 29
 historical, 2
 physical, 2
Environmental
 agreements, 5, 21, 23, 100, 113
 border improvement projects, 30
 Commission for Environmental Cooperation, 22, 29, 110
 degradation, 18
 disputes, 3, 29, 76, 110-112, 184
 laws, enforcement of, 22, 109-12
 food safety, 98
 human health protection, 112
 impact, 5, 168
 interest groups/movement, 7, 8, 168
 issues, 2, 27, 103, 168, 182
 laws, 22, 27, 109-12
 NAFTA components, 5
 non-governmental organizations (NGOs), 73
 North American Agreement on Environmental Cooperation (NAAEC), 5, 27–28, 109-12, 180
 North American Development Bank (NADBank), 11, 29-30
 pollution, 22
 projects, 30
 protection, 73-74, 99, 109-12, 137, 170
 regime, 7
 sanitary and phytosanitary measures, 73–77, 100, 103
 Sanitary and Phytosanitary Measures Committee, 98
 standards, 7, 109, 112, 137
 tariff/tax, 22
 technology, 13

Equilibrium model, 158
Established enterprise exception, 52
Estoppel, 71
Europe, 5, 14, 15, 16, 19, 142, 162, 165, 175
European Commission, 11, 124-26, 150, 164
European Court of Justice, 29, 40, 45, 56, 58, 97, 107, 127, 186
European Customs Union Study Group, 14
European integration, 2, 14
European Union/EEC/EC, 1-6, 9, 11-12, 14, 17, 20, 30-31, 35, 38, 42-46, 55-59, 63, 73, 89, 91, 95, 99, 107, 116, 119-37, 141, 149, 151, 153, 157, 159, 161, 167-70, 172-73, 181, 184-86
and NAFTA, 119-38
foreign affairs opinion, 128
European Union, Treaty on, *see Maastricht Treaty*
Evaluation Committee of Experts (ECE), 114
Exchange control, 56
Exchange of information, 1
Exon-Florio Statute, 149, 163
Export balancing requirements, 57
External access to U.S. market, 15
External commercial policy, 2, 5, 30-32

"Fabric forward", 145
Fair Trade Center (Japan), 140-41
Fast-track legislation/rules, 21, 180, 182 184
FCN treaties (Treaties of Friendship, Commerce and Navigation), 115, 132-33, 148-49, 162-63
Financial services, 48–49, 52, 80–85, 125, 132-34, 145, 150
banking, *see Banking*
Canada, 127, 129
Committee, 98
insurance services, 87, 125, 135
investments, *see Investments*
market access, 49, 52

modes of supply, 48
Financing, 17
Finland, 120
Ford, President, 8
Foreign direct investment, 18, 123, 127, 131, 134-136, 139, 144, 149-50, 161-63, 173, 182
in Mexico, 18, 123, 127, 131, 136, 141
National Commission of Foreign Investments, 135
Foreign Investment Act (1993 Mexico), 57, 92, 125, 135, 149-50, 163
Foreign investors, 131, 134-35, 161, 163
Fortress Atlantic, 138
Fortress Europe, 120, 136, 138
Fortress North America, 136, 138
France, 15, 121, 132-33
Freedom of establishment, 131
Freedom of expression, 187
Free market economy, 175
Free movement of labor, 2
Free Trade Commission, 28, 97, 183, 185
FTAs (generally), 41, 54, 67, 72, 91, 124, 155, 166
economics of, 172-73
non-members of, 38

GATS (General Agreement on Trade in Services), 3, 5, 32, 34, 47-54, 79-80, 82, 86-92, 95, 125, 133-34, 137, 149, 162
GATT, 2-6, 10, 12, 24-28, 32, 35, 36-37, 39-46, 58-59, 61-64, 67-69, 71-77, 91, 98, 100, 102-07, 116, 124-25, 127, 129, 136-38, 143-45, 147-48, 151, 156-57, 166-67, 173
Trade Policy Review Mechanism, 41
Gephart, Congressman, 22
Germany, 15, 121, 132-33
Global
economic warfare, 156, 165, 170
economy, 15, 16, 170-87

integration process, 169
regulation of trade, 35
resources, allocation of, 36, 44
trade policy, 13
trading system, 5, 36, 59, 127, 150, 166-67, 169-70, 186
Government procurement, 55, 72–73, 82, 130
Gravity flow model, 158
Greece, 121, 133, 168
Grenada, 177
Growth dividend, 155
Guatemala, 177-78
Guyana, 177
Group of 3, 178

Health, 22, 73–77, 97, 112
measures, 100
protection of, 22, 73–77, 99, 112
and safety, 22, 73–77, 99, 112
Hemispheric free trade area, 154, 183
Hemispheric negotiations, 19
Historical environment, 2
Homogenous social environment, 2
Honda automobiles, 68
Honduras, 177
Hong Kong, 10, 160
Hub and spoke system, 4, 181
Human rights, 12, 175

ICSID, 102
Illegal immigration, 17, 18
Imported goods, free circulation of, 39
Import substitution, 18, 19, 179-80
Imports, surges of, 21, 22
India, 19, 41
Indonesia, 10, 13
Industrial Structure Council (Japan), 140-41, 147-48
Industrialized countries, 1, 32
Information exchange, 1, 99
Input procurement, 15
Insurance
companies, 46
services, 46, 125, 135

Institutional structure, 1, 2, 28-30, 97-102, 184-86
Institutions, multilateral, 2
Integration, economic, 2, 14, 49–54, 177
Integration process, 1, 2, 4, 6, 14
Integration, regional, 1, 3, 6, 13, 35, 64, 151, 161, 171, 184, 186
Intellectual property
agricultural products, 93
audio visual services, 96
broadcasting, 93-94
cable service, 94
cinema, 94
copyright, 93-94
copyright protection under NAFTA, 93-94
cultural industries, 94-96
discriminatory regimes, 95
enforcement of rights, 93
film industry, 93
geographical indication of origin, 93
industrial designs, 93
integrated circuit layouts, 93
inventions, 94
Japan report, 148
market access, 95-96
NAFTA provisions, 79, 92-96, 148
neighboring rights, 93
patentable inventions, 94
patents, 93-94, 125
pharmaceuticals, 93-94
pipeline protection, 93
protection, 5, 47, 79, 92-95
rights, 3, 5, 47, 79, 92-93, 95, 162
rights enforcement, 93
satellite signals, 93
theater/movies, 94
trademarks, 93
trade secrets, 93
Inter-American Development Bank, 178
Interest groups, 2, 7, 59, 91, 98, 158, 168, 182
Internal preferences, 44
Internal sales tax(es), 44
Internal services regimes, 48

International Court of Justice, 30
International law of treaties, 26, 108
International legal personality, 30, 56
International organization(s), 35-36, 137, 169, 185
International standards, 74-75
International Trade Commission (U.S.), 22, 62, 124
International Trade Organization (ITO), 166
International trading system, 2, 5, 6, 13, *see also Global trading system*
Inter-regional tensions, 142
Inter-state political linkages, 14
Intra-regional trade, 49, 72, 167, 186
Investment, 5, 13, 18, 23, 83-84, 102, 125, 131-36, 145-46, 159, 162, 164
    access, 151
    air transport, 149
    direct, 15, 123, 127, 132, 144, 149, 162-63, 173
    diversion, 161
    equity ownership, 83
    flows, 160-61
    in financial services, 81
    foreign, 18, 123, 127, 131, 134, 144, 149, 161-63, 173
    international trade barriers to, 44
    issues, 178
    liberalization, 83-87, 92, 135
    limitations in Mexico, 18
    limitations in U.S., 162
    measures, 25, 56-57, 83-90
    performance requirements, 83
    promotion, 23
    protection, 151
    public utilities, 149
    reform, 178
    restrictions, 81, 144, 163
    shipbuilding, 149
    third countries, 125, 159
    water transport, 149
Investors, foreign, 18, 123, 127, 131, 134
Ireland, 121, 132

Italy, 121, 132

Japan, 4, 5, 6, 9, 12, 16, 17, 19, 41, 67, 92, 94-95, 119, 121, 123, 127-28, 139-51, 153, 162, 182, 186
    automobile industry, 142, 144
    computer industries, 142
    economic competition, 139
    economic interests, 143
    economic view of NAFTA, 145-47
    exclusive dealing practices, 139
    Fair Trade Center, 140-41
    Industrial Structures Council, 140-41, 147-48
    interlocked corporate relationships, 139
    internal flexibility, 140
    market access, 139, 143
    market protection, 140
    -Mexico treaty, 147
    Ministry of Finance, 149
    Ministry of Foreign Affairs, 140-44, 147
    MITI (Ministry of International Trade and Industry), 142-45, 147
    MITI White Paper, 140
    NAFTA implications, 149-51, 153
    political perspective/NAFTA, 141-42
    restrictive distribution system, 139
    social relationships, 140
    textiles, 142, 145
    trade disputes with U.S., 143
    University of Tokyo, 140
Johnson, President L.B., 8

Kantor, M., 8, 146
Korea, North
    nuclear threat, 142
Korea, South, 10, 12, 127, 151, 155

Labeling of Textiles and Apparel Standards Subcommittee, 98
Labor/labor issues, 1, 113-15
    agreements, 21

basic principles, 113
Commission for Labor Cooperation, 22, 29, 113
cooperation, 22, 29, 113
disputes, 22, 114-15
dispute settlement, 22, 114-15
enforcement, 113-15
free movement of, 2
groups, 177
health and safety, 22, 73-77, 99, 168
laws, 113-15
Mexican standards, 114, 144
minimum standards, 113-37
Ministers, 29, 113
NAFTA approach, 5
National Administrative Office (NAO), 113-114
North American Agreement on Labor Cooperation (NAALC), 5, 29, 97, 113-15, 180
principles, 113
standards, 113-15, 137, 144
unemployment benefits, 22
unions, 7, 8, 168, 180
worker adjustment, 30
worker (re)training, 22
Land Transportation Standards Subcommittee, 98
Language, 17
Language barriers, 17
Latin American Free Trade Association (LAFTA), 176
Latin American Integration Association (LAIA), 177
Latin American countries, 9, 30, 126, 128-29, 141, 144, 151, 154, 164, 175-77, 179-81, 185, 187
Leather goods, 154
Legal services, 90, 135
foreign consultants, 90, 135
Liberalization
agreements, 51
of capital movement, 132
economic, 1, 180
of investment, 83-87, 92, 135
of services, 3, 47, 50-52, 54, 84, 87-88, 90-92, 95, 133
of trade, 2, 50, 53, 166, 170
of transportation services, 87-88
Licensing requirements, 46
Living standards, Mexico, 124
Local content requirements, 57, 146, 173
Local producers, 12
Lóme framework, 120, 130
Luxembourg, 121, 133

Maastricht treaty, 2, 30-31, 35, 38, 107, 115, 120, 131-32, 134, 172, 184
Machine tools, 150
Malaysia, 10
Macroeconomic
policies, 13, 161, 176
structure, 181
Maquiladora, 18, 69, 145
Maritime transportation services, 80, 87-89, 149
Market access, 10, 12, 17, 48-49, 52-53, 80, 90, 95-96, 120, 125, 129-37, 139, 143, 149, 162-65, 181
Market closing forces, 9, 169-71
Market growth, 68
Market opening, 9, 10, 11, 18, 19, 170-71
Market opportunities, 146
Market protections, 140
Market restricting, 9
Marketing requirements, 44
Marketing Standards Working Group, 98
Marshall Plan, 14
Matsushita, M., 141-43
Matsutomo, K., 141
Merchandise trade flows, 16
MERCOSUR, 176-79, 181-82, 185
Mexico
agreements, 31
Canadian expansion in, 19
cultural industries, 95
direct investments, 18, 144

economic growth, 18, 23, 150, 164-65
economic policy, 14
economy, 18
emigration to U.S., 18
environment, 18
environmental regime, 7
Foreign Investment Act (1993), 57, 92, 125, 135, 149-50, 163
foreign investment in, 18, 123, 127, 131, 144, 161
foreign ownership in, 135
illegal immigration from, 17, 18
import substitution, 18, 19
infrastructure, 19, 144, 150
interests in NAFTA, 18-19
insurance, 135
investment limitations, 18
labor standards, 114, 144, 168
legal services, 135
Maquiladora, 18, 69, 144
numerical limitation, 90
and OECD, 32
open market economy, 18, 19
petroleum industry, 135
political instability, 144
political reform, 18
political ties with U.S., 19
preferential treatment, 18
restriction of opportunities, 15
standards of living, 124
stock market offices, 135
telephones, 135
unregulated production, 7
Military conflict, 14-15
Minimum standards, 49, 113, 132, 137
Ministry of Finance (Japan), 149
Ministry of Foreign Affairs (Japan), 140-44, 147
Ministry of International Trade and Industry (Japan), 142-45, 147
Modes of supply, 51-52, 88, 133
Monopolies, 44
Montevideo, Treaty of, 176
Montserrat, 177

Most favored nation, 12, 36-37, 40, 43-45, 48-50, 54, 63, 76, 80-81, 83, 95, 103, 148, 166
Multilateral
   institutions, 2
   integration process, 4
   Investment Fund, 178
   liberalization, 186
   organization(s), 108
   trade agreements (MTAs), 3, 36, 55
   trade ideal, 4
   Trade Organization (MTO), 35
   trade regulation, 36
   trading system(s), 4, 6, 108, 137, 161, 165, 166
Multilateralism, 4, 166-167

NAFTA
   accession, 28, 59, 155, 164, 181-85
   and other agreements, 23-28
   Agricultural Subsidies Working Group, 98
   antidumping and countervailing duty (AD/CVD), 101-02
   approval process, 4, 5, 7-22
   arbitration, 102, and see Dispute settlement
   Automotive Standards Council, 98-99
   Automotive Standards Subcommittee, 98
   balance of power, 164-65
   Canadian interest in, 19-20
   Committee on Small Business, 98
   Committee on Standards-Related Matters, 98-99
   Committee on Trade in Goods, 98
   Committee on Trade in Worn Clothing, 98
   and CUSFTA, 5, 23-25, 65
   developmental effects, 167-68
   dispute settlement, 3, 5, 26-30, 33, 97, 100-17, 126, 127

dispute settlement panels/ procedures, 28-30, 100-17
economic(s)/perspective 6, 155-61
enforcement of laws, 97
environmental provisions, *see Environment and Environmental*
European Union and, 5-6, 9, 11, 20, 119-38
external personality, 30-32
external policy, 30, 120
Financial Services Committee, 98
formation process, 14, 98
Free Trade Commission, 28, 97, 183, 185
GATT and, 23-28, 102-09
global trading community and, 7-13
goods provisions, trade in, 61-77
impact on third countries, 153, 161, 164
impact on WTO, 4, 31-32, 56-60, 166-71
implementing legislation, 21, 24, 30, 68-69, 99, 116
institutions, 28-30, 55, 97-117
intellectual property provisions, 79, 92-96
investment provisions, 33, 79-92, 112
Japan and, 9, 139-51
Labeling of Textiles and Apparel Standards Subcommittee, 98
labor and, *see Labor/labor issues*
Land transportation Standards Subcommittee, 98
market access, 162-65
Marketing Standards Working Group, 98
Mexican interest in, 18-19
and multilateralism, 166-67
political integration, 23
regulatory framework, 5, 97-117
Rules of Origin Working Group, 98

sanitary and phytosanitary (SPS) measures, 73-77
Sanitary and Phytosanitary Measures Committee, 98
self-executing effect and, 116
services provisions, trade in, 17, 79-92
social integration, 23
standards compatibility, 98
standards enforcement, 98
standards-related measures, 98-99, and *see Technical standards, and Sanitary and phytosanitary measures*
structure, 13, 20, 23-33, 55
subsidiary entities, 97
Supplemental Agreements, 2, 5, 29, 97, 109-15, 180
tariff, 12, 130, and *see goods provisions, trade in*
technical standards, 73-77
Telecommunications Standards Subcommittee, 98
Trade and Competition Working Group, 98
trade creation, 6, 23, 159-61
trade diversion, 6, 159-61
trade effects, 159-61
trend implications, 165-69
U.S. interest in, 15-18
welfare effects, 165-69
working groups, 28, 98-99
WTO priority and, 26-28, 102-09
and rest of world, 153-73
National Administrative Office (NAO), 113-14
National Commission on Foreign Investment (Mexico), 135
National enterprises, 99
National security, 149, 155, 162-63
National treatment, 36-37, 43-46, 48-51, 54, 58, 72, 76, 80-81, 83, 87, 94-95, 132, 134, 148, 162-63
Natural resources exploitation, 149
Negative listing, 80

Netherlands, 58, 121, 123, 133
New world order, 166
New Zealand, 10, 141, 155
Nixon, President, 8
Non-discriminatory access/treatment, 48, 82
Non-tariff barriers, 1, 44, 63, 143, 148
North American Agreement on Environmental Cooperation (NAAEC), 5, 29, 97, 109–12
North American Agreement on Labor Cooperation (NAALC), 5, 29, 97, 113-15
North American Development Bank (NADBank), 11, 29-30
Norway, 120
Notification, 48, 82
Numerical limitation, 90

OECD, 32, 55, 87, 129, 160-62
    Code of Liberalisation of Capital Movement, 162
Open market, 9, 10, 11, 18, 19, 170-71, 186
Originating good(s), 61, 65, 129-30, 172

Panama, 178
Papua New Guinea, 10, 13
Paraguay, 176-77
Performance requirements, 83, 125, 135
    prohibition of, 83, 125, 135
Peru, 177
Petroleum sector, 83
Philippines, 10
Physical environment, 2
Phytosanitary measures, 73–77, 98, 100, 103
Political
    developments, 1
    integration, 23
    linkages, 14
    prisoners, 12-13
    sensitivity, 103
    tension, 17, 151
Portugal, 45, 121, 168

Positive listing, 80
Preferences, 120, 130-31
    British Imperial, 157
    European Union, 153
    tariff, 12, 38-39, 43, 65, 67, 69, 125
    trade, 131, 159
Preferential arrangements, 42, 51, 140
Preferential/favourable treatment, 18, 38-39, 44, 51, 65, 67-68, 71, 125, 130, 154
Preferential regional agreements, 41, 140, 142
Presidents/administrations
    Bush, 8, 9, 18, 21-22, 128, 153-54, 178
    Carter, 8
    Clinton, 8, 9, 10, 11, 12, 21-22, 153-54, 165, 180
    Ford, 8
    Johnson, 8
    Nixon, 8
    Reagan, 8
    Salinas, 18, 154
Primo Braga, C.A., 158-61, 179, 186
Privatization, 175, 178
Productivity advantage, U.S., 16
Products originating, 37-38
Professional (and legal) services, 89-91, 150
    engineers, 89
Protectionism, 15, 151, 161
Protectionist (and approach), 9, 11
Protection of animals, 24, 73-74, 99
Protection of health, 24, 73-74, 99
Protection of human life, 24, 73-74, 99
Protection of plant life, 24, 73-74, 99
Public utilities, 149

Quantitative restrictions, 44, 147
Quota(s), 44, 54, 63, 145, 160

Railways, 88
Reagan, President, 8
Real estate, 132, 146

Reciprocity, 54, 166
Recognition, 48
Red Cross, 12
Regional, *see Regional integration arrangements* and specific headings
Regional integration arrangements (RIAs), 1, 3-6, 9, 13, 20, 31, 33-60, 68, 77, 95, 107-09, 136, 148, 151, 155-59, 166-70, 181, 183-84, 186
Regional market, structure, 140
Regional organization(s), *see Regional integration arrangements*
Regional value content, 65
    net cost method, 65
    transaction value method, 65
Regionalism, 4, 164, 166, 186
Regionalization, 13, 140, 165, 167, 169-71
Regionally-produced goods, 44-45, 65-72
Regionally-transformed goods, 68
Regulations of commerce, 38-39, 43-44, 64, 67-68, 71-72
    elimination of, 37, 61, 64, 71-72, 91
    restrictive, 38, 64, 67, 70-72, 91, 145
Republican party, 8, 9, 11, 180
Residency requirements, 89, 162, 181
Restrictions on non-party countries, 17
Riesenfeld, S.A., 166
Rio Group, 177
Risk assessment, 74-75
Roads, construction of, 90
Roessler, F., 41, 68, 107
"Roll-up" rules, 147
Rules of origin, 5, 16, 38-39, 41, 61, 65, 69, 125, 130, 144-49, 153-54, 173

Safadi, R., 158-60, 179, 186
Safety measures, 22, 73-77, 99, 112
Salinas, President, 18, 154
Sanctions, 59, 111-12, 114
Sanitary and phytosanitary measures, 73-77, 98, 100, 103
Sapir, A., 161

Sectoral coverage, 51, 79, 90
Senate, U.S., 11
Sensitive sectors, 135
Services, 17, 47-54, 79-92, 131-35
    barriers, 1, 16, 36, 51, 53, 79, 151
    construction and engineering, 89-90
    exports and imports of, 122-23
    liberalization, 3, 47, 50-54, 79-81, 84, 87-92, 133
    licensing, 46, 90
    market access, 17, 48, 90, 120, 163
    market integration, 91
    preferences, 49
    providers, 16–17, 46-50, 52-53, 79-82, 87, 89-91, 131, 134, 150-51
    regulation of/regulations, 46, 50, 90-91
    sector, 120, 125, 139, 163
    union, 53
Shipbuilding, 149
Singapore, 10, 160, 168
Snapback(s), 41-42, 63-64, 145
Social
    charter, 2
    developments, 1
    environment, 2
    framework, 2
    infrastructure, 19
    integration, 23
    provisions, 2
    security, 86
    welfare, 6, 15, 18, 119, 136-37, 156, 158, 168, 171-72, 180, 187
Southern Cone bloc, 181
Soviet (bloc) countries, 162, 175
Spain, 121, 133, 168
Srinivasam, T.N., 157-58
St Kitts and Nevis, 177
St Lucia, 177
St Vincent, 177
Standstill commitments, 134
Structural evolution, 1
Structural Impediments Initiative (SII), 139

Structural regionalization, 13, 165, 171
Subsidization, 54-55, 125
Substitution, 18, 19, 179-80
Sumitomo cases, 163
Supplemental Agreements, 2, 5, 29-30, 97, 109-15, 174
Sweden, 120
Switzerland, 122

Taiwan, 4, 10, 12, 19, 155, 160
Tariff Act (1930), 46
Tariff(s)
  applied rates of, 40
  barriers, 1, 44, 143, 145, 165, 173, 180
  change in classification, 65
  collection, 130
  common customs, 38
  common outer, 129, 172, 177
  double payment of, 70, 130, 173
  elimination, 12, 24, 37-39, 44, 61-64, 91-92, 148, 172
  free entry, 145, 154, 164
  high, 125, 150
  inter-constituent, 39
  maximum single, 39
  non-members, 38
  preferences, 12, 37, 49, 150
  preferential, 12, 38-39, 43, 65, 67, 69, 125, 130-31
  rates, 40, 63, 70
  reductions, 39, 44, 61-62, 64, 91, 177, 180, 182
  schedules, 61, 130
  wall, 38, 172
Tariff rate quota (TRQ), 62-63
Taxation, 15, 44
  direct, 44
  indirect, 44
Technical barriers to trade rules, 55, 73-77, 97-100, 106, 112
Technical cooperation, 98
Technical standards, 5, 55, 73-77, 97-100, 106, 112
Technological advantage, U.S., 16

Telecomunications, 13, 46, 80-85, 121, 130
Telecommunications Standards Subcommittee, 98
Telephone
  equipment, 146
  services, 80, 84-85, 135
Television, 136, 147
Texas, 17
Textiles and apparel, 66, 129, 142, 147, 154
  "fabric forward", 145
  fiber comprising yarn, 66
  trade diversion, 154
  "yarn forward", 66, 145
Thailand, 10, 12, 19, 76
Third countries, discrimination against, 12, 36, 50-51, 115, 125, 127, 142, 145
Third country enterprises, 52, 81-82, 92, 102, 115, 127, 133, 162
Third country trade, 10, 31, 38, 51, 67-71, 115, 125, 129-31, 159-60, 165, 172
Third World, 32
Tokyo Round (1979), 527, 55, 106
Trade, and *see* specific headings
  agreements, multilateral, 3
  concessions, 40, 59
  creation, 6, 23, 126, 156-57, 159-61, 169, 173
  diversion, *see Diversion, trade*
  flows, 16, 157
  in goods, 5, 16, 32, 36, 37-45, 47, 54, 61-77, 91, 125, 129-31
  ideal, 4
  international, 4, 54, 92, 143
  liberalization, 2, 50, 53, 166
  -related intellectual property rights (TRIPS), 3, 5, and *see Intellectual Property*
  -related investment measures (TRIMS), 3, 5, and *see Investment*
  in services, 3, 5, and *see Services*
  surplus(es), 16, 119, 122, 139

Trade barriers, 19
    disguised, 112
    elimination of, 36, 53, 130-31, 176
Trade and Competition Working Group, 98
Trade policy
    Japan, 151
    Mexico, 31
    Review Mechanism (GATT), 41
    U.S., 4, 10, 13, 15, 31, 137, 182, 184
Trading system
    global, 5, 6, 36, 59, 127, 150, 166-67, 169-70, 186
    international, 2, 5, 6, 13
Transfer of technology, 13
Transformation, 65-67
Transparency, 48, 137
Transportation services, 13, 84, 87–89, 91, 150-51
    air, see Air transportation/aviation services
    bus companies, see Bus companies
    liberalization, 87, 88
    railways, see Railways
    trucks/operators, see Trucks/operators
    water, see Maritime transportation services
Treaty of Rome (1957), 89, 91, 132, and see Maastricht Treaty
TRIMS, 3, 5, and see Investment
TRIPS, 3, 5, and see Intellectual Property
Trucks/operators, 88
    liability concerns/insurance, 89
    liberalization of restrictions, 88–89
    ownership, 88-89
Tuna imports/Panel, 47, 73, 76

UNCITRAL, 102
Understanding on Dispute Settlement (WTO), 36, 57, 102-04
Unemployment benefits, 2
Unitary entity, 50

United Kingdom, 121, 123, 133
United Nations Organization, 30
United Nations Charter, 30
United States
    anti-discrimination law, 149
    Asia-Pacific relations, 13
    automobile industry, 7
    balance of payments, 165
    Caribbean Basin Free trade Agreements Act, 154
    defence expenditures, 122
    Democratic party, 8, 9, 11, 180
    direct investment, 15
    economic growth, 23
    economy, 15, 16, 61, 122-24, 128, 153, 165
    environmental movement, 8
    environmental standards, 7
    Eurocentric policy, 10
    external economic relations, 119
    federal livestock grazing land fees, 11
    foreign commercial relations, 32
    House of Representatives, 9, 11, 21, 61, 153
    international bargaining position, 164-65
    investment in Mexico, 18, 123
    -Japan trade imbalance, 143
    military conflict with Mexico, 14
    military presence, 142
    NAFTA policy, 15–17
    political insensitivity, 141
    productivity advantage, 16
    protected growth, 15
    Republican party, 8, 9, 11, 174
    Senate, 11
    service sector, 16, 17
    sphere of influence, 128
    taxation of business, 15
    technological advantage, 16
    trade deficit, 122, 128
    trade and economic policy, 4, 10, 13, 15, 30, 119, 129, 137, 182, 184

trade surplus, 16, 119, 122
trading partners, 119, 122
unemployment, 128
wages and benefits, 7
United States International Trade Commission, 22, 62, 124
Uruguay, 176-77, 182
Uruguay Round (GATT), 2, 9, 11-12, 35-38, 73-74, 92-93, 95-96, 124, 127, 129-31, 137, 143, 150, 159-61, 170
    Understanding on the Interpretation of Article XXIV, 37, 39, 40-43, 55

Value-added imports, 19
Value added in manufacturing, 16
Vandenbergh Resolution, 14
Venezuela, 177-78, 182-83
Vienna Convention on the Law of Treaties (1969), 26, 108
Vietnam, 19
Viner, J., 155-56
Violence, 1, 182
Virgin Islands, 178
Visa requirements, 45

Wage rates, lower, 12, 18, 19, 168
Wages, worker, 7, 18, 144
Waiver(s), 40-41, 45, 49, 70, 108
Welfare
    benefits, 155-56
    effects, 158-61, 168
    policies, 15
Western Hemispheric Free Trade Area (WHFTA), 4, 6, 19, 154, 181, 184, 186
Western Hemispheric integration, 31, 164-65, 175-87
    structural issues, 183-85
    and the WTO, 186-87
Western Hemispheric RIA(s), 4, 6, 31
Whalley, J., 157-58
Wooten, I., 157-58
Worker adjustment assistance programs, 30

Worker (re)training, 22
Worker wages and benefits, 7, 168
Working conditions, 168, 170
Working Group on Agricultural Subsidies, 98
Working Group on Rules of Origin, 98
World economy, integration of, 6
World Trade Organization (WTO), 2-6, 26-28, 31-60, 64, 69, 71-77, 89, 95-109, 133-34, 136-38, 143, 147, 151, 166-67, 169-71, 186-87, and see specific headings
World trading system, 6

Yarn, 127
"Yarn forward", 66, 145
Yeats, A., 158-60, 179, 186